CALLED TO AN EXTRAORDINARY ADVENTURE IN FAITH

Isabelle Smyth, MMM

Loving wishes & prayers
Isabelle
19.01.25

PACEM IN TERRIS PRESS

Devoted to the global vision of Saint John XXIII,
prophetic founder of Postmodern Catholic Social Teaching,
and supporting the search for a Postmodern Ecological Civilization
that will draw on all the eco-spiritual wisdom traditions
of our global human family.

www.paceminterrispress.com

2024

ISBN: 979-8-9912115-0-5
English Language Paperback Edition
Cover photo: the Virunga volcanic mountains in Rwanda
taken by Sister-doctor Geneviève van Waesberghe MMM

Pacem in Terris Press publishes scholarly books directly or indirectly related to Catholic Social Teaching and its commitment to justice, peace, ecology, and spirituality, and on behalf of the search for a Postmodern Ecological Civilization.

In addition, to support ecumenical and interfaith dialogue, as well as dialogue with other spiritual seekers, Pacem in Terris Press publishes scholarly books from other Christian perspectives, from other religious perspectives, and from perspectives of other spiritual seekers that promote justice, peace, ecology, and spirituality for our global human family.

PACEM IN TERRIS PRESS
is the publishing service of

PAX ROMANA
Catholic Movement for Intellectual & Cultural Affairs
USA

1717 K Street NW, Suite 600
Washington DC 20006, USA
www.paceminterris.net

A new command I give you:
Love one another as I have loved you.

JOHN 13:34

A hundred thousand men and women,
fired with the zeal of holiness,
fortified with eternal faith in the Lord,
and nerved to lion's courage by their sympathy for the poor
and the fallen and the downtrodden,
will go over the length and breadth of the land,
preaching the gospel of salvation,
the gospel of help, the gospel of social raising up,
and the gospel of equality.

SWAMI VIVEKANANDA

This book is gratefully dedicated to all who have shared my journey on the different stretches of life.

TABLE OF CONTENTS

PREFACE

IT IS BOTH A PRIVILEGE AND A CHALLENGE for me to write a short introduction to this remarkable book. I suppose it is not surprising that the book is remarkable because the author, Isabelle Smyth, has lived through such a variety of interesting experiences and has been personally involved with so many outstanding people.

She provides a very accurate record of her immersion in many different important movements and events; but this book is far more than a memoir. What we have here is a book that gives us fresh insight into a wide range of many of the most important issues in today's world — and which does so by linking each of them concretely with her own personal experiences and reflections.

A particularly interesting feature of the book is that each chapter is built around one or two outstanding leaders, several of whom Isabelle has not only met but with whom she has worked closely. Perhaps the most significant of these leaders, from Isabelle's point of view, is Mother Mary Martin, the foundress of Isabelle's religious congregation, the Medical Missionaries of Mary.

In her second chapter Isabelle gives us a deeply insightful and moving account of Mother Mary's early life and final illness. She focuses particularly on the gift of empathy which Isabelle sees as an outstanding feature of Mother Mary's character. She spells out the remarkable parallels between Mother Mary's life and that of her contemporary Saint Edith Stein, whose major philosophical legacy is her study of empathy, to which the reader is introduced in the opening chapter.

Among the other topics which Isabelle covers in this book are the value and excitement of interfaith dialogue; the wonderful expansion of primary healthcare in the global south; the valiant effort of the great Julius Nyerere to pioneer a just and sustainable economic system in Tanzania as an alternative to exploitative capitalism; the development of liberation theology and especially of its feminist dimension; the effective work in literacy and the education of poor people pioneered by Paulo Freire and developed so successfully by Anne Hope and Sally Timmel; the emergence of a rich ecological spirituality, culminating in the concept of 'The Cosmic Christ'; the challenge of responding to the horror of human trafficking; and the extraordinary advances in artificial intelligence with all its advantages and its dangers.

I feel sure that most readers will find, like myself, that this book offers new and important reflections on these topics and puts them in touch with sources of further information on all of them.

I am astonished at the variety of personal experiences Isabelle has had on all these issues—and the skill with which she succeeds in bringing technical knowledge 'down to Earth' by relating it to her own direct involvement. Not only that, but on most of these issues she fills us in on the history of how she and a host of others became involved and responded to these human stories of challenge and success.

Donal Dorr

PART 1

MY EXTRAORDINARY ADVENTURE

Listen daughter, and pay careful attention:
Forget your people and your father's house,
Let the King be enthralled by your beauty.
Honor him for he is your Lord.

PSALM 45: 10-11

CHAPTER 1

EMPATHY: A MEDITATIVE TASK

IT WAS A SUNNY MORNING IN 1963 when I was introduced to the story of Edith Stein. I was among a bunch of eighty young women from half a dozen nationalities, who shared the same crazy notion which we had tried — but failed — to shake off. To get this far we had already paid a price, said farewell to family and home, let all the gorgeous guys we'd met and might have married go their way.

The Constitutions of the Medical Missionaries of Mary told us we were called to 'an extraordinary adventure'. It would be an adventure in faith. Our vocation was 'to be contemplatives who are active in the world.' As soon as we were ready, we would be missioned to bring healing and development to places of great need.

On that sunny morning our Director of Formation called me to her office. She told me it would be my turn to read in the dining room when we had silent meals during the coming week. Making good use of silence was among the tools of our trade in the 1500-year-old monastic tradition of St. Benedict in which our work was grounded. I was handed an early account of the life of Edith Stein. Thus, I was introduced to the concept of empathy.[1]

This was a fairly new word, only coined in the late 19th century when psychologists began to investigate the older concepts of compassion and sympathy. The word 'compassion' had been around for a long time — since about the 14th century. If I have compassion for you, it means I am with you in what you are suffering. I care about you. Even though I may not know you personally, I will probably want to do something to help your situation. That action might energize me. But it wouldn't mean that I feel what you are feeling.

Then in the 16th century the word 'sympathy' became popular. It could be used instead of 'compassion' but it could also cover something wider than some personal pain or grief you are suffering. It could mean I support a cause you have adopted. And in expressing my sympathy I want you to know that I am supporting you and am in sympathy with your cause as best I can be.

In the second half of the 19th century in Germany, philosophers. psychologists and artists began exploring 'sympathy' — its application and its effects. It is from this psychological curiosity that the word 'empathy' came. As I become aware of your emotional experience, I can try to take it into myself. I can distance

---

[1] Published by Sheed & Ward in 1952, *Edith Stein* was written by Sister Teresia de Spirito Sanctu ODC, Prioress of the 'Regina Pacis' Carmel in Cologne and is referenced today under her surname, Posselt. It was translated by Cecily Hastings and Donald Nicholl from the original German version that had been completed in time to mark the tenth anniversary of Edith's perpetual vows in the Cologne Carmel on May 1, 1948. The book is dedicated to the Carmelite communities at Cologne and Echt. It was not intended to be a biography, but a summary of Edith's life. With extensive quotations from Edith's hand, in places it is autobiographical in character.

my attention from everything else except what you must be feeling. We are actively sharing each other's experience. Scholars wondered what is happening in our brain cells as we do this. Experience is the essential ingredient of empathy.

Visual artists invite me to feel what they are feeling or what concerns them as I view a painting. An example might be Picasso's horror of war depicted in *Guernica.* Similarly, a ballet or a theatrical production, a musical recital or perhaps a circus could evoke the same emotion in me as the artist expresses. This could also happen in liturgy.[2] Much research is still taking place to explore what exactly is happening in our brains when we embrace the pain or the joy of another to the point of being deeply moved by it.

Some people seem to be gifted with empathy, even though they may have never heard the word. We have examples of people from earlier centuries who have inspired us in this way. However, most of us have to work to develop our sense of compassion to the point where we can experience how another person is feeling and respond in practical ways.

While developing her theory on empathy as a social, ethical and aesthetic phenomenon, Edith Stein also discussed whether we could experience the feelings an animal is having. Charles Darwin had already explored this idea. Edith believed our capacity for this is limited because our bodily capacities are different. Animals have their own ways of sharing their feelings with us. I observe this in my own city garden – visiting foxes, and resident squirrels; cats of course, as they dream about the

---

[2] Pope Francis' Apostolic Letter in 2022, *Desiderio Desideravi,* does not use the word 'empathy' but his message is shot through with the same concept in a spiritual context. He says that every time we go to Mass we are drawn there by the desire of Jesus for us as expressed at the Last Supper before he suffered and died. Cf *Desiderio Desideravi* par 6-11, 33ff.

birds queueing for our bird feeder; big seagulls and flying geese overhead, tiny ladybirds; field mice, slugs, and snails; butterflies and occasionally a healthy hedgehog and his wife and family who've set up home under our garden shed.

Our fifteen thousand bees flying to and fro from their hive don't pause to be observed except when they know that the time to swarm has come. Do they realise, I wonder, that their species as Irish black bees is threatened with extinction and that is why they have been invited here to increase and multiply as they enjoy the safety of our neighbourhood? Do they know that we know that we cannot survive if they do not? And if so, how do they know? By some bee version of empathy, I suppose.

Although we may not be able to feel exactly how an animal is feeling, we can observe how they let us know how they are feeling. I had a handsome grey cat for nineteen years whose name was Smokey. One day two young women knocked on our door asking for a donation for a cause they were supporting. We invited them in to tell us about their cause, sat down with them at the kitchen table and made a pot of tea. We never suspected they were thieves. In turn, each asked if she could use the bathroom. Smokey was in another room. Not a bit like him, he gave a loud meow as they passed the door. We paid no attention, but one of them said "Oh you have a cat, I'd love to see him". She was ushered in to the room where he was. When she returned, the other one said she wanted to see the cat too. Smokey howled as we continued our tea in the kitchen. But we ignored him. It was only when they had gone that we realised the cash was taken.

As kids, when we were packing for our annual summer holiday at our grandmother's house overlooking the spectacular seafront and cliff walks in Tramore, our little Cairn terrier,

Jessie, always picked up the excitement several days before we were due to go. Year after year, as soon as the trunk and suitcases were taken down from the attic and dusted off, she would pick up the clues and remind us every hour that this was a time to be extra happy. She wasn't a water dog, but we were all good swimmers. She would sit contentedly and guard our clothes on the pier watching our feats in the water below. Then when it was all over and we were back home in Dublin, and our school bags replaced the holiday luggage in the hall, she would sit on the mat inside the door and sulk for several days – letting us know that she would put up with a walk if that was all we could offer. She knew, too, that well managed sulking can be very therapeutic.[3]

Indeed, at a time of family bereavement, a pet animal may reveal the feeling it shares. I can vividly recall such an experience the day my father died in 1990. Another Cairn terrier, Terry, jumped up on the armchair and ever so gently nuzzled close, wanting to let me know he understood the feelings we all had. Many years later when Terry had to be put to sleep because old age brought on repeated fits, with breathing difficulties, I was deeply distressed. Terry belonged to my brother and sister-in-law who were abroad on holidays, so he was staying with us when he began to get seizures. For several days I brought him with me to my office to keep an eye on him. A visitor who called to see me on some business was an experienced dog handler. She observed how he would seek an empty room to be alone. She said to me: "That little dog is telling you he feels that death is calling him. Can't you see the way he is separating

---

[3] I discovered this on a visit to our community in Appalachia. In the wisdom of the local culture, people build a special nook called a 'Pouting House' near their home where you go and remain alone when you feel the need to pout. And when you are finished, you will be welcomed back to the community and gifted with support.

himself from the pack?" I phoned my brother with the awful news. They agreed I should do whatever the vet advised.

Next day as I drove him to the vet on that final journey to Dun Laoghaire, he lay quietly on the cushion beside me. When we parted I headed immediately to Galway to be comforted by my younger brother and his family. Tears were still streaming down my face as I drove past the fields of Athenry. In my brother's home they were expecting me. I knew I looked a sight. They had a magnificent pedigree sheepdog called Megan. She had a haughty air about her as if she was aware of her awesome appearance. She was usually quite aloof. Incredibly that day, as soon as I entered the house, she picked up my sorrow. When I sat down, she slowly and gracefully made her way across the room and put her head gently on my knee engaging me with her soulful eyes to let me know she understood my feelings. Did she experience the same feelings? Maybe not, but she knew about mine and seemed to understand their significance.

One of the local veterinary community in Galway felt Megan's aloofness might be due to depression. She thought this could be helped if a little mongrel terrier in their rescue centre - called Mollie - joined the family. We don't know what trauma Mollie may have suffered in her early life, but she never disguised her need to love everyone she met and to experience that she was loved in return. She was the cuddliest little dog – among many – that I ever met. I'd be sitting there with my laptop on my lap doing something I thought was important, and without realising it after a few minutes I would notice that Mollie had managed to snuggle her little self under my elbow. It was an amazing experience repeated every time I sat down anywhere in that house. Mollie seemed to understand, too, why she had been adopted into this family. She alone could break through the barrier of Megan's aloofness. She would entice her out to the back garden where they would chase each other around and rub noses as they wagged tails and enjoyed a great frolic. Their growing relationship also enhanced the experience of the humans who watched these antics from the patio.

On Whose Shoulders Do I stand?

Looking back now over the decades that have passed, thinking of the great people who have inspired me, Edith Stein stands out among them. She was one of the leading scholars who developed the understanding of empathy from within the discipline of philosophy. She lived and worked among the greatest thinkers of her generation.

Edith was the youngest of seven children in a Jewish family in Germany.[4] She admitted that she felt more at home in school than in their family home. She loved history and literature and was seldom without a book in her hand. In March 1911, at nineteen years of age, she entered the University of Breslau. Most biographers record that since she was fifteen, she had secretly become an atheist but continued to accompany her mother to the Synagogue. Frau Stein knew well that her youngest daughter, like her two older brothers, had given up her faith but they never spoke about this. They remained devoted to one another.

When she was fifteen, she had taken a break from school and travelled to Hamburg to stay with her oldest sister, Else and her husband, Max Gordon. She would help Else care for their toddler daughter and newborn son. In her book *Life in a Jewish Family* where Edith writes about the eight months she spent in Hamburg, she wrote: "Deliberately and consciously I gave up

---

[4] Edith's mother, Auguste Stein, had given birth to eleven children, four of whom died in infancy before Edith was born.

praying here." Reflecting on this memoir, Edith's niece, Susanne Batzdorff, gives us a different view on the question of atheism:

> *From this one sentence several biographers and commentators have deduced that Edith Stein became an atheist at age fifteen. I would submit that this gives too much weight to one brief remark. First of all, Edith only tells us that she stopped praying. We do not know what sort of prayers she had been accustomed to until then. Were they the prayers of childhood, which would suddenly no longer appear meaningful or appropriate to the adolescent away from home for the first time? Besides, a thoughtful young woman, who is searching for the truth, as Edith was fated to do all her life, is bound to struggle with doubts and uncertainties, especially during her teenage years. In the process of growing up, Edith was destined to experience a number of shifts in her thinking. That a fifteen-year-old does not pray is probably much more common than that she should observe this fact in herself and comment upon it.*[5]

Reading this, I recall that at the age of fifteen my doubts and uncertainties were more about the sanity of my parents than anything else. How could they not understand that it was *not* too cold in March to go camping? I mean, we didn't live at the North Pole exactly. How could they not grasp what my friends would think if I wasn't able to go away with them for St. Patrick's weekend? How could I possibly sit at home when all my friends were away? Could they not experience what I was feeling? I could show you the spot in our neighbourhood where I blackmailed my mother saying I would never pray again if she failed to persuade my father on this issue. She usually took my

---

[5] Batzdorff, Susanne M., *Aunt Edith, The Jewish Heritage of a Catholic Saint,* p 67, Springfield, IL, Templegate Publishers

side in a predominantly male household, and luckily, she won that toss! Off I went to camp, and I never used that threat again.

When Edith began her university life in 1911 in Breslau, she took courses in several subjects. These included psychology, which was invaluable to her in the later development of her thought. But she became unhappy with this discipline. In 1913 she moved to the University of Göttingen, where Austrian-born Edmund Husserl, the 'father of phenomenology', was teaching. Edith became engrossed in what she was learning. One hundred years ago, the relationship between philosophy and psychology was very different to what it is in our times. Edith wrote:

> *All my psychological studies had led me to the view that this science had not got beyond its infancy, that it still lacked the essential, clear, basic concepts, and that it was in no condition to work out these basic concepts for itself. And what I had so far learnt about phenomenology had captivated me precisely because it set itself this task of classification and was fashioning the very conceptual tools one needed.*[6]

When Edith reached Göttingen she found the philosophy lectures took place right up under the roof of the new Seminar Building, whereas the Psychology Institute was entirely separate being situated in the area of St. John's Church, a little west of the marketplace in an old house with worn steps and narrow rooms. She wrote: "This spatial separation in itself indicated clearly that philosophy and psychology had nothing to do with each other in Göttingen".[7] She loved this magical time, of which she later wrote:

---

[6] *Edith Stein* op. cit. p.22
[7] Ibid, p 25

Dear Göttingen! I do believe only someone who studied here between 1905 and 1914, this short flowering of the Gottingen School of Phenomenology, can appreciate all that resonates in that name. I was twenty-one years old and looked forward full of expectation to all that lay ahead.

Before going there, she had been told by a tutor in Breslau who had spent a semester studying with Edmund Husserl: "In Göttingen all you do is philosophize, day and night, in the streets, at meals, everywhere. All you talk about is 'phenomena'.[8]

Phenomenology as developed by Husserl is a way of exploring *how* we know *what* we know. This method of investigation differed greatly from the analytic school of philosophy that dominated thought in the English-speaking world at the time[9]. It also differed from earlier German philosophers who sought to understand *how* we know *what* we know about others.

In the hundred years since Edith's time, the answer to this question would become very important for research in the disciplines of sociology, psychology and healthcare as they developed. Researchers today look to Edith's work on the question of empathy as foundational to the study of social cognition.

Edith's doctoral dissertation *The Problem of Empathy*[10] says: "The goal of phenomenology is to clarify and thereby to find the ultimate basis of all knowledge."

---

[8] Cf Susanne Batzdorff, op. cit., p.112

[9] Philosophers like Ludwig Wittgenstein and Bertrand Russell worked from a study of linguistics, sometimes invoking mathematics, to study *how* we know *what* we know.

[10] The title of the treatise originally was *The Empathy Problem as It Developed Historically and Considered Phenomenologically.* In the opening chapter she traced the work of philosophers of the 18th and 19th centuries on this topic, but this chapter has been lost.

Many of her predecessors understood that the way we know the relationship between a physical body and that person's internal psychological states is by inference, i.e. applying reason to arrive at further conclusions from what is already known. Edith saw it differently. We know these things by empathy, she understood. In an empathetic experience we are presented with persons, not just with bodies. These persons may be angry, or grieving, or joyful. Persons and their mental states are observable, presenting us with something akin to perceptions. How to clarify these perceptions was the big challenge.

Edith would claim that engagement in empathetic acts also enhances our self-knowledge. Empathy is essential to understanding one's own set of values. Empathy reveals to me what kind of person I am. Together with self-knowledge we also have an important aid to self-evaluation.

She devoted much thought and research into developing a successive step-by-step methodology on two inter-related levels in order to reach the experience another person is having. Students today, like those of Edith's generation, continue to explore this aspect of understanding in the fields of cognitive science, sociology, and psychology. Empathy, as she developed it, is understood as a theory of the emotions. Our emotions are responsible for grasping information about the world. They give us a valuable perspective on what matters.

Just as her theory of empathy draws the disciplines of philosophy and psychology closer to one another, so also it invokes the praxis of social care. Through empathy she wants us to ask ourselves what leads us to respond with sensitivity and care to the suffering of another. Thus, she sees empathy as one of the key constituents in an ethics of care.

Husserl's thought process was very complex, but this is the thing: when studying phenomena, the researcher must focus solely on the experience being researched, nothing else. This means that when looking at a situation the researcher must refrain from judgement and bias and opinion in order to wholly focus on and seek to understand the experience. Husserl developed a very detailed procedure for this. Others, like Martin Heidegger who followed him, developed different procedures. To this day researchers are refining this task and coming up with new methods, but all derive from one or other of the two streams developed by Husserl and Heidegger.

As a process, phenomenology has been likened to Yoga. It is a meditative task. The best explanation I've come across for focussing on an experience is the analogy of a microscope[11]. When one focusses the microscope on an object – say, a part of an insect – one is directing attention to one object alone in what would otherwise be a wider a field of vision. It is somewhat similar when our minds zoom in on an experience to be studied in phenomenology.

In 2021, a step-by-step guide to assist doctoral students today in presenting their research in the fields of social science and healthcare was published by Katarzyna Peoples of Walden University.[12] As well as providing insight into the thought of Husserl, Heidegger and later philosophers, this book gives the student detailed guidance on interview processes. She writes: "Philosophical research questions have one unwavering rule.

---

[11] R. Puligandla, *Phenomenological Reduction and Yogic Meditation*, Philosophy East and West, Vol 20, No. 1 (Jan. 1970), pp 19-33, University of Hawaii Press *http://www.jstor.org/stable/1397657*

[12] Katarzyna Peoples, *How to Write a Phenomenological Dissertation*, (2021), Sage Publications Inc. This author had completed her early studies, and obtained her Master's and Doctorate at Duquesne, where Adrian Van Kaam had introduced phenomenology to the Department of Psychology.

The inquiry must always be about experience as lived." She gives the example: "How do teenage girls describe friendship in high school?"

This is not a phenomenological question since opinions and descriptions are the focus. A phenomenological question could be created by changing the focus to experience: "What are the lived experiences of friendship among teenage girls?" In drawing up their interview questions, students must only ask about experiences, not about thoughts, feelings, or perceptions. When analysing the data, students need to slow down and live through their participants' descriptions as if they were their own.

War

When war was declared in 1914, Edith felt her country needed her. She paused her studies and with the Red Cross in Breslau trained to nurse sick and wounded soldiers. This included spells in different hospitals under the direction of the nurse in charge. There were so many volunteers applying to the Red Cross that it was not until April 1915 that she received her assignment. She had hoped to be sent to a field hospital at the war front. Instead, she was assigned to a hospital where 4,000 men with infectious diseases were receiving treatment near Mährisch-Weisskirchen, about 300 km south of Breslau. The soldiers there were suffering from cholera, typhoid, diphtheria and venereal disease.

It was a new world to Edith, and she sometimes found the rough-and-tumble behaviour of the soldiers quite upsetting. She wrote: "I got the impression that the sick were not used to getting loving attention and that volunteer helpers therefore could find endless opportunities to show their own compassion and love of neighbour in these places of suffering." Her patients, co-workers, nurses, and doctors viewed her as a warm person, a gentle carer, a person who was able to form friendships easily. This is evidenced in Edith's own memoir of those days which is included in her *Life in a Jewish Family*. She describes her work on the typhoid wards in great detail.

The hospital's patient cohort changed radically following the launch of the Gorlice-Tarnów offensive which began on May 1, 1915, some 250 km further east. Edith would not have known that her fellow-philosopher, Ludwig Wittgenstein, was a soldier on this battlefront. A few weeks earlier on the Western front, the German army had made the first ever large-scale use of chemical weapons. Following the destruction of Ypres and having crushed Belgian and French fortresses, they used 500 trains to urgently transport troops and equipment to the Eastern front.

The ground battles of the new offensive were enhanced with air attacks and an effective mobile field telephone service. In the first three days of battle, the captured Russian soldiers were estimated to number 12,000 men. By May 3rd, Gorlice was in ruins. Successive offensives between May and October 1915 caused the total collapse of the Russian lines.

The new cohorts of wounded men now came from the many different cultures that made up the Austro-Hungarian Empire. Edith was re-assigned to the Operating Room in her block, where she quickly became responsible for the sterilisation of surgical instruments, ensuring the surgeons had what they needed at the three operating tables. Her memoir also records her first experiences of attending young men at the hour of death.

By autumn, however, as one German victory followed another, her contract as a Red Cross volunteer was coming to an end.

She struggled with the decision to return to her studies. She knew there were very many women volunteering for the work she was doing. She informed the Red Cross that she was available to take up a further assignment, but she was not called up for this. She returned to her studies, knowing from experience how empathy was not only a tool of research about human knowledge, but also a tool in the human encounter and understanding of pain and loss.

Like all young men and women of her generation, the First World War ended the carefree lives Edith and her friends had enjoyed.[13] Many of the young men in her circle left to train for battle. She sent parcels to the warfront for Hans Lipps,[14] one of the men in the group of young people who were exploring the ideas of Husserl and their application in various disciplines. Hans had been studying medicine and natural science as well as philosophy.

Edith's niece, Suzanne Batzdorff, tells us that Edith seemed to have had serious feelings for Hans and kept a photo of him on her desk. He later married in 1923. When his wife died in 1932, he proposed marriage to Edith, but by then it was too late. She had 'found another path', as her niece records.[15]

Edith's doctoral dissertation was written during the years when her religious belief was in some kind of suspension. In the very last section important questions arise. She asks:

> *Is it essentially necessary that spirit can only enter into exchange with spirit through the medium of corporeality?...*

---

[13] Details of how the war affected young people on the other side of that war are famously recorded by Vera Brittain who writes about 'the lost generation', cf. *Testament of Youth*, Penguin Classics.

[14] During the second world war, Hans was conscripted again. He was killed while serving as a medical doctor on the Russian front in 1941.

[15] Suzanne Batzdorff, op. cit., pp 184-185.

> *There have been people who thought that in a sudden change of their person they experienced the effect of the grace of God, others who felt themselves to be guided in their conduct by a protective spirit ... Who can say that there is genuine experience present here ... the study of religious consciousness seems to me to be the most appropriate means of answering our question, just as, on the other hand, its answer is of most interest for the domain of religion. However, I leave the answering of this question to further investigation and satisfy myself here with a* 'non liquet'. *It is not clear.*

While trying to complete her dissertation, she was feeling a sense of her own spiritual poverty. Like many who embark upon doctoral studies, she began to despair of ever understanding the task she had undertaken. Her level of depression became quite serious. An important person in her life at that time was Adolf Reinach, one of the tutors who explained Husserl's thinking to students at Göttingen. He came from a prominent Jewish family. He was a very revered scholar whom Edith asked to look at the work she had written with much self-doubt. Seeing Edith's desolation, he invited her to stay with him and his wife, Anna, at their home.

This in itself was a lesson in empathy. They challenged her to cope with her self-doubt and depression. They told her that they were in the process of preparing for their baptism in the Lutheran faith. Looking back on that experience, Edith later wrote that she was transformed almost without knowing it. It gave her the stability to finish and present her doctoral thesis, which was granted *summa cum laude.*

Edith followed Husserl who moved from Göttingen to Freiburg and embraced the role of his assistant after Adolf Reinach left for war service. Husserl, too, had been born into a Jewish family, but in his late twenties he had been baptized in the

Lutheran community. Without any initiative on his part, many of Husserl's students converted to or rediscovered Christianity.

Being Husserl's assistant was not an easy job! In fact, it was very messy. All his notes were written in a form of shorthand known as Gabelsberger stenography. This was widely in use among scholars at that time. It was also used by Martin Heidegger. In order to decipher Husserl's thoughts Edith had to master this 'language' in addition to her mastery of French, Latin, and Greek as well as having a good command of English.

During the war paper became very scarce. Later researchers estimate that Husserl's writing was on some 40,000 pages, often written on scraps of paper, even on the back of receipts. He left her at her task, without personal involvement while he got on with more writing. This was not what Edith was expecting when she offered to become his assistant. She found it a lonely task and would like to have been writing herself.

From her frank personal correspondence with tutors and friends, we get a good insight into how difficult and frustrating this was. Students were travelling to Germany from many countries to learn this new approach to research and she knew that if she did not do this work, valuable ideas would not be accessible to them. Worse still, much of Husserl's thought would be lost to the scholars of future generations who would stand on his shoulders.

Edith also became good friends with Husserl's wife, Malvine[16] to whom she referred as "my staunch patron". Edith expressed

---

[16] From helpful footnotes in the publication of Edith's letters by ICS Publications in 1993, we learn that in 1940, two years after the death of her husband, Malvine Husserl was helped by a Franciscan priest, H.L. Van Breda, to bring her husband's entire literary legacy to Belgium where it was placed in the Catholic University at Leuven. She herself was hidden from

her frustrations about the work in several letters to her friend, Roman Ingarden, the Polish philosopher whose doctoral thesis was also under the direction of Husserl. She wrote in January 1917:

> *The Master's latest prognosis for the production of* Ideen: *first of all, I am to stay with him until I marry; then I may only accept a man who will also become his assistant, and the same holds for the children. Highly* impropitius! *Even apart from the time, the requisite preconditions are absent. For if, in the long run it is not entirely beyond the realm of the possible that someone could be found who would not shy away from an alliance with me (and vice versa), I deem it essentially impossible that a man could be his assistant ... we hardly talk together anymore. For me this is very painful, for matters are very complicated and the material I have in hand is altogether incomplete. However, I am working pretty independently now and that is, of course, very enjoyable, but some exchange of ideas could be very beneficial. So I would have a great deal of use for you now, and in all likelihood you would get more from me on a philosophical plane than in the terrible time during which I had become a semi-imbecile from getting the manuscript notes in order.*

And in February 1918:

> *I can only continue with this occupation if I do something original on the side. I am curious what he will have to say to that... I can place myself at the service of something, and I can do all manner of things for the love of someone, but to be*

---

the Nazis by Catholic religious brothers and sisters. She kept up correspondence with Edith until her deportation to Auschwitz. Malvine also became Catholic. In 1945, she was able to join her surviving son and daughter in America, returning to Germany a short time before her death in 1950.

at the service of a person, in short – to obey, is something I cannot do. And if Husserl will not accustom himself once more to treat me as a collaborator in the work – as I have always considered our situation to be and he, in theory, did likewise – then we shall have to part company. I would regret that, for I believe there would then be even less hope of a connection between himself and 'youth'.

While experiencing great difficulty in her work situation, Edith continued to greatly respect and value 'The Master', as everyone called Husserl. By agreement, they ended the arrangement that she work as his assistant in 1918. Writing to her contemporary, Fritz Kaufmann[17] in November 1919 she admitted that during the two years of her personal relationship with Husserl, it was not easy to maintain the right attitude:

One must keep reminding oneself that he himself suffers most because he has sacrificed his humanity to his science. That is so overpowering and the amount of gratitude we owe him for it is so incalculable that, in view of that, any kind of personal resentment should not even arise. For me, he will always remain the Master, whose image cannot be blurred by any human weakness.

Grief in Process

In 1916 and again in 1917 Edith visited Pauline Reinach, a sister of Adolf. By this time, they had become close friends. Pauline later became a Catholic and a Benedictine nun in Belgium. Writing her memoir in the 1930s, Edith could not recall on which of these occasions they visited the Cathedral in Frankfurt together. While there, Edith observed a woman coming in

[17] Despite Edith's reservations about a man being able to work with Husserl, Fritz Kaufmann worked as his assistant until 1938, the year Husserl died, and the year Kaufmann was able to emigrate to America.

with her market basket and kneeling down in one of the pews to say a prayer. Edith later recalled:

> *This was something entirely new to me. To the Synagogues or to the Protestant churches which I had visited, one went only for services. But here was someone interrupting her everyday shopping errands to come into this church, although no person was in it, as though she were here for an intimate conversation. I could never forget that.*

Later, Pauline led her along the River Main to visit the Liebig Institute where they stopped at a 16th century sculptured group. The artist's work was empowered with empathy. Edith later described "the Mother of God, and John in the center; Magdalen and Nicodemus on either side. There was no longer an image of Christ in the group. These figures had such an overpowering effect on us that, for a long while, we were unable to tear ourselves away."[18]

In November 1917, the dreadful news came that Adolf Reinach was killed during the fighting at Flanders. He was thirty-three years of age. This brought untold grief to his many friends and former students. Husserl asked Edith to represent him at the funeral. She was totally distraught. Anna Reinach, coping with her personal bereavement, asked Edith to come to their home and sort all Adolf's papers. The fortitude and serenity of this young widow amazed Edith. She later acknowledged: "That was my first encounter with the Cross and the divine power it bestows on those who carry it ... That was the moment my unbelief collapsed, and Christ shone forth."

During her time in Göttingen, Edith had become close friends with the couple Theodore Conrad and Hedwig Martius, both well-known philosophers. In the summer of 1921, she was

---

[18] This visit is described in detail in *Life in a Jewish Family.*

staying at their home in Bergzabern where they managed an orchard to supplement their income. Lots of philosophers gathered there. Most biographers tell of the evening the couple had to leave Edith alone in their home. Before going out, Hedwig brought her over to their bookcase and suggested she pick something to read. Edith chose the autobiography of Saint Teresa of Avila and sat up all night reading it.

Another account of this experience is recorded by Pauline Reinach in her submission for Edith's canonization process. She says she definitely recalls that the above incident happened when Edith was staying with Anna Reinach. Whichever version is the correct one, it is clear that on completing the story of Teresa of Avila Edith felt 'this is the truth'. She realised that God is not knowledge. God is love.

A soul is not a phenomenon as she had assumed. It is perceptible in the same way that light is perceptible, though its source may be unknown. God does not respond to intellectual search, but to the soul that surrenders to God's embrace. Next morning she went out and bought a copy of the New Testament and began to study it. She soon found that resting in God offered a break from her intellectual activities.

For the first time Edith went to Mass at St. Martin's Church in Bergzabern and immediately asked the pastor there to arrange her baptism. A dispensation was procured so that Hedwig Martius, of Protestant faith, could be her sponsor. On New Year's Day of 1922, Edith was baptized in the Catholic faith. She took Teresa Hedwig as her baptismal names. She received her first Holy Communion on January 2nd and Confirmation a month later.

Frau Stein had long known that Edith was not observing the Jewish practices, but this was a much bigger blow. She and other members of Edith's family viewed Catholicism as a superstitious sect. There were no Catholics among their acquaintances. Most of them in Breslau belonged to the lowest strata of economic life.

Having been denied a university post due to her gender and her Jewish origins, Edith took up a teaching post at a boarding school for girls in the town of Speyer on the Rhine. It was run by Dominican sisters. Edith had accommodation in the convent quarters. She lived and worked there from 1923 until 1932 when she became a lecturer at the Institute for Pedagogy in Münster.

Here also she was able to live at the Marianum convent. From her youth, she had been committed to feminism. As a teenager, she participated in the Prussian Association for Women's Suffrage. She believed in the equal but complementary status of women and men. She advocated for sexual education in the school curriculum for both girls and boys alike. She was particularly concerned with women's access to all branches of education. She pointed to the special expertise women would have in law-making concerning women and children.

During these years she was frequently invited to speak to the Catholic Women Teachers' Association. Unlike other feminists who campaigned for equality with men, she emphasised the distinctiveness of women, who are essentially different from men and who have a critical social role as educators. A woman is more than a helpmate for a man. She has her own specific talents to bring to social and political life. In her public talks she discussed the feminine energies that would come from the ordination of women as priests and the fact that there is no dogma preventing this.

At the same time, she was translating from English to German some of the writings of Cardinal John Henry Newman and the work of Thomas Aquinas on *Disputed Questions on Truth.* She was enthralled to find that this described not only the relationship of faith and reason but showed the way to a mystical union with Truth. In 1927 in the autumn, she went for retreat to a Benedictine Monastery at Beuron on the Upper Danube. With guidance from the young Abbot, Dom Rafael Walzer, her ability to pray deeply for hours was honed. But her attraction to the Carmelite way of life was not diminished by this experience of Benedictine spirituality.

In 1933 Hitler became German Chancellor with almost dictatorial powers. The Nazis launched a deeper offensive against the Jews. Early that year, Edith wrote to Pope Pius XI requesting an audience. It was not granted. She decided to put in writing what she would have said if she had been granted an audience. During the Easter holidays she would visit Beuron and ask her spiritual director, Abbot Walzer, to forward the letter to the Vatican. With this in view, she did not date the letter at the time of writing, and it eventually was sent to the Pope Pius XI undated. Edith never received a personal reply. Abbot Walzer was thanked in a letter from the Secretary of State, Eugenio Pacelli, who became Pope Pius XII. It said: "I leave it to you to inform the sender in an opportune way that her letter has been dutifully presented to His Holiness ...". Edith's letter remained in the Vatican archives for seventy years until 2003. It is published in full in the second edition of the work of her niece, Susanne Batzdorff, *Aunt Edith: The Jewish Heritage of a Catholic Saint.* The pain caused by the lack of response to the letter is revealed in the final chapter of that book.

As Hitler's grip tightened, Edith's employers at Münster felt they could no longer have a Jewish-born person on the staff.

Edith felt this was her opportunity to fulfil her dream of becoming a Carmelite. She was almost forty-two years of age but was welcomed by the community at Cologne. Frau Stein, now eighty-four years of age, felt her daughter was deserting the Jewish community in their hour of greatest need. Edith had to draw deeply on her faith during this very dark period. She knew the Cologne Carmelites had planned to establish a new community in Breslau and she requested from the beginning that she would be assigned there in due course, hoping for closer contact with her mother. Meanwhile, as recorded by the Prioress at Cologne in the opening of her book:

> *Week by week, usually on Friday morning, there was a knock at the door of my cell. At my 'Come in', Sister Benedicta would enter with a letter addressed to 'Frau Auguste Stein, Breslau, Michaelisstrasse 38'.*

For a long time, the heart-broken Frau Stein could not bring herself to reply. Edith's request to be transferred to the new Carmel in Breslau was not granted.[19] But when the construction work for the new monastery had begun, in the Autumn of 1935 her mother went over to that part of the city and stood observing the site. We can only guess her feelings! From that time on she added a few lines at the bottom of Rosa's letters to Edith. Rosa also wanted to become a Catholic, but seeing her mother's desolation at Edith's decision, she waited until after her mother's death to be baptised.

In the new year of 1934, the Cologne Carmelite community were preparing for the 300th anniversary of the founding of their monastery. Edith was very happy when her older sister, Rosa, decided to become a Catholic too. But the situation in

---

[19] When that foundation took place, it was decided that having a community member of Jewish origin living there would be too dangerous.

Germany for people of Jewish origin was becoming ever more dangerous. Edith began to think about death. She saw her future as the way of the Cross and accepted this. She could see that Hitler wanted a wider war than just exterminating the Jews and other peoples he considered of lower status. His sights were on conquering the whole of Europe.

By the end of 1938 the time had come to get out of Germany. On New Year's Eve, Edith bade goodbye to her community in Cologne where Christmas celebrations that year had been muted. Under cover of darkness, she was driven one hundred and nine kilometers across the border into The Netherlands, to join the Carmelite community at Echt. It was still safe there, but Edith knew it would not be for long. She wrote "I joyfully accept in advance the death God has appointed for me".

In 1939, Rosa was able to reach Echt via Belgium. Edith was very happy to be reunited with her sister, but they were warned that Echt would not be a permanent solution to their problem. Rosa requested to become a Carmelite at Echt but at 56 years of age she was not accepted. However, she was welcomed to remain with the community as an Extern, and work as portress.

In 1940 Hitler conquered The Netherlands. When the community at Echt had begun preparations to mark the fourth centenary of the birth of St. John of the Cross in 1542, Edith was asked to write about his legacy. She took the Cross as the centre of her study of his life and works.

By 1942 a ghetto of 14,000 Jews had been established in Amsterdam. Concentration camps were built throughout Holland. Thousands of Jews were deported to Buchenwald, Mounthausen, and Auschwitz. Edith had the opportunity to transfer to a Carmelite community at Le Paquier in Switzerland where she would have been safe. But there were administrative difficulties that prevented her sister, Rosa, from being accepted and Edith would not go without her. Those difficulties were resolved afterwards, and they were both granted entry to Switzerland, but by then it was too late.

During that summer the Catholic Bishops of The Netherlands, together with leaders of other Christian faiths, attempted to intervene with the Nazis on behalf of the people of Jewish origin. These efforts were rebuffed. Consequently, a pastoral letter was read in all Catholic churches in the Netherlands on 26th July 1942 which asked God "to strengthen the people of Israel so sorely tested these days..." This was the last straw for the Nazis. On August 2nd all Catholics of Jewish origin were rounded up. At 5 pm, Edith had read the opening prayer as the community began their evening hour of meditation. Then a loud banging on the front door resounded through the cloister. The prioress was told to summon Edith and her sister Rosa. Through the grille they were ordered to be ready in five minutes.

They were driven by a squad car to a camp in Amersfoort, a journey of 164 km. With the help of dogs and clubs, more than 1,000 Jews were herded roughly into their quarters. Two survivors testified that Edith tried to be cheerful as she helped with the children. Two of her friends were among the crowd. Fifteen members of religious communities including two priests began the Rosary and other prayers. Forms had to be filled out and signed. Husbands and wives were separated, and relatives had to say goodbye to one another.

Enormous efforts were made to establish what exactly happened to Edith and Rosa after that, much of which is recorded in the large body of literature that has since been published. Survivors remembered how during those few days Edith took care of those she could, helping to wash clothes and clean the barracks into which they had been crowded.

They were told they would be moved to Westerbork and could write letters. Edith wrote to Echt requesting toiletries and blankets, which the community despatched quickly by car. The drivers met Edith and Rosa. Edith told them they expected to be taken to work in the coalmines. But not so. Early next morning a siren wailed to awaken the prisoners. They were herded into a goods train that would take them on the long slow journey of 1,184 km to Auschwitz, crawling through Cologne, stopping at Schifferstadt, not far from Speyer. Station officials opened the doors of the train to relieve the stench.

Edith called out to the Station Master on the platform and was seen dropping a note on the tracks which was picked up by a priest and delivered to the Dominicans in Speyer. It read: "Greetings from Sister Teresa Benedicta a Cruce. En route for the East."[20]

When the train reached Breslau on 7th August, it pulled up alongside another train waiting for signalling clearance. On board that train was a group of conscripted postal workers. When a security guard opened the door of the wagon opposite, one of them noticed a woman dressed like a nun. The stench from the wagon was overwhelming and the awful degradation of the occupants listlessly squatting on the floor could be observed.

The postal worker, who is named as Joannes Wieners, had some conversation with her. She looked into the distance and told him this was Breslau, where she grew up and which she would never see again. He offered to organize some food and

---

[20] Quoted by Peter Tyler in *The Living Philosophy of Edith Stein*, Bloomsbury Academic Series.

drink for the prisoners, but she replied: "No thank you, we won't take anything." Author Peter Tyler movingly tells readers: "These are the last recorded words that we have of Edith Stein: philosopher, women's rights activist, Jew, Catholic, Carmelite and saint."

Edith's death is officially recorded as 9th August 1942.[21] Despite tireless investigations, it still remains uncertain as to when, where, and how Edith and Rosa died. It is known that industrialised extermination was seen as economical, using gas to choke the prisoners in groups and then burning their bodies in ovens. In the postscript printed in the 1950 edition of *Edith Stein*, a parish priest in Württemberg reports what he was told by a parishioner who had been a guard in Auschwitz. The priest is quoted:

> *I am very much inclined to accept his version, because he quite spontaneously claimed that he recognized the Sister the very moment I showed him the picture, and before I had explained my reasons for showing it to him. He would not have it that Sister Benedicta must have been wearing prisoner's clothes when she arrived; that was not the case with any of the transports to Auschwitz. On the same day at the beginning of August – he cannot remember the exact date – two transports arrived from Holland, one of men in the morning and one of women about ten at night. Both were ticked off at the guardhouse as transports of insane people ... The train had taken him further into the camp than he was usually supposed to go. Finding himself alone he risked going further still and noticed the Sister in the middle portion of the train;*

[21] Her older sister, Frieda Tworoger, born in 1881, died in Teresinstadt in 1942; their older brother, Paul, born in 1872 and his wife, Trude born that same year, also died in Teresinstadt in 1943; Eva, born in 1915, daughter of Edith's brother, Arno, also became a victim of the Holocaust in 1943.

around her were people who seemed to know her, but who were not wearing religious habits. Possibly there were more Sisters further forward. At other times lists of people for working parties were drawn up even from transports of women, but no one from this transport was noticed in the following days; it was therefore believed that all these victims had stripped off their clothes at the usual spot and then been herded naked about a quarter of a mile to the place of slaughter. Here they had been burnt in the crematorium – immediately after they had arrived.[22]

Back in Echt, in Edith's room the community found the open manuscript of the study of John of the Cross upon which she had been working. She had read how all that is mortal is consumed in the fire of eternal love. She noted how John of the Cross uses the night symbol to describe the journey through which the soul must pass to reach union with God. She understood that the human spirit is destined for immortal being.

Edith's writings from 1933 were not published until after her death. On January 6, 1945, the community at Echt were forced to flee ahead of bombings by the Allied forces. Three days later one of the community managed to return to Echt and salvaged two sacks of Edith's papers which they had carefully put in order after her death. There was no space to store them safely in the tiny convent at Herkenbosch where they were sheltering.

After the capture of the Netherlands by the Allied forces, huge efforts were made to retrieve her writings. The Franciscan professor, Fr. Hermann Van Breda of Louvain, and the Carmelite Prior of Geleen borrowed a military vehicle and searched in vain in the ruins of the bombed Carmel at Echt. They drove on, through snow bound roads, for twenty kilometers to

---

[22] Op. cit., p.237

Herkenbosch and there found the two sacks, 'three-quarters of which were scattered about, very dirty and torn.' [23]

Edith's last major philosophical work was *Finite and Eternal Being*. As soon as the war ended, dedicated researchers began to piece together all she had written. Scholars today say there is still much to be done to unpack the depth of this work.

The core of this writing is the fruit of her reflection on 'the meaning of being'. Having written about being which is finite, she then reflects on that which is eternal. She draws upon the thinking of Thomas Aquinas but goes beyond it. She wants to understand how finite beings can have a share in Divine being. She reflects on the relationship between the Second Person of the Trinity - the Divine Word - and creation. She concludes that all finite being is rooted in eternal being. She also considers how the relationship between the Creator and creation differs from relations among the Trinity. She concludes that the way of faith gives us more than philosophical knowledge - it reveals to us the God of personal nearness.[24]

Unknown to Edith while she was studying the legacy of St. John of the Cross in 1940, in the town of Gemert sixty-four kilometers to the north of Echt, a twenty-year-old Dutchman was preparing for profession of vows in the seminary of the Holy Ghost Fathers. His name was Adrian Van Kaam. He would later be trapped behind Nazi front lines in the western Netherlands when he went there on retreat in 1944. Although starving himself, Van Kaam took any food he could procure to Jews who were in hiding. This period permanently affected his

---

[23] Op. cit., p.226

[24] Cf Alex Terego, *Edith Stein, Philosopher, Mystic, Martyr, Feminist*. Kindle Edition 2013. www.alexterego.com

health, making it impossible for him to serve abroad as a missionary.

After his ordination to the priesthood, he became a seminary professor, eventually being assigned to America to teach faith formation at Duquesne University run by the Spiritans. Before long he was asked to move to the psychology department and began work for his doctorate on *The Experience of Really Feeling Understood by a Person.* Van Kaam's work put the study of phenomenology at the core of the psychology department at Duquesne, where scholars continued to explore and develop its use. Van Kaam was later involved in creating the Institute of Formative Spirituality. This played an important role in the future of Catholic spirituality after Vatican II.

Pope John Paul II had good reasons to follow closely the cause for beatification prepared by those who had been influenced by Edith Stein. Growing up in his native Poland he understood the conflicts and struggles of the war years and the reality of the Shoah. He had many Jewish friends from his young schooldays into his adult life. Like all his contemporaries, he suffered from the harsh restrictions of the Gestapo once they occupied Poland in September 1939. When they forced his university to close down, he had to take up menial and laborious work. His efforts to help Jews during those years is well documented.

He later studied philosophy under Roman Ingarden, the Polish Catholic phenomenologist who was one of Edith's close friends from her student years. Like Edith, after his ordination, Karol Wojtyla studied the writing of Thomas Aquinas and the philosophy of Max Scheler, obtaining doctorates for his development of the ideas of both these thinkers.

As Pope, he was intent upon furthering reconciliation between Christians and Jews as well as between Christians and Muslims. He saw that Edith Stein could be a figure to bridge the centuries-old strain between Christians and Jews. But there was little he could do that would pour balm on the wound that was felt when Edith's letter to Pope Pius XI was not acknowledged to Edith personally and was filed away for seventy years.

Perhaps there is little Pope Pius XI could have done in 1933 that would have put a stop to Hitler's vendetta; by speaking out he might even have made matters more difficult for Jews who had become Catholics. But not communicating to Edith some kind of concern for the issues she had raised left a very deep wound, not just to her personally but to the Jewish community who came to know these facts later.

At the beginning of Mass, Catholics often pray the '*confiteor*'. This prayer asks pardon for 'what we have done and what we have failed to do'. For most of us, what we have failed to do is likely to have caused more pain and lasting harm than anything harmful we have ever done.

The final chapter of *Aunt Edith: The Jewish Heritage of a Catholic Saint* is given the heading *A Letter Long Delayed*. This revelation of the pain caused by the failure to acknowledge to Edith her detailed plea for intervention on behalf of the Jewish people makes very difficult reading.

More positively however, in the previous chapter, there is a detailed description by this observant Jew of her aunt's canonization in Rome in 1998. She tells us of the effect of this event on her extended family, of whom 97 travelled to Rome for that ceremony. They came from the United States, Germany, Switzerland, Colombia, South America, and Israel. Four generations were involved, and they included Jews, Catholics, and Protestants. The event affected them in different ways, some very positively, some otherwise. Her brother Ernst, who had declined the invitation to attend the Beatification in Cologne Cathedral back in 1987, came to Rome for the Canonisation, but only to use the opportunity to make a protest.

Edith had been devoted to her family all her life. One of the fringe benefits of the family gathering at her canonisation, her niece felt, was that some members of the younger generation who met in Rome became friends and are continuing to keep in touch. But, on a wider stage, she notes:

> *The dialogue continues, not just among family members, but also among the faiths. Controversies and misunderstandings continue to happen, but people of good will try to overcome conflict with free-wheeling discussion to create better understanding.*

Susanne Batzdorff writes that naming Edith as one of the three women patron saints of Europe can be, "a permanent goad to Europe's conscience".

That is exactly what many German people have been during the past eighty years. As soon as they got back on their feet after the war, groups of concerned people looked far beyond their national boundaries to respond to those in great need. In 1957 the global relief of contagious illnesses like tuberculosis and Hansen's disease was addressed.[25] As needs arise they still finance efforts to eradicate Buruli ulcer, Chagas disease, yaws, lymphatic filariasis, schistosomiasis and other neglected tropical diseases. In 1958 the Bishops of Germany built upon the already existing efforts of Catholic communities to form the

---

[25] See Deutsche Lepra-und Tuberkulosehilfe e.V.

organization we know as *Misereor.*[26] Based in Aachen, this is a generous and knowledge-based agency of the church's global *Caritas* network.

As Europe – like other continents – now copes with unprecedented change, perhaps we can hope that Edith Stein as Patron of Europe offers us something more than a goad to conscience. The number of scholars who continue to explore her writing gives rise to reading groups and eager students around the world who are exploring her legacy. Some focus on her philosophical investigations; others reflect on her spiritual writing; those drawn to contemplative prayer study her insights on finite and eternal being. What if we could all learn from her to step back and take the time to focus deeply on what other people are experiencing wherever they are? What if we could make it a lifetime's ambition to become accomplished in the essence of empathy? [27]

---

[26] See www.misereor.org.

[27] I feel deeply indebted to Thomas Szanto and Dermot Moran for their detailed research. Cf. "Edith Stein" in The Stanford Encyclopaedia of Philosophy (Spring 2020 Edition). Also, to Elisa Magri and Dermot Moran, *Essays on Edith Stein's Phenomenological Investigations,* Center for Advanced Research in Phenomenology, Vol 94. My study of Edith's thinking has also been greatly helped in conversation with Fr. Thomas Tusuubira who introduced me to the recent work of Íngrid Vendrell Ferran.
See https://www.jstor.org/stable/22475460 and also Fredrick Svenaeus. https://doi.org/10.1007/s11097-017-9544-9 and the thoughts of Kris McDaniel *Ten Neglected Philosophical Classics,* ed. Eric Schliesser, Oxford University Press.

CHAPTER 2

A LIFE LIVED IN EMPATHY

MARIE MARTIN WHO FOUNDED the Medical Missionaries of Mary[1] was born in Glenageary in the suburbs of Dublin on 25th April 1892, just six months after Edith Stein had been born on 12th October 1891 in the town of Breslau, then part of Germany[2].

Edith's birth was on the feast of Yom Kippur, the holiest day of the year in Judaism. It was a most significant day for her mother. I am fascinated by the amazing complementarity about the way these two women who never met came to understand empathy – despite their widely differing personal gifts.

The keynote in Marie's growth from adolescence to maturity was the way she developed empathy as a personal attribute. It didn't matter whether people were wealthy or poor, if they were suffering, she would be moved to respond as if their suffering were her own.

There were remarkable coincidences in the young lives of these two women. Edith was the youngest of eleven siblings though

---

[1] Baptized Marie Helena Martin, she became known as Mother Mary Martin after her religious profession in Nigeria in 1937.

[2] Located on the Oder River, during Edith's youth it had a population of half a million people. In August 1945, Breslau became part of Poland, after the Soviet army had defeated the Nazis. It is now called Wroclau.

her parents had lost four children in their infancy before Erna, the second youngest was born, with Edith coming just eighteen months later. Marie was the second of twelve children and, like Edith, had a very close relationship with her mother.

Edith's father died when she was two, leaving the widowed Frau Stein, then aged just 44, to run the family lumber business. She was a merchant's daughter. She possessed all the talents needed to turn around what had been a debt-ridden business even though, at that time, it was uncommon for a woman to have this responsibility.

Her own siblings advised her against this. But she made a success of it. Her eldest daughter, Else, helped Frau Stein in caring for the younger members of the family, especially Edith and Erna. Her eldest son, Paul, after completing his apprenticeship, was drafted into the business.

It was known that Frau Stein had acquired such technical knowledge that she had only to pass by a wooded area to make an accurate estimate of its value as timber. She bought up whole forests in Croatia, had the wood sawn up on the spot, and then brought to Breslau as it was needed.

Marie's father died tragically when she was fourteen. The widowed Mrs. Martin, aged 41 and pregnant with her twelfth child, leaned a lot on her eldest daughter to help care for her younger siblings. Marie did so lovingly. Like the Stein family, the lumber trade underpinned the wealth of the Martins.

During the previous century, the family owned the first fleet of Tall Ships on the River Liffey, all vessels with a distinguished history[3]. They included *The Howth, The Fingal, The Dunboyne*

---

[3]Cf Flood, Patrick, (2021), *Aspects of Irish Maritime History both at Home and Abroad.* Self-published

and more. The Martins imported timber from Canada and Scandinavia and exported it to Australia, where they had offices at St. Kilda, near Melbourne, allowing the wood to mature on the long slow voyage. Marie's inheritance from this wealth was invested in establishing the health services to which she would devote her life.

Edith and Marie shared a keen sense of what they wanted and what they did not want. As young women, they both suffered fragile health. In their correspondence with family and friends, they both used expressions like 'terribly kind' and 'awfully good'. This would have drawn the wrath of teachers by the time I was learning to write!

Unlike Edith, Marie did not like school. In the Martin household in Dublin, the six resident-staff included a German governess who provided the four girls and eight boys with their early education.

As a teenager, Marie was sent to boarding school first with the Sisters of Mercy in Scotland and then with the Congregation of the Holy Child Jesus in England - but homesickness was always a big problem. Marie would pester her mother to let her return home. In April 1910, when Marie was eighteen, Mrs. Martin took her to Germany, to join two of her cousins at a residential finishing school in Bonn.

Marie thought travel was a great form of education and discovery. Travel would be her school for the rest of her life. She would learn all she needed to know through connecting with the people she would meet and listening to what they would tell her. It was not long until she found her way to an agent and booked tickets to Oberammergau for the Passion Play for herself and other family members. She also visited cities like

Munich and Cologne. She shared her mother's deep commitment to her Catholic faith.

Over the next few years, she studied the entire spiritual writings of Dom Columba Marmion, the Irish Abbot of the Benedictine monastery at Maredsous in Belgium. The Benedictine way of seeking God made a lot of sense to her.

A few months after Marie left Germany, her Uncle Charlie who was grieving the death of his wife, took his young niece with him on a cruise to the West Indies. This gave her the opportunity to witness another culture and meet more people. In those days, few Irish women of nineteen years of age would have travelled so much or have witnessed how people live outside their own family environment.

Like Edith and her friends in Germany, the war that broke out in 1914 changed everything for the Martin family. The tennis parties and dinner dances at their home in Monkstown suddenly stopped. Just as Edith had trained to nurse wounded Austrian soldiers, Marie and her younger sister, Ethel, volunteered for training with the Voluntary Aid Detachment of the Red Cross to nurse soldiers who were wounded while fighting the German army.

Marie's older brother, Tommy, who had recently graduated from Trinity College Dublin, joined the Connaught Rangers while her younger brother, Charlie, still an undergraduate, enlisted with the Royal Dublin Fusiliers.

In October of 1915 Marie sailed for Malta aboard the hospital ship *Oxfordshire.* At St. George's Hospital[4] with a bed comple-

---

[4] As Marie finished her time in Malta, the future British journalist Vera Brittain, was assigned by the Red Cross to St. George's Hospital. Like Marie, she later worked in France in a hospital on the coast of *Pas de Calais.* Her detailed descriptions of life as a VAD nurse throw much light on the

ment of 1,000, she soon became expert in the treatment of scabies, which the soldiers developed in the trenches. When winter really hit, as well as those wounded in the fighting, many developed frostbite and needed hospital treatment.

Malta became known as the 'Nurse of the Mediterranean'. Every large building was converted into a hospital. The work was nothing short of hard labour. As well as providing nursing care, the Red Cross volunteers were expected to do all the scrubbing and cleaning that would have been unknown to Marie from the gentle life of her early upbringing.

The Army discipline was a lot more rigorous than anything she would have known at school or at home. Marie adapted to this, not just willingly, but gratefully and joyfully. She discovered that it was not what was easiest that would make her happiest.

At Christmas of 1915 she was very involved with the other nurses decorating the wards. They planned entertainment to help the sick and wounded soldiers whose morale was very low. Then, on December 27th the most dreaded news arrived.

Her beloved younger brother, Charlie, was reported missing in action in Serbia. Following the disastrous and badly planned attempt of the British army to land troops, including the Royal Dublin Fusiliers, on five beaches of the peninsula of Gallipoli in April 1915, Charlie and his comrades had survived the second attempt in August, this time from Suvla Bay.[5] But as the total failure of that campaign began to be acknowledged, Charlie's battalion had been withdrawn to Serbia in October.

---

challenge of these assignments. See her autobiography *Testimony of Youth,* (1978), Virago Press, London.

[5] See Philip Lecane, (2015), *Beneath a Turkish Sky: The Royal Dublin Fusiliers and the Assault on Gallipoli,* The History Press Ireland

For the remaining four months in Malta, Marie used all her contacts, and all her off-duty time, trying to find out what had happened to Charlie and where he might be. She scanned the daily lists of wounded men. She watched out for each hospital ship docking in the port at Valletta, hoping Charlie might be on it. She found out where soldiers of Charlie's regiment were being nursed in Malta.

Then she travelled all over the island to talk to men who were with Charlie during that last battle. From them she learned how brave he had been as their Lieutenant and how well respected he was by all the soldiers he commanded, though he was a very young officer. She telephoned to the war-front office at Salonika to make enquiries, all to no avail.

Though often exhausted from her work and her strenuous efforts to get news, she would send her mother whatever scraps of information she could glean. They lived in hope and tried to keep their spirits up.

Marie was developing her gift of empathy. Though it was not part of her job description, she would sit up late at night to write to the wives and mothers of soldiers in her care who had died from their war injuries or illnesses. She could personally experience each mother's pain.

When her six-month contract in Malta was up, Marie sailed for home. She arrived as Dublin's city centre lay in ruins following the Easter 1916 rising against British rule, which led to the execution of sixteen leaders of the rebellion. After a month's rest Marie was reassigned to France. Under army rules, she could not tell her mother the name of her location, so she decided to give her three clues. Put this together: the opposite of 'soft', add the fifth letter of the alphabet, and the man in the Bible whose wife was turned into a pillar of salt[6].

July 2nd was the busiest day ever, the day the first casualties from the Somme arrived at Hardelot. Marie was very late getting off duty. When she did, she opened a letter from her mother confirming that Charlie had died in December, two days after he was captured and six months before his twenty-first birthday[7]. If there was any comfort in her grief, it was that Charlie had been spared the terrible suffering she was witnessing among her young patients.

When the Germans began using mustard gas - the first chemical weapons of warfare - Marie's days were devoted to the very patient, long-term recovery that the soldiers needed till their lungs healed enough to breathe once again. The doctors Marie worked with were experts in respiratory medicine. But in a letter home, Marie revealed that she could be the only nurse on duty in her tented ward of fifty-four patients, with just one orderly to help her. Echoing the words of Edith Stein in her correspondence of the time, Marie's letters were asking 'Will this war ever end?'

Years later, when Jean Paul Sartre was thinking about the meaning of being, he wrote that presence is important to our understanding of being, but he also discussed absence. He

---

[6] The military hospital was in Hardelot in Pas de Calais, the medical wards were set up in tents on the sand dunes overlooking the coast. The surgical wards were located in what had been the Aviation Hotel, so named in honour of Louis Bleriot who learnt to fly on the long beach at Hardelot and became the first pilot to complete the flight across the Channel in 1909.

[7] It was later established that, though shot in the arm and leg, Charlie continued defending the position while his men retreated to safety, for which he was posthumously awarded. Another bullet then lodged in his spine, leaving him paralyzed. He was taken to a Dressing Centre by the Bulgarian army, where he died on December 10, 1915.

imagined a situation where someone is expecting to find a person, whom he names Pierre, in a café. In fact, Pierre is not there. But the expectation of finding Pierre causes the absence of Pierre to be a real event.[8]

During the Battle of the Somme Marie had this experience. The love of her life was a young Irishman, Gerald Gartlan. When her mother asked her to which of the young men in the trenches she should send food parcels, Marie chose Gerald. Many years later she would admit: "He was the one I most loved in all the world". Each day she would scour the published lists of soldiers who had been wounded in the hope that she would *not* find Gerald's name there. For her, this absence would be an important fact.

But Gerald's mother had written to tell Marie that he had been wounded. Then she received a letter from him saying he was not too bad. His nerves had been affected but he was ready to return to the trenches. He hoped they could meet at a spot in Boulogne when he was on his way back and he gave her the date. Marie arranged her weekly half day off duty for that date. We can imagine her feelings as she boarded the tram for the 15-mile trip to Boulogne. They failed to meet. The absence of Gerald was a real event.

Something similar is revealed in the correspondence of Edith Stein about Hans Lipps. In May 1918, she wrote to a friend: "Lipps (100th *Leibgrenadier* Regiment, 1st Battalion) was slightly wounded a while ago and, on his return trip to the front, came through Göttingen on the very day I left. Since he knew nothing of my impending departure and I nothing of his presence, he slept through the few hours we might have spent together!"

---

[8] *Being and Nothingness*, p. 278

Three months later the experience of Hans' absence is also highlighted. She wrote to the same friend: "Lipps, who took part in the Battle of the Marne, recently announced he would be visiting me. Hering and I, however, have been waiting for him in vain for all of ten days."

The Impact of Grief

Edith developed an insight similar to the thinking of Sigmund Freud but arrived at independently. She described how an experience which took place in the past can exist in the background of present experience and still have an effect. This is very evident in the life of Marie Martin and indeed in Edith's own life.

The death of twenty-year-old Charlie Martin on 10 December 1915, following his capture two days earlier on the plains of Serbia, and the death of thirty-three-year-old Adolf Reinach in battle at Dixmuide, Flanders, on 16 November 1917, had profound life-changing effects on Marie and Edith respectively.

Marie's entire worldview was totally changed by the death of Charlie. The whole course of her life was impacted as she came to terms with this grief. Her war experience taught her that empathy and the work of healing was a sign of God's love. In the Gospel stories, she saw that these gifts were used by Jesus as a tool of his mission on Earth.

Back home from the war front, during 1917 while Marie was at prayer in her parish church at Monkstown, she came to realise that God was offering her a different path in life. She understood that her vocation was not to marriage. She must let Gerald go. In her diary she noted that she put on her new navy suit and white spats and set out to explain to him that they must say goodbye. She did not know what the future would entail.

All she knew was that the social life she used to enjoy no longer mattered. She would sacrifice the joy of motherhood for which she had hoped so much. The great influenza epidemic of 1918 soon reached Dublin, and she devoted all her time to helping her local doctor to cope with his large workload.

Marie felt God was calling her to establish a group who would employ healthcare as a tool of mission but her search for implementing this was deeply frustrating. In the 1917 Code of Canon Law, it was laid down that women or men in religious life could not become engaged in surgery or obstetrics.

In 1920, one of the presbyteries of her parish in Monkstown was a rented property at 16 Longford Terrace, overlooking Dublin Bay. Here lived one of the local curates, Fr. Tom Ronayne[9]. He had given Marie her first copy of the Bible. In 1920 he told Marie that he had been granted leave of absence from Dublin Diocese to go to Nigeria. He wanted her to meet Bishop Joseph Shanahan, who had recently been ordained Bishop and appointed Vicar Apostolic of Southern Nigeria.

Marie went to the Presbytery at Longford Terrace where she met the newly ordained Bishop. She gladly told him of her ideas about a medical missionary congregation of women and they agreed that she should qualify in midwifery at the National Maternity Hospital and go to Nigeria as a lay missionary as soon as she was ready.

When the *SS Elmina* docked at Calabar on 14th June 1921 and Marie prepared to disembark, Fr. Tom Ronayne rushed up the gangway to inform her that she must register with the immigration authorities as a teacher. This is how she discovered

---

[9] Later, at the age of 51, Fr. Ronayne joined the Spiritan Missionaries and became Bishop Shanahan's secretary. He died on Christmas Day in 1965 and is buried at the Cathedral in Onitsha

that she could not become involved in healthcare after all. Bishop Shanahan had realised that he needed to be careful with the colonial authorities. They were most anxious for him to develop the schools, but healthcare was in the hands of Protestant missionaries. He must not interfere with that. This was long before the era of ecumenical collaboration.

If Marie had been informed of this before sailing, she might have decided not to go to Africa at all, but to follow her earlier plan to join Lady Frances Moloney to whom she had also been introduced in the Presbytery in Monkstown by Fr. Ronayne. They both trained in midwifery at the National Maternity Hospital in Dublin, before Lady Moloney founded the Columban Missionary Sisters for work in China and the Far East. But she was already in Calabar when she was given this information.

Marie was totally unqualified to be a schoolteacher but the companion who had sailed with her to Calabar, Agnes Ryan[10], had three degrees in education, so Marie took on the administration of the mission school for girls while Agnes organized the teaching.

Marie shared Edith Stein's passion for the education of women. In Calabar, in the cool of evening, she would invite the young women who did the catering and housework at the mission to go out with her and learn to ride a bicycle. In the large port of Calabar in 1921, the sight of women riding bicycles was something new! The colonial wives did not do such things. Bicycles were for men.

Like Edith, Marie believed women should be freed from their subordinate role in society and this should be tackled from as many angles as possible. Marie wanted to understand the new

---

[10] Agnes Ryan later became one of the founding members of the Missionary Sisters of the Holy Rosary

Code of Canon Law which by then was reaching remote parishes. The well-known Irish theologian and writer, Fr. Edward Leen, was on a two-year assignment to south-east Nigeria at the time.

He and Marie became great friends, and she asked him to direct a 30-day retreat for her. She also told him she would make a bargain. If he would explain the new Code of Canon Law to her, in return she would teach him how to darn his socks and bake scones. If women were to move into wider roles, then men would need to learn some new skills too.

Marie felt she needed to know what plans Bishop Shanahan had in mind for the future of health care. To see him she would have to travel to Onitsha. How she researched that journey of 175 miles is a mystery to us, though in her correspondence with her mother we can read the outline of her plans. Within Nigeria telephone calls and cables were the frequent means of communication, but it seems unlikely that she told the bishop she was coming! She asked three young local women to accompany her on this two-week adventure.

By December 1921, when the school closed for Christmas holidays, they were ready to set off. They set out by canoe heading for Nwaniba. The boatmen would have to be careful to get into the most westward of the rivers that formed the delta that met the Cross River as it flowed into the Port at Calabar. The travellers slept in makeshift huts in the bush until they reached the road that would take them to the Government Rest House at Nsukara, and from there on to Owerri. Marie had shared her plans with the doctor's wife there who offered to provide a car to take them on the last 50 miles to Onitsha.

Bishop Shanahan explained to Marie that for now, all she was permitted to do was to respond to an emergency with nursing care, but nothing formal could be established. It is likely that, busy with Christmas preparations, he arranged a car and driver to take them back to Calabar.

At last, in April 1922 Bishop Shanahan came to Calabar. For eight hours every day, Marie would sit on the veranda of the mission with him and with Fr. Leen, and Fr. Ronayne. They were working on a document that would become the first constitutions of the Medical Missionaries of Mary at some future - still unknown - date. They all hoped that before long the ban on religious men and women practising obstetrics and surgery would be lifted. All around them the needs for modern healthcare were pressing. Alas, that would require much patience.

Just as Edith had found her work with Husserl somewhat frustrating, Marie had similar experiences with Bishop Shanahan. After the work on the Constitutions at Easter 1922, he disappeared back to Onitsha, and she heard no more for many months. Marie knew from her wartime nursing that patience was a discipline that lies at the heart of empathy, but she was in the doldrums.

At the end of 1922, Bishop Shanahan had visited the Superior General of his congregation in Paris, Archbishop Le Roy. Thus, he heard of plans to establish a congregation of Holy Ghost Missionary Sisters in France. Archbishop Le Roy wanted any recruits to be directed there instead of founding another congregation. Bishop Shanahan asked Marie what she thought. He got a very direct answer, based on Marie's awareness of the rigidity of Jansenism[11] which still had a lingering influence in some French circles.

---

[11] Jansenism was a 17th century heresy which had a big influence in France. Its legacy also affected many churches in Europe. It emphasised the

We would always be under a French rule and Spirit, which I am and have been all my life against ... They are very narrow in themselves. This reacts in all their works, and they are not able to cope with the broad work of a missionary life. They forget Christ's beautiful prayer for His disciples, a thing that strikes me very much when he prayed, 'I pray not that Thou shouldst take them out of the world, but that Thou shouldst keep them from evil'.

As the new year of 1923 dawned, Bishop Shanahan was sending more potential recruits to join Marie in Calabar, not all of whom she found suitable for the difficult life. Mrs. Martin was given the job by Bishop Shanahan of interviewing young women who volunteered for the work in Nigeria. Marie wrote to her mother about those who should be accepted:

The bishop is making a big mistake sending out girls without trying them hard at home first ... Only an exceptional girl will stand the strain of living here as a religious and according to rule ... They must not be timid but must have a bright cheery character, with plenty of common sense, but above all to realize the work here is beyond any individual human power. God's grace alone can do the work. We must just be a tool in His hands.

In 1923 Bishop Shanahan went to Rome and obtained permission from Pope Pius XI to establish the new Sisterhood, but the Pope stipulated that the candidates must spend some time in Ireland before going to join the Novitiate in Nigeria. At the beginning of 1924, Bishop Shanahan called Marie back to Ireland to join the Missionary Sisters of the Holy Rosary. Marie very reluctantly accepted his advice but found that healthcare was

---

depravity of human nature and did not allow for the freedom of the human will to cooperate with Divine grace.

not the priority. It risked being assigned to a secondary place with so many educational needs demanding attention. Besides, the novitiate formation was under the direction of the Dominican Sisters whose special charism was education. After completing her novitiate,[12] Marie contacted Fr. Pat Whitney who was working towards the establishment of St. Patrick's Missionary Society. He collected her from Killeshandra.

She travelled to Leisin in Switzerland to take care of her younger brother, Desmond, who was suffering from tuberculosis. While there, she heard that Bishop Shanahan was in the southern Swiss town of Sion, so she went down to visit him. Disappointed that she had left the new novitiate, he impressed on her that she could never return to Nigeria as a lay missionary.

She decided to join the Glasgow-based initiative of a Jesuit priest and doctor, Fr. Thomas Agius, called the *Institutum Deiparae.* It was supposed to be a training ground for medical missionary work in Africa - but that experience did not have a happy outcome and Marie returned home, her health greatly depleted. Soon afterwards the *Institutum Deiparae* was disbanded by the Archbishop of Glasgow.

Bewildered about her future, like Edith, Marie turned to the writings of Teresa of Avila, in search of her future direction. She also studied the writings of the newly canonised Thérèse of Lisieux. She began to wonder about the contemplative life as a Carmelite. She received all the votes of the community at Hampton on the north side of Dublin, but Mother Dympna, the Prioress, advised her against joining them. She should pursue her desire about the medical work on the overseas missions. In

---

[12] This served for the Canonical requirement of becoming professed as a Medical Missionary of Mary later.

her diary, Marie wrote extensive notes on the pros and cons of both options.

In 1933, at the very same time that Edith was writing to Pope Pius XI hoping to visit Rome and speak about the problems Hitler was creating, Marie was also thinking of writing to the Pope. Her request was about lifting the restriction regarding obstetrics and surgery. But she was luckier than Edith! She realised, as she said, that 'Rome had come to Ireland' in the person of the newly appointed Apostolic Nuncio, a Franciscan Friar, Dr. Paschal Robinson. By coincidence, Marie's doctor was the physician to the new Nuncio too. He offered to give her an introduction. Thus began a long friendship that was as inspiring as it was fruitful.

The new Nuncio was born in Dublin in 1870 but grew up in New York when his parents emigrated. His appointment as Apostolic Nuncio to Ireland, on November 27, 1929, was considered a delicate one. Ireland was still in need of healing from the civil war that had ended just seven years earlier. There had been no Apostolic Nuncio in Ireland for three hundred years since the time of Cromwell.

It was a winter's night when Archbishop Paschal Robinson arrived in Dublin. The Pro-Cathedral was thronged as the people, led by Archbishop Byrne, gave him the warmest welcome anyone could desire. Despite his often expressed wish to retire to some quiet monastery to spend his last days in peace and prayer, he was nevertheless happy to be back in the city of his birth. It was here that the experienced and erudite scholar would serve the Church for the last nineteen years of his life.

The young Monsignor Antonio Riberi from Monte Carlo, who was Auditor at the Dublin Nunciature in 1933 was present each time Marie went to the Nunciature. He would play a key role in the years ahead. Sometime after this he was appointed Apostolic Delegate with responsibility for missions in East and West Africa, residing in Mombasa, Kenya. Later he became a Cardinal.

When Marie was leaving the Nunciature after their first meeting, Paschal Robinson said: "I trust you will not hesitate to call on me for whatever aid I can give in connection with the very difficult task you are so anxious to undertake". Marie took that literally. He became for her the kind of friend to whom you relate all your movements, with whom you share all the happenings in your life, all the developments in your plans, the advisor whom you feel you can pester, even while you reverence their knowledge and high office. He didn't seem to mind one bit. He was a very busy man. But he took on her project to establish a medical missionary congregation with an enthusiasm and dedication to match her own.

Benedictine Life at Glenstal

One afternoon in September 1933, Marie was shopping in Dublin's Grafton Street. There she bumped into her Aunt Jenny, who had just been visiting the Central Catholic Library. She told Marie that she had been speaking there to Dom Gerard François, prior of the new community of Benedictine monks who had come to Glenstal from Maredsous six years previously. He had poured out his problems to Aunt Jenny, relating how the school was going well academically but the domestic arrangements were in chaos. The monks were at risk of having to abandon the Irish foundation and return to Belgium.

Marie - the problem solver - knew instantly what she would do! Going in haste, she crossed the mile or so to the Central Catholic Library in Merrion Square and found Dom Gerard still there. She told him about her plans, and that she already had one or two candidates, who could go with her to Glenstal and solve their domestic problems in return for spiritual formation. Dom Gerard promised to consider the matter and to consult the Archbishop of Cashel, in whose diocese Glenstal was situated.

Familiar with the writings of Dom Columba Marmion, Marie thought this was just great! Through her frequent contacts with Fr. Pat Whitney, who had recently founded St. Patrick's Missionary Society at Kiltegan, she had come to know his secretary, Nora Leydon. With Fr. Whitney's encouragement, Nora became the first candidate to share the dream. Marie kept her new friend, the Papal Nuncio, fully informed of all she was doing and he, too, felt the invitation to Glenstal was providential.

On 21st March 1934, Marie and Nora took the train to Boher Railway Station where they were met by a monk with a pony and trap for the four-mile drive to the Priory. Their spiritual formation was placed in the care of Dom David Maffei, the Novice Master. He later described the conditions under which Marie and Nora lived:

> *Glenstal was then at its beginnings; all was primitive ... The rooms where Miss Martin's companions lived were directly under the roof, they were small and poorly ventilated and not heated in wintertime. Miss Martin herself had a very small room on the ground floor which had been used as a storeroom or pantry in the time of the Castle. It was barely large enough to hold a small bed and a small table, and the unpolished glass of the little window gave it the appearance of a prison cell... All this could look romantic at first sight but was very hard ... especially during winter.*

In February 1936, while Marie was making a retreat at the Benedictine Abbey at Kylemore, news was published in *The Irish*

Catholic that Pope Pius XI had signed the necessary decree permitting religious women and men to be involved in all branches of healthcare and calling for new religious communities to be established for this purpose. But despite the appeal from the Pope, every Bishop in Ireland that Marie approached declined to welcome such an initiative. They needed all the resources they had for the educational and healthcare needs in their own dioceses. What was happening in faraway countries was not on their agenda!

By this time the future Bishop James Moynagh, had been appointed to the Prefecture of Calabar, which would soon become a Diocese. He agreed to let them make the foundation there although he was very nervous about the fragility of it all. He regretted that while on leave in Ireland, in the kitchen of his home he had mentioned the new venture to his mother. His sister overheard him. He had not anticipated that she would immediately decide to join Marie too!

On a dark night, 29th December 1936, when Marie and her first two companions arrived at the quayside in Dublin to board the ship that would take them to Liverpool, three men who shared their dream were waiting to give them their blessing: the retired Bishop Joseph Shanahan, who was then living at Blackrock College; Fr. Pat Whitney, Superior General of the newly founded Missionary Society of St. Patrick at Kiltegan; and Monsignor Giuseppe Bearzotti, Auditor at the Nunciature in Dublin.

Marie's frail health soon became a problem. Malaria led to cardiac complications. The future Bishop Thomas McGettrick, then a young curate at the mission in Anua, records in his memoirs how on that Holy Thursday, he carried her down the stairs and put her in the car to take her to Port Harcourt. As soon as they had gone, he proceeded to have her coffin made.

Archbishop Antonio Riberi had arrived in Nigeria from Mombasa. In Onitsha he made frantic efforts to communicate to the Vatican the urgency of issuing approval for the establishment of the new missionary Congregation. Everyone was silently wondering what would happen if the future foundress died?

When news of the approval came there was huge relief, but it created great urgency with all that had to be done to make preparations. The Missionary Sisters of the Holy Rosary in Emekuku and the Sisters of the Holy Child in Ifuho were roped in to provide the essentials for the ceremony. They would have to be the witnesses too. The weather was bad and the roads treacherous. Getting to Port Harcourt would not be all that easy. 'What's she going to use for a habit?' is one of the questions recorded in the Archives of the Holy Child Sisters. And the lamentation afterwards: 'There was no holy water'.

Monsignor Moynagh arranged that the foundress would pronounce her vows before the Offertory at the Low Sunday Mass of 1937, which he would celebrate beside her hospital bed where she would be propped up. And so, it was.[13] The fragility of the birth of the Medical Missionaries of Mary was well captured a long time later in the lines of a Nigerian Sister[14]:

> *I keep imagining her sick, weak, frail*
> *yes, I imagine her lying on that hospital bed*
> *in one of those pokey cubicles.*
>
> *I imagine her feverish, nauseous, aching*
> *taking one bitter medicine after another*
> *drinking syrups and soups trying to keep her energy up*

---

[13] She took the name Sister Mary of the Incarnation, and soon became known as Mother Mary Martin.

[14] Dr. Ekaete Ekop is an MMM Obstetrician and Gynaecologist.

clutching at straws of hope.

And then the good news arrives!
Is it possible that nineteen years of waiting
have come to an end?
that the dream had been given a chance to become reality?

But what a chance!
How could she take such a step
when she was hovering between life and death?
when her very life seemed to be sucked out
slowly by illness?

What would the future be? Did she have a future?
Dare she make such a bold step
when frail health and circumstances all screamed against it?

Frail health and circumstances had never been her masters
frail health and circumstances had played insignificant roles
during the waiting years.

She had always coasted on the wings of faith and trust
these had led her and would lead her still.
Her eyes on the Lord
her mind on his promises being fulfilled
now she went on.

She stood alone, on a firm faith
a lone MMM she grasped Love with both hands
she summoned all her strength
and declared to the hearing of six witnesses
MMM is born.

As Archbishop Riberi was heading back to Mombasa, Monsignor Moynagh made arrangements for Marie to return to Ireland on the next boat. His sister and the other would-be novice[15] would have to be sent to the Holy Child Sisters in Ifuho to begin their Novitiate. On April 22nd, as the Consultant Physician, Dr. Eldred Braithwaite,[16] watched the Elder Dempster liner *Accra* sail out of Port Harcourt for Liverpool he said: "Let me never see that woman in Africa again." Once more, Marie's mother was preparing to welcome her back to her original home in Monkstown.

In Dublin, on the last day of 1937, the property that had been bought with Marie's family inheritance as a house of studies for the new missionary Congregation was occupied for the first time. On New Year's Day, Marie took up residence in the new house called 'Rosemount' – the first property the Medical Missionaries of Mary would own.

As 1938 unfolded, the infant missionary society began to grow. A family of O'Sullivans had moved from Cork in 1934 and bought a house called 'Springville' on Cross Avenue just around the corner from Rosemount. All through 1938, Maureen O'Sullivan would watch Marie at early morning Mass in Booterstown church.[17] She was eighteen and would soon be leaving school. Learning about what was going on, she decided she'd give the new venture 'a go'. Like many of the residents of Booterstown, her parents were already enthusiastic supporters of Marie. Everyone loved to see the young student sisters tearing up and down Booterstown Avenue on their bicycles, en route to the University in Earlsfort Terrace or the nurse training school at St. Vincent's Hospital.

---

[15] Sister Magdalen O'Rourke. All the other early candidates were still studying in Ireland.

[16] The role of this dedicated colonial doctor is described in *A Faith Shared*, marking the centenary of the first Mass celebrated in Ogoja at Pentecost 1921.

[17] My uncle, Fr. Paddy O'Flynn, was a young curate in Booterstown at the time and recounted hilarious stories to us of those fragile early days.

Maureen joined MMM on 6th January 1939 and became the eighth professed sister. When she moved to Rosemount and began her nurse training at St. Vincent's Hospital things were still very sparce in the student residence. If unexpected visitors arrived, while someone entertained them in conversation, Maureen would run up to Cross Avenue and borrow saucepans and recipes from her mother.

One morning a phone call came from the Archdiocesan offices to say Archbishop Byrne would be visiting later that day. Maureen was a quick thinker. She dashed up home again and got her six young brothers to carry the table and eight chairs from their dining room down to Rosemount. They would need a room where the archbishop could sit down properly and have a cup of tea. You couldn't ask him to sit on a kitchen stool or an upturned crate. The boys got there in the nick of time. When the Archbishop was gone back to Drumcondra and well out of sight, the young O'Sullivans returned and carried the furniture back home.

A few months after Maureen came, the new venture was blessed with the arrival of Margaret Mary Nolan, the first doctor to join MMM[18]. Born in 1896, she was twenty-third on the

---

[18] Margaret Mary Nolan became a legendary figure in Nigeria. Her presence, along with a very committed team of nurse tutors and others put the MMM flagship hospital at Anua on the map of the colonial world, gaining recognition in Britain for training qualifications for its nurses and graduate doctors. The people had such faith in her that when they heard that Pope Pius XII died in October 1958 they cried: 'Why didn't they send for Sister Doctor?' She received an OBE from Queen Elizabeth and was decorated with the *Order of the Niger* by the Government of Nigeria in 1965. The stories about her are legendary, noting that she was as good in community relations as she was in the operating room. She also served for three of her older years as Medical Secretary in the Catholic Secretariat in Lagos. Margaret Mary died in Drogheda in 1984.

register of new members. She gained her Fellowship of the Royal College of Surgeons in 1932 and became a Member of the British College of Obstetrics and Gynaecology in 1933. When she obtained her Fellowship in Obstetrics in 1949, she was the first woman in Britain to hold a Fellowship in Surgery and another in Obstetrics and Gynaecology.

Before entering Medical School, Margaret Mary had obtained a BA at UCD in 1918. She also held two professional qualifications from the Trinity College of Music in London, a Licentiate in the Art of Pianoforte Playing, and a Teacher's Diploma in the Art of Teaching and Musical Rudiments, both awarded in 1918.

Born in Co. Kildare, she was a fluent Irish speaker. A handwritten account of the history of the Irish harp is among her personal papers housed in our Archives. In 1925, when women in India could only attend women doctors, she registered with the Countess Dufferin's Fund. She appears to have been the only Irish woman among the forty-one volunteers with this organization.

In 1927 she returned briefly from India to follow a number of hands-on post-graduate courses at the University of Paris, obtaining certificates for thoracic surgery, gynaecological surgery, surgery of the digestive tube, oto-rhino-laryngology, ophthalmology, and serology. She returned to India in 1927 but came back to Europe in December 1931 to gain further experience at the University of Berlin. The 50th Jubilee report of the Countess Dufferin's Fund published in 1935 shows that she wrote the annual report from Ishwari Memorial Hospital, Benares, in December 1934.

Having read the entire works of Dom Columba Marmion in a French edition, in 1939 she felt called to become a Medical

Missionary of Mary. Because her mother was a widow and an invalid and Margaret Mary her only child, it was arranged that Mrs. Nolan would come too, and be cared for by the young student MMMs. Mrs. Nolan was ready to do anything that would make her daughter happy. In Rosemount, she grew to love the young community and they loved her in return. Margaret Mary also brought along her little car called 'Dolly' which was a great asset.

For Marie this was the beginning of a difficult but satisfying journey that has been told elsewhere [19]. Very quickly enquiries from prospective candidates were coming in. The problem was where could they live? Rosemount was only approved as a house of studies and only one professed sister was permitted to live there. Well, there were only three professed sisters in the Congregation anyway, two of them in Nigeria. Marie decided to ask two of the women who had been in Glenstal with her, Honora Murphy and Nora Leydon, to postpone their novitiate and go to Anua to help get the hospital on its feet.

They made private vows, with Fr. Hugh Kelly SJ officiating. He had been Marie's spiritual director for many years and continued to be so all her life. Honora and Nora set off for Nigeria. Due to the war they had to remain there until 1945 when they could come back to start their novitiate training. Sister Magdalen O'Rourke, who was one of the two who had completed her novitiate in Ifuho, was asked to come back to Ireland to help Marie get things going.

Fr. Hugh Kelly advised Marie to write to Cardinal MacRory[20] in Armagh. When he asked her why she had gone to Nigeria

---

[19] Cf Mary Purcell "To Africa with Love" and Isabelle Smyth et al. "If you only knew the Gift".

[20] Joseph MacRory (1861-1945) became Archbishop of Armagh in 1928 and was raised to the Cardinalate the following year. Like Bishop James

to make the new foundation, she told him she had not found a Bishop in Ireland who would accept the new initiative. He replied: 'but you didn't ask me'.

Thus began the long story of the relationship of MMM with the Archdiocese of Armagh, ever challenged by the contagious spirit of St. Patrick and the inspiration of the Irish martyr, St. Oliver Plunkett, whose National Shrine is in the Church of St. Peter in Drogheda. A house called 'Elm View' was purchased in Collon, Co. Louth. There were five young women ready to begin their Novitiate training. But the house was unfurnished!

By now Michael Byrne and his young wife Betty, had moved into the Gate Lodge at Rosemount from where they became an indispensable part of the running of MMM for the remainder of their lives. Michael recorded in his memoirs all that happened on the day he set out for Collon. Driving through Dublin he saw traffic lights for the first time.

> *There was a man we knew with a lorry who used to help us sometimes. He was Mr. Smith. He came along and himself, his helper and I loaded the lorry, and we started out for Collon… we had some very odd pieces of furniture on the lorry and gardening tools… after a very good supper that was provided for us, we headed for home.*

That first meal at Collon was cooked on an open fire by Gertrude Davis, the first English woman to become a Medical

---

Moynagh, on a visit to his family in Dungannon he spoke about the new missionary congregation in his diocese. His grandniece, eleven-year-old Maureen Ita, was listening. She made up her mind: 'when I grow up that is what I will do'. Many years later, when she was on sabbatical leave from her work in Ethiopia, I shared a room with her for a year in Maynooth. She later went to Boston to study Clinical Pastoral Education and on return worked at Cluan Mhuire, an Alcoholic Rehabilitation Centre in Newry.

Missionary of Mary. She had been a member of The Grail Movement in London. She told us later about 'the large ginger pussy cat, half Persian', that looked on as she cooked that meal. That pussy became a permanent member of the new household.

With the centuries-old Martin instinct for business and trade, Marie knew how to handle the media! When the first Novitiate was opened and blessed by Cardinal MacRory on 12th December 1938, the members of Drogheda Corporation attended in their full ceremonial robes. The Drogheda Brass Band in their uniforms entertained the large crowd. The national newspapers had been invited to send journalists to cover the event. Before long, many young women who read the newspaper account of the day were making enquiries. The idea was catching like the 'flu.

In 1950, Archbishop Richard Cushing of Boston was leading a pilgrimage on a visit to the Shrine of Oliver Plunkett in Drogheda. The parish priest invited Marie to his house to meet him. He warmly invited her to open a Novitiate in his Archdiocese. At 11.30 am on the 5th of July that year, Marie was thrilled when she boarded the tender at the quayside in Cobh that would take her to the *Mauritania* out in the bay.

Shipping was part of her DNA. In her cabin luggage she had carefully packed the two large round tins that contained the film *Visitation* that she had made in Nigeria three years earlier.[21] It took her no time to find the ship's Purser, Mr. Thomas, and establish that there was a 35mm projector on board. In her luggage she also had a personally printed invitation for the Captain and his crew to view the film and sent him a copy of

[21] To achieve this, she had made her first visit to Africa by air, a journey that took three days as the plane had to land for refuelling so many times.

the book about the making of the film, signed by the Director, Andrew Buchanan. The ship's doctor and nurses, the Chief Engineer and his staff, were also invited. And of course, there was a special invitation for the staff of the Purser's office who arranged for the showing of the film on the final day of the voyage, Monday, July 10th.

A novice and medical student, Sister Stella Phelan, who accompanied Marie on this trip, kept a diary:

> *Distributed literature to the people as they went in. Full house with only standing room. People seemed very interested and many suggested that we should have a collection.*

Archbishop (later Cardinal) Cushing told her he could make available a house that belonged to the Archdiocese at 36 Commonwealth Ave, but it would not be available until September. No need to hang around Boston until then. They headed back to New York, got an appointment with Cardinal Spellman and learned about the Missionary Cooperative Plan. They visited the dioceses of Newark, Trenton, Camden, Wilmington, Baltimore and Philadelphia. They met the two other great missionary foundresses of that era, Mother Anna Dengel of the Medical Mission Sisters and Mother Mary Joseph Rogers of the Maryknoll Sisters.

They went to Washington DC and then on to North Carolina where Bishop Waters had requested MMMs for his diocese of Raleigh. Regretfully, he was told this would not be possible as the focus was on places where the Church was very young or not yet established at all. After a tour of his huge diocese, the bishop very kindly booked a flight for them to their next stop, Chicago.

Everywhere they could, they looked at hospitals and noted new ideas. From Chicago they travelled to Rochester, Minnesota to see the renowned not-for-profit Mayo Clinic. After that they went to Detroit, Cleveland, Buffalo, Rochester NY, Syracuse, Albany, Springfield. Back in Drogheda, the editor of the monthly magazine opened a letter telling her to inform the readers that they were now 'very glad at last to be on the way back to Boston, our future home in the United States of America'.

On October 3rd, 1950, which was then the feast of St. Thérèse of Lisieux, the house at Commonwealth Avenue was formally opened by Archbishop, later Cardinal, Cushing.

Before they returned to Ireland at the end of October, the US première of *Visitation* had been arranged for New York, with the introduction to be inserted recorded by Bishop Fulton Sheen – the famous church personality known to media circles worldwide. It would not be long before more young American women were making enquiries. As happened in Ireland, England, and Scotland a decade earlier, the idea was now catching like the 'flu in America too. The house at Commonwealth Ave wouldn't hold them all.

In 1954 Marie returned to the United States to make a fund-raising tour right across the country. Thanks to generous financial support from Archbishop Cushing, a large, secluded property had been bought at Winchester where the novitiate was now flourishing. Sister Teresa Connolly - who had pioneered the leprosy work at Ogoja in Nigeria in 1945 - was now assigned to tell the MMM story in schools and parishes all over the United States. An experienced driver, years later she showed me her diary and told me how they left Winchester at 7.40 on 4th June 1954 at the start of their fund-raising journey:

We drove along the Connecticut River into the Mohawk Trail and reached Albany in upstate New York at 1 pm for a meeting with Fr. Brennan, Director for the Propagation of the Faith in Albany Diocese. He promised to think of MMM in his plans for the following year.

An hour later, they were on the road again for Rochester, where they stayed with the Sisters of St. Joseph. Next morning after Mass at 6.45 am they left for the Canadian border, entered Ontario, and then returned across the border to Buffalo. They reached Chatham that night and stayed two nights at the Motherhouse of the Sisters of Mercy. June 6th was Pentecost. They did not travel on Sundays so that evening, having had a tour of Mount Carmel hospital, they showed *Visitation* to the community. Sister Teresa who starred in the film, was right there with them to answer questions.

Next morning after 6.30 am Mass, they headed for Detroit, Michigan where they met the Secretary for the Propagation of the Faith, who also promised to remember MMM in their plans the following year. They met Cardinal Mooney briefly, then on to New Buffalo where they were given permission to send sisters to do promotion work. They also met a Mr. Simms of the American Automobile Association, who planned the route they would take from there to Los Angeles.

About 1.30 pm they took the road to Dubuque through prairie land. Called to see Fr. Godfrey CP, crossed the Mississippi at 9 pm and arrived at St. Joseph's Hospital, Dubuque at 10 pm. On June 9th, once again Mass was at 6.30 am. After breakfast Marie wrote letters before they set off through cornlands. They reached Cedar Rapids at 1 pm, had lunch, and distributed leaflets to curious people to wanted to know who they were. At 8 pm they crossed the Missouri at Blair, they were now in Nebraska. They stayed that night at the Erin Hotel in Fremont.

On June 10th, after 8 am Mass they had breakfast with the Sisters of St. Francis and then ran into a bad sandstorm. Driving was slow and at times they could not see the road. They reached the Ursuline Convent, North Platte[22] by suppertime, and drove on till they arrived in Sidney at 9 pm. As they had crossed the time zone, they put their watches back one hour.

Their next goal was to reach Cheyenne and Rock Springs in Wyoming. It was now June 11th. Monsignor Lenk gave them advice about the journey ahead. At this point the diary noted 'the Sisters we met everywhere were kindness personified'. Next morning, they left at 9 am driving through cattle ranching areas. They called at De Paul Hospital in Cheyenne. Sister Teresa had slipped on a stairs, and at the hospital Sister Joan of Arc insisted that she have her finger x-rayed, but luckily no bone was broken. She was pronounced fit to drive on. After a lovely lunch they set off for Rock Springs, where they called on Fr. Butler, a native of Thomastown, Co. Kilkenny.

On June 12th they proceeded as soon as possible after Mass, driving by hill and plain to Ruper in Idaho. They received a great welcome from Fr. McNeill, a native of Collon, Co. Louth. They had dinner there and were taken to Mrs. Heinchild who was providing hospitality for them for the weekend. They made arrangements to hold church collections at Masses next day. Sister Teresa would go to 7 and 9 am Masses at Burley. Marie would do the 8 and 10 am Masses at Rupert. Needless to say, the people were very very generous. As well as Fr. McNeill, they met Fr. O'Driscoll who was from Waterford,

---

[22] My grand-uncle, Monsignor Thomas Murray, who baptised me, was parish priest of North Platte at that time.

both priests very helpful. After dinner they showed *Visitation* to an interested parish group.

Next stop was Ely in Nevada, and from there on June 15th they drove through the mountain desert area on poor roads with no habitation for hundreds of miles till they reached Las Vegas where they booked into a hotel. Next morning, they left at 4.40 am, entering California at 5.15 am. There was a rule at the Customs Office that Californian fruit should be protected from disease. They did not think they had any fruit to declare, but a decayed pear was found by the Customs Officer. They could not remember in which of the ten states they had visited they had been given it. But they were let through!

They arrived in Los Angeles at 1.30 pm and got a wonderful welcome. After this whistle-stop twelve-day drive, the diary simply noted: 'We were thankful to God to be safely arrived at our destination'. The call of the West had been answered.

Following the meetings in Los Angeles, Sister Sheila Hogan was asked to resign from her duties as senior radiographer at the hospital in Drogheda, and she accepted the assignment to California to initiate decades of fund-raising there. Later, Sister M. Andrew Phillips, a native of Conway, Michigan, would devote most of her life to co-ordinating the extensive promotion work all along the West Coast. She became leader of a small community of sisters established at Oakland.[23]

Through the decades that followed, all Marie's efforts, successes and failures, were supported by her family and her countless friends and benefactors in Ireland, the UK and USA.

---

[23] I once had the opportunity to stay with this community while facilitating meetings for another Congregation. Sister Andrew took time off to drive me through Napa Valley and proudly showed me the magnificent wine groves of her native land.

She made many visits to mainland Europe, to Lisieux, Lourdes, Rome, and took on the management of the very successful *Clinica Mediterranea* in Naples where the miracle attributed to the then 'Blessed' and later Saint Oliver Plunkett was recorded. She accepted to provide sisters to staff the initiative with the *Clinica Moscati* in Rome, from which it later became necessary to withdraw. Meanwhile more films were made in East Africa, as communities were established in Tanzania, Uganda, Ethiopia, Malawi and Kenya, and in Angola in West Africa.

Invitations to make new foundations were arriving in Drogheda from Bishops in many parts of the world. In 1959, with so many invitations and a limited number of sisters, Marie decided she would have to visit the places to where she was invited before making a decision. She also felt she needed advice about a number of things at the Vatican department then known as *Propaganda Fide.*

She set off from Drogheda on 25th September 1959. When she arrived at Winchester on 13th April 1960, it was Wednesday of Holy Week. She had visited every community in Africa and every diocese to which she had been invited. Details of this lengthy trip were logged in a diary, mainly by Sister-doctor Maura O'Donohue whom she asked to join her for the rest of the journey when she reached Anua.

Just as well she brought along the doctor! On 5th March at 1 am they left the Nunciature in Addis Ababa for the airport to catch their flight to Hong Kong. The toll of the long working days and extensive travel of the previous months finally showed. During that flight Marie collapsed in heart failure. Maura had an emergency kit and gave initial treatment. Then she called the hostess and asked her to arrange an ambulance to meet the plane. However, that proved impossible, but a taxi was brought to the steps of the plane. Marie was conscious as she was carried down the steps.

Maura arranged for her to rest in the medical center at the airport while she went to the reception desk to enquire about a hospital. She was informed there was no hospital in Kowloon. The taxi took them to the Four Seas Hotel where Marie was confined to bed. She asked Maura to share her room, so she was able to monitor the situation.

Maura was most anxious to contact the Columban Missionary Sisters. Hong Kong was the only place where they were not listed in the telephone directory under their own name, but under the name of the hospital where they worked. Maura later told me how alone she felt with this responsibility. She had just reached her twenty-seventh birthday that week.

After an effort that took four days, with the help of Air India, Maura was able to locate the Columban Sisters. Mother M. Stephen - who was also a doctor - came on the Star Ferry from Hong Kong Island bringing their car. At Ruttenjee Sanatorium run by the Columbans, Marie was able to rest. She was already improving after her stay at the Hotel. Early on the morning of 11th March, Mother M. Stephen drove them to the airport and helped Maura to organise that oxygen would be available on the flight to Taipei. The crew of Cathay Pacific gave them a special compartment to themselves.

When they landed at 11.30, they were taken to the Benedictine convent, where the busy round of looking at potential sites for a new mission began all over again.[24] Later when I reviewed

---

[24] An MMM foundation was made in Taiwan soon after that, but at the General Chapter of 1974, the community of five sisters drawn from USA and Ireland told the delegates that if MMM was not able to establish a novitiate in Taiwan, they did not see any point in remaining there. That would require at least five more sisters to be assigned to Taiwan, some of

the diaries and reports and mapped that 1959-60 journey, I counted 91 locations visited in 22 countries.

Despite her fragile health, Marie lived into her 83rd year. During the final seven years her physical and mental condition declined progressively. At times she would be found weeping. Once, when asked 'why the tears' she replied: "I can't help it. I want to say something and the words that come out are not the words I want, not what I meant. It's so frustrating not to be able to explain things … I feel so very lonely."

There were moments of clarity too when she would reveal that she had a sense of what was happening. In December 1967 when Cardinal Antonio Riberi died, she was considered too ill to be informed. But sometime later when her brother, Desmond, was sitting at her bedside thinking she was asleep, she suddenly opened her eyes and said: "Next time we are in Rome, Desmond, you and I must visit Dr. Riberi's grave." Another day she told the sister who was nursing her: "The Nuncio will be coming to visit me today."

When he got out of bed that morning Archbishop Gaetano Alibrandi had no notion of visiting her. But he had some business with Cardinal William Conway in Armagh. The road back to Dublin would take him through Drogheda and, as he approached the town, he decided to call in to visit Marie. She was awake and bright when he arrived, and she welcomed him saying: "I knew you would come today, I told sister."

In 1972, five years after Marie had given up any active role, the Central Leadership Team of MMM decided to fulfil a dream she had nurtured for several decades – to establish a Novitiate in Africa. It would mean that African women would no longer

---

them with qualifications in spiritual formation, and that was just not possible at that time.

have to travel to Europe to begin their 'extraordinary adventure'. Their early formation could take place in a more appropriate milieu of mixed cultures.

Bishop Richard Finn of Ibadan extended a warm welcome to his diocese which included the most densely populated city on the continent of Africa. Sister JoAnne Kelly who had been appointed to open the new Novitiate called to visit Marie the evening before she left for Nigeria. Marie was unresponsive when the nurse told her the visiting sister had come to say goodbye. JoAnne sat by the bedside for a long-time hoping Marie might wake up. Eventually she touched Marie's hand and said, 'I am going now'. Marie opened her eyes and said: "Dear, there will be times when you will not understand them, and they will not understand you, just be patient." Then she closed her eyes again and said no more. Her final message about empathy was clear. Human in-depth encounters, especially when they involve intercultural communications, need patience.

Marie had to endure the loneliness of her mental condition for a further three years. In the end, her death came quietly, peacefully, and with no warning in the small hours of a winter morning, 27th January 1975. Shortly after midnight, the sister nursing her transferred her from her chair to her bed. She spent a few minutes brushing her hair as this always had a very relaxing effect. Marie took her right hand in both of hers and gave her a big kiss on it and said, "Thank you, Dear" and went off to sleep very peacefully. At 2.40 am she showed signs of restlessness. The nursing sister put her hand on her arm and asked was she alright or did she want anything. That sister recorded:

> *She opened her eyes, put out her hands, smiled beautifully, looked up to heaven and was gone there in a matter of*

minutes. Of all the many deaths I have witnessed, hers was the most beautiful, calm and serene.

Condolences

I was our Congregational Secretary at that time, so I was wakened immediately to inform the news media of the death of Mother Mary Martin, as Marie was known since her religious profession. As dawn broke over Drogheda, her remains were brought to repose in a large room just inside the front entrance of the Motherhouse. The community of more than one hundred sisters were able to come and pray privately throughout the morning.

In the afternoon, the former President of Ireland, Eamon de Valera, came to mourn her passing. That evening, her coffin was removed to the Motherhouse oratory. By then there was a growing stream of people coming from far and near. The community arranged that the hours of the Divine Office would be sung throughout the vigil. During the next three days crowds of people ignored the wintry cold and pouring rain to pass the open coffin and join the sisters in prayer. There were people in wheelchairs, toddlers, and babies in their parents' arms.

Books of condolence were signed by more than 4,000 people, but many more came who could not wait in the long queues to sign the books. From many countries, telegrams of condolence piled high. People of all ranks and from many parts of the world recalled what the blessing her life and work had meant to them personally and to their town or country. It became obvious that big numbers would gather on 30th January for her funeral in the nearby parish church of Our Lady of Lourdes. As Marie had been granted the Freedom of Drogheda, she was given the equivalent of a State Funeral. During the days of the vigil, army personnel came to Drogheda to arrange the details and the security.

As the Founder of a religious congregation, Marie would have to be buried in three coffins which would be placed in a brick-lined vault in the nearby parish cemetery, St. Peter's. The vault had been discreetly constructed several years earlier during her long illness. It had been announced on local media that the oratory would be kept open to visitors until 9 pm on the night before the funeral. Up to the last minute, people were coming.

When all had left, the undertakers were joined by workmen who had served from its earliest days in the Lourdes Hospital which Marie had established in Drogheda. Called the International Missionary Training Hospital, it served as a training centre for work in the global south. The undertakers closed the coffin and placed it inside the second coffin which was made of lead. The outer coffin was also wooden. The chairs and the Paschal Candle that had been in place during the Vigil were pushed aside as the workmen prepared to seal the lead coffin.

Just then a phone call came from the printers in Dublin, who had been working for three days to get the booklet with the funeral ceremony designed and printed in time. They had recommended that it be printed on a special quality of paper that would not make noise when people turned the pages during the funeral Mass. Now, at the eleventh hour, the printers wanted to come personally from Dublin and say goodbye themselves. I asked them to stay on the phone while I went to the oratory to consult the men who had already begun their work. The clock was showing 9.45 pm. They put down their blow lamps and chisels as the senior among them replied: "We would not want to deprive any other workers of the chance to say goodbye to her". Their empathy touched me deeply.

While the team from the printers got into their cars to make the thirty-mile journey from Dublin, the workmen moved the lead coffin out of sight, reopened the wooden coffin, replaced the Paschal Candle and chairs. I made them a pot of tea and we chatted quietly until the printers arrived. Thus, the people who were the last to say goodbye were simple working men and women who had embraced Marie's vision with so much devotion. As the printers were leaving the Oratory, I bent over and kissed her forehead and signalled to the men that they could now complete their work.

Next morning, the town of Drogheda closed its schools, shops, and businesses. Dignitaries began to arrive. Joining the Martin family were the President of Ireland, Cearbhall Ó Dálaigh and his wife, Máirín. The Mayor and Corporation of Drogheda were present in their robes. A single red rose lay on top of the coffin – a symbol of Marie's devotion to St. Thérèse of Lisieux, who on her deathbed said she would send 'a shower of roses' spending her heaven doing good on Earth.

Student nurses formed a guard of honour to the cemetery, the Drogheda Brass Band playing the sombre funeral march. One of the student nurses[25] echoed the thoughts of many when she wrote:

> *Love lingered in her presence.*
> *Her passing from us is like the passing of a great light,*
> *of which we have seen but a shadow.*

---

[25] Sheila Conachy.

CHAPTER 3

THE CRISIS OF CAPITALISM

THE LITTLE ELDERLY LADY CARRYING HER PITCHER became mine more than fifty years ago in Tanzania. She is carved in the tradition of the great Makonde artists of East Africa. I was bound for Ireland that day. I wanted to buy some small souvenirs for my family and friends. In Arusha, I stepped from the bright sunshine into a dark cavern of amazing treasures. The smell of wood assailed me. The silence absorbed me. I was the only customer in this exotic treasure trove.

From the back of the cavern, the owner appeared and eagerly welcomed me. She told me they would ship my purchases to anywhere in the world. She nodded compassionately when I explained I was not a tourist, but a volunteer missionary worker and my budget was quite tiny. Still, she proudly showed me the pieces that gloriously revealed the gifted art of the Makonde people. I gazed admiringly at the depiction of their ancestry, the ornaments, and the pots.

She also stocked the work of other artists - small tables and large trunks, the carved forms of the Big Five[1] who roam the nearby Serengeti plains. The batiks enthralled me - oh such wonderful batiks - in orange and purple and turquoise, the

[1] These include lions, leopards, elephants, buffalo, and rhinoceros – four of which I have encountered on different journeys. Giraffes and ostrich were also frequently met on the roadsides of Tanzania and Kenya.

deep, deep blues, the yellows and greens and pinks and reds, and the carefully chosen spots where the wax was peeled off to reveal pure sparkling white.

I bought a pair of bookends supported with polished brown elephants, a family tree, and a few small batiks. 'That's all I can fit in my luggage', I explained apologetically to the owner, as I unrolled a wad of smelly twenty-shilling notes.

'But you'll have room for this', she said. 'This is from me to you to help you to remember us' and she handed me the slim brown woman walking with her pitcher. The little lady was old when she was carved, eight inches tall. But she's still upright on my mantelpiece today. Every day I look on her when I get out of bed - and yes, I do remember.

I was leaving Tanzania reluctantly. I had been recalled to work in Ireland, after just two short years. What excitement I had felt when I received my letter of assignment as business administrator to Makiungu Hospital. It is in a semi-desert area on a plateau of the Great Rift Wall that runs from Cairo to Cape Town. That letter of assignment came back in 1970. I was a student at Maynooth working on my master's thesis on 'Responsibility and Revolution'.

I told my friends how much I looked forward to working in the Tanzania of Julius Nyerere. It was just three years since the publication of the *Arusha Declaration,* the short document that set out Nyerere's policy of self-reliance for the people of Tanzania. It called for an ethic of longer working hours and dependence on food production rather than the expectation of major foreign aid to fund development.

Now, as I sat in the small departure lounge of Arusha airport - this was long before the Kilimanjaro International Airport was built - my thoughts returned to the *Arusha Declaration.* I had come to know the Bank Manager in Singida, the town 20 miles from our hospital compound. Of Indian origin, he trusted me every time I called in to assure him that I would soon have more funds coming to complete the building of our new midwifery training school. When the banks were nationalised, I discussed with him the possibility of introducing a savings scheme among the hospital employees.

Development is what President Nyerere was calling for, and I wanted to do my bit. Even though some of our workers were barely literate, they were enthusiastic when I met with them to explain the concept of a bank account and a savings scheme. The Bank Manager arranged to send a jeep with armed security to the hospital compound one afternoon every two weeks. Employees who wished, lined up to open an account, and their salaries were paid by cheque for the first time.

Whether or not they could manage to save a little was not my business - I left it to the Bank staff to explain privately to each individual what that would involve.

A Flight to Remember

The plane that would take me to Nairobi on the first leg of my journey to Ireland was on the runway now. It looked enormous after the small planes that landed regularly at the airstrip of our hospital.

Usually, we knew when they were coming. Every day at 1 pm one of us would go to the radio room and call the Flying Doctors at Nairobi: 'Foundation Control, Makiungu calling, over'. That mantra would not be easily forgotten. And the friendly voice from the Africa Medical & Research Foundation[2] would

---

[2] Known as AMREF. *www.amref.org*

come crackling in with any news they had for us about upcoming specialist team visits, or news from any of our other three hospitals in Tanzania, or from our seven mission outstations in the Turkana Desert in Kenya, which were supported from the hospital which we staffed at Lodwar.

Occasionally we would hear a small plane overhead that we were not expecting. It had to be coming to us, as no other aircraft would have any business in the skies overhead. 'Wonder who is coming to visit us' we would ask ourselves. Someone would grab the keys of the Land Rover, drive up the sandy path to the airstrip, and shoo away any goats that might have wandered into the path of the plane that was about to land.

How could I ever forget the unexpected little plane that came one Sunday morning! It brought our Swiss-born architect from Dar es Salaam, and the Indian building contractor for our new midwifery training school. By the time they had completed their inspection, a thought had entered my head.

I had been due to visit Dar es Salaam earlier that week, but cancelled my overnight trip by train from Itigi when I learned that the representative from Oxfam whom I was to meet had postponed his visit to Dar. My long shopping list had gone back on file. Most items could wait, but there was some urgency about getting the vaccines from the Department of Health's medical stores.

'Could you give me a lift to Dar?' I asked the architect as we finished lunch. 'What weight are you?' he asked, 'are you more than 130 lbs?' 'No, but I will have to bring an overnight bag and some large flasks' I replied. He looked at the Indian builder. 'Are you OK on the dickie if we bring her?' I hadn't realised it was just a two-seater. It was flying with the code name

'November Victor'. We took off without delay. We would have to be on the ground in Dar by sunset.

It felt like no time at all until we were landing at Dodoma for refuelling. Even before the door was opened, the fuel tank was being wheeled towards us. 'You can get a cold drink in the Waiting Room' the architect indicated. Just before I headed up the path, I caught him saying to the man at the pump 'eight and eight'. Eight what — I wondered with some anxiety — is it litres or gallons? Dar es Salaam was 500 miles from Makiungu, and we had only flown a short distance.

As we took off again, I gazed at the two fuel gauges in front of me in the passenger seat to the right of the pilot. Each tank had a capacity of 25 gallons, but neither was anything like full as we left Dodoma. Soon we were winding our way through spectacular mountains. Sometimes I thought the wing tips would touch the trees.

The pilot read my thoughts. 'Don't worry', he said, 'we can't fly higher because of the extra weight'. Silently I asked myself 'does he mean me, or the flasks'. I had to bring them to ensure the cold chain would not be broken once I picked up the vaccines at the Medical Stores. The ice would last just about long enough to get me back on the overnight train from Dar to Itigi. The slightly built Indian seemed secure and unconcerned in the dickie seat behind us. He was Muslim and he had said his prayers.

My anxiety did not lessen when the pilot flicked the control from the empty right hand tank over to the left one. By then the sun was lowering in the sky behind us.

'November Victor, November Victor, give your bearings' came the voice from the Control Tower. The pilot responded calmly.

But he pointed to the fuel gauge when it was showing just 5 gallons. 'Hope it is enough to get us there' he said.

Options

'What will you do if it is not?' I asked, with more than curiosity. 'Oh, we'll come down on a road', he replied, like as if it is what you do any Sunday afternoon when you're stuck for fuel. I gazed down, but there was not a road in sight. Not even a path. Not a village anywhere. Just forest. I envisaged myself dangling from one of those trees as I said goodbye to life. So be it.

My only concern was for my father. My mother had died after a long illness just three weeks earlier. I had received her last letter to me two days previous to this flight when the bus from Singida brought our postbag. It would be good meeting her soon in heaven. But how would my Dad cope with losing his only daughter, the other most loved woman in all the world?

'November Victor, November Victor, show you lights'. Each time the voice from the Control Tower sounded more insistent and more impatient. In response the pilot showed our lights and recited our co-ordinates into his hand-held mike. But there was no sign of a city on the farthest horizon. The sun was sinking fast.

There was less than a gallon of fuel showing on the gauge when we eventually saw the lights of Dar on the eastern horizon. We could make it yet, I told myself ... just about.

Due to our arrival after sunset, the pilot was called to the Control Tower for a caution as soon as we landed. Three cautions and his licence would be suspended. This was only his second. I insisted that our Indian friend would take the front passenger seat as we relaxed into the pilot's gorgeous Mercedes. I can still feel the luxury of having four wheels beneath us as we sped into the city. The pilot's teenage daughters had been waiting for their Dad to get home to bring them to a movie, so I tagged along too. I was game for anything so long as it was at ground level!

I always enjoyed the busyness of the large port at Dar es Salaam. There were the big cargo ships and the small fishing vessels and the ferry that plied over and back to Zanzibar. I remembered what I had been taught – always walk on the shady side of the street and keep out of the sunlight whenever you get the opportunity. I bought a ticket for the overnight train journey back to Itigi. That was about sixty miles from Makiungu, so I phoned AMREF in Nairobi asking them to let the hospital know I would need the Land Rover to collect me from the train on my return.

I did my general shopping before heading to the Medical Stores to collect the vaccines that I had ordered. I was dismayed to find many shelves in the supermarket were empty. But I could buy as much toothpaste or as many toilet rolls as I wanted, all made in China. I was familiar with the cohorts of Chinese workers in various parts of the country, assigned to various public projects, the most spectacular being the building of the Tan-Zam Railway. This would provide a link from landbound Zambia to the Indian Ocean at Dar es Salaam.

Julius Nyerere was a leader who showed concern not only for his own people, but for the peaceful development of the whole of Africa. But for his involvement with China, he paid a high price.

Change of Assignment

It was about a year later that I received the letter changing my assignment back to Ireland. I wasn't ready for it. Now sitting at Arusha airport, my thoughts were urgently ushered back to the present when the flight to Nairobi was called. While I watched my luggage being towed out to the plane that would carry me away from Tanzania, I was unaware that something much more precious would also travel with me - indeed would remain with me for the rest of my life - the mystique of Julius Nyerere, the man who famously reminded everyone 'I am a teacher first, a President second.'

Five years would pass before I would be in Tanzania again. This time I arrived by bus from Nairobi, lugging my suitcase through the border village on the sturdy metal wheels I had purchased in Dublin. Luggage with in-built wheels was still an invention of the future. I was only coming for a business meeting, but as I entered Tanzania my load felt lighter, and I had a warm sense of homecoming despite the horrendous paperwork at the border. The East African Community, comprising Kenya, Uganda, and Tanzania, had been disbanded when Idi Amin came to power in Uganda. What a loss that was.[3]

I reached Arusha in time to join our community for Evening Prayer. It was the first time I heard the opening hymn 'You shall cross the barren desert, but you shall not die of thirst ...' Later during that visit, in a small bookshop in Dar es Salaam, I picked up a booklet, not much more than a pamphlet, and quickly took it to the cashier. Written by President Julius Nyerere, it set out the mistakes he could see he had made since the publication of the *Arusha Declaration* ten years earlier.

Where else would I find a political leader so ready to acknowledge his mistakes and share them with all who could read and write? By then it was widely acknowledged that his economic policies were failing. Rich western countries

[3] Years of preparation to establish a new East African Community came to fruition in July 2000

declined to provide the capital that was essential to industrial development. Not surprisingly, China was very pleased to take up Nyerere's socialist ideas and pour in aid, at their own price. Nyerere, a staunch Catholic[4], a Christian of deeply held beliefs and practice, was labelled a communist by capitalists of the Western world.

The Young Nyerere

Still today my thoughts eagerly wander back to accounts of his younger days. I feel greatly indebted to the late Fr. Arthur H. Wille of the Maryknoll Missionaries for his personal memoirs. In 1955, when he was assigned to open a new Catholic mission among the Zanaki people in north-western Tanganyika, he was told to seek out Julius Nyerere who would teach him the Zanaki language.

The young teacher was overjoyed at the news that a mission was to be established among his own people. He offered to move with his wife, Maria, and the two children they had at that time, Andrew and Anna, into Musoma town on the shore of Lake Victoria and find a place to stay while he taught his native language to Fr. Wille who recalled:

> *In the afternoons after teaching me, we would drink tea together. It was at this time that he told me much about himself, his childhood, his family and especially what he hoped to accomplish when he led the country to independence. He never had any doubts that Tanganyika would become independent from the colonial power.*

---

[4] On May 15, 2005, Pope Benedict XVI declared Julius Kambarage Nyerere 'Servant of God' which is the first step in the process towards beatification and eventually sainthood, a process that is now being pursued under the guidance of the Tanzania Episcopal Conference.

When the country merged with the island of Zanzibar in 1964 it was renamed Tanzania.

Fr. Wille records that the rains were very heavy on the day Nyerere was born in March 1922 in Butiama Village. The infant was given the name 'Kambarage', after an ancestral spirit who lives in the rain. His father, Burito Nyerere was one of the eight chiefs of the Zanaki, a small ethnic group of less than 50,000 people. Burito Nyerere was polygamous, and Mugaya, the baby's mother, was the chief's fifth wife.

According to Zanaki custom, the husband builds each wife a house, usually mud and wattle with a grass roof. Each wife would have fields to raise food to support herself and feed her children. As the boy grew, he tended his mother's goats, spending the whole day in the fields.

After World War I, when the British had taken over German East Africa and named the country Tanganyika, they opened a boarding primary school at Mwisenge in Musoma town to educate the sons of the chiefs. Burito Nyerere was not eager to send his sons to this school. However, when he was busy with his duties as a chief, he would ask Julius to entertain important visitors.

When the chief of the neighboring Ikizu Ethnic Group came to visit Burito, Julius engaged him in the African game called 'soro' in the Zanaki language - or 'bao' in Swahili. This is a difficult game, involving the planning of many moves ahead and remembering them. One day, after Chief Makongoro was defeated by the young Kambarage at 'soro', he persuaded Burito Nyerere to send his bright son to school. There was no stopping the child's intellectual development after that.

Those who taught the future President had an enormous influence on the growing boy. 'Mwalimu', the Swahili word for 'teacher', was the most prized title he would ever hold and by which he is affectionately remembered.

This talented youth won a scholarship to go to middle school and after that, another to attend the highly regarded Tabora Boys' Secondary School. And then, not surprisingly, he won a scholarship to Makerere University in Uganda, established by the British to educate an elite cohort of people to serve in East Africa.

Before going there, Kambarage asked to be baptized. He had studied the catechism for ten years and knew it well. Yet, he accepted the requirement that he be prepared for baptism by a humble catechist with little education. At the age of twenty, he was baptized Julius Kambarage Nyerere on December 23, 1942, and received the sacrament of Confirmation on May 30, 1944.

Julius Nyerere mastered English to the point of translating Shakespeare's *Merchant of Venice* and *King Lear* into Kiswahili. On graduation, he was offered two posts in Tabora. The headmaster of the government Tabora Boys Secondary School made a bet with Fr. Richard Walsh, the headmaster of St. Mary's Secondary School that Julius would choose the government school. He was wrong.

When Julius chose St. Mary's, the government advised him by letter that at a mission school he would not get the same salary. Also, if he later transferred to a government school, he would not be able to count the years spent teaching in a mission school towards his pension. Julius was furious at this and replied in a letter: 'If I ever hesitated, your letter has settled the matter. The mission teachers are doing as much as the government teachers are'.

The friendship Julius developed with Fr. Walsh was to last a lifetime. I recall a morning when I was working back in Ireland in the mid-1970s. A phone call came through to my desk in Drogheda from the Embassy of Tanzania in London. The message conveyed that a representative of the Government of Tanzania would arrive in Drogheda next day to attend the funeral of Fr. Richard Walsh, who had died at the Lourdes Hospital the previous day. A magnificent bouquet of flowers was delivered, sent by Mwalimu Julius Nyerere.

Back in the days when Fr. Walsh was headmaster at St. Mary's Secondary School in Tabora, he had raised funds among his friends in England for scholarships to get higher education for his staff. Twice his offer of a scholarship was turned down by Julius Nyerere. He was afraid that studying in Europe would make him less African. Fr. Wille writes: 'He loved his culture. He loved his roots. He loved who he was.'

But Fr. Walsh continued to urge him to go abroad. In 1949 he arrived in Scotland to begin his studies in history and economics at Edinburgh University. He didn't look for accommodation among the better off students, but moved in with a Scottish family who were miners. He discovered that not all Europeans were like the well-off colonials whom he observed in Tanganyika but white people too could be at the bottom of the economic ladder.

At one point Julius wrote to Fr. Walsh telling him that he was thinking about becoming a priest as it would give him an opportunity to do a lot of good for people. The reply, based on Fr. Walsh's insight that this man was interested in politics and the independence of his country, advised him that he did not have a vocation to the priesthood, and Julius accepted this advice.

While in Scotland, Nyerere was influenced by the work of the Fabian Society, the socialist organisation established by British intellectuals in 1884 and which founded the London School of Economics and Political Science in 1895. The goal of the Fabian Society was to advance the principles of democratic socialism through reformist efforts rather than by revolutionary overthrow. Today the Society functions primarily as a think tank. It is among the twenty-one socialist organisations affiliated with the British Labour Party which developed from the original Fabian Society.

On return from Edinburgh in 1952, Julius married his fiancée, Maria Waningo Gabrieli, fondly known by the people of Tanzania as 'Mama Maria'. He took up a teaching post in Dar es Salaam at the elite secondary school known as St. Francis' College at Pugu, run by the Irish Spiritan Fathers. Julius Nyerere was the first of his nation to hold a master's degree in education. In the ensuing years he became involved in the political organisation of the people and their yearning for independence. Eventually he reluctantly accepted that to devote himself to the political goal, he would have to retire from teaching.

Like many African people, Nyerere's mindset was influenced by the ancient philosophy of Ubuntu. It values a way of life that reveals to me the importance of the other person as giving meaning, formation, and quality to my life. Ubuntu accepts that everybody makes mistakes, but mistakes should be seen as lessons, sometimes even as life lessons. It is only through erring that many people learn[5].

---

[5] This was most impressively expressed in the forgiving attitude of Nelson Mandela who showed no bitterness or hatred after being in prison for so many years as a political prisoner.

This view of life requires identifying with the problems and sufferings of others in an understanding way. However, caring for society means it is unacceptable to be patient with social misbehaviour or injustice. In a work environment, people of all ranks are treated equally. For example, in an office or a factory, the person who makes the tea and the manager are treated equally, but the fact that they fill different roles is understood. Seniority of age is respected, even if the role is a minor one. The Extended Family system can be found in many parts of Africa. It seeks to link the value of family with an understanding of society.

Under the influence of Ubuntu philosophy, Nyerere believed that people become true persons within a community, starting with the family. His concept of *Ujamaa* (extended familyhood), found in traditional African villages before the arrival of the colonizers, could become the basis of a system wherein wealth would spread horizontally, not vertically. But not everyone was eager to adopt the communal villages that were established. The system failed to boost agricultural output.

My grasp of Ki-Swahili was limited, but I had tried to listen carefully at meetings of the ten-cell system through which representatives of each household were encouraged to take part in local decision making. I sensed that a missing link in Nyerere's policy was a plan for the ongoing education of local leadership in his philosophy and method. I could hear that many people were reluctant to embrace the communal farming that was encouraged. But rural people were glad to use the communally owned machinery available to do much of the work that had involved hard manual labour before.

By 1976, the forced collectivization programme was discontinued. By then Tanzania had dropped from being the largest exporter of agricultural products in Africa to becoming the largest importer of agricultural products. But while the economic policies of Nyerere's socialism failed, other policies succeeded. Literacy and health care surpassed anything most African countries had achieved at that time. At the time of Independence in 1961, the literacy rate was only 15%. When Nyerere stepped down from the Presidency in 1986 it had reached 91% and nearly every child was at school. In 1961 there were two trained engineers in the country and twelve doctors. Nyerere claimed that during his Presidency, thousands of engineers, doctors and teachers were trained.

Education for all was Nyerere's great ambition. But a candidate for university education must first prove himself or herself in the countryside, living on communal farms, showing their talent for hard work and community service. On such candidates, university education would not be wasted. National youth service was a requirement that showed the young men and women what hard work and fitness involved. As the Arusha Declaration proclaimed: The development of a country is brought about by people, not by money. Money, and the wealth it represents, should be the result and not the basis of development.

Nyerere resisted the demands to establish a television network throughout the country. It would be better to wait until every home had a radio before they would invest in television. He resisted the demands of foreigners to build luxury hotels in Arusha so that income could be generated from rich tourists anxious to view the Big Five on the Serengeti Plains. No, he felt. The people are still poor. How would they feel with wealthy tourists crossing the land carrying expensive cameras to take home pictures of us and leave little behind?

The survival of the country's wildlife was also greatly valued. Nyerere said "these wild creatures amid the wild places they inhabit are not only important as a source of wonder and inspiration, but are an integral part of our natural resources and our future livelihood and wellbeing ... We will do everything in our power to make sure that our children's grandchildren will be able to enjoy this rich and precious inheritance."

The leadership code in Nyerere's plan is also worth recalling. Party and State leaders were prohibited from ownership of company shares, from taking directorships in private enterprises, from receiving two or more salaries, and from owning property for the rental market.

In 1985 Nyerere fully accepted that his economic policies had failed. It was probably a lost cause from the start since the Western countries were determined to withhold financial support for his ideas. He announced that he would voluntarily resign from the Presidency. He continued to play a significant role in the international political arena, especially in relation to Africa and the Organization for African Unity.

Two years before his death, Julius Nyerere asked people to look upon his ideas as a source of inspiration for the future, but to consider his legacy critically in order to best understand the way forward. "Tanzania", he said, "can learn from my mistakes as well from our aims and achievements."

When he died in 1999 at the age of 77, his legacy was described as rich, generous, and varied. An obituary in *The Economist* concluded: "He was a magnificent teacher: articulate, questioning, stimulating, caring. He should never have been given charge of an economy."

Indeed, it is in the field of economics that his legacy is viewed most negatively. However, Canadian Professor of Economics, Gerry Helleiner, who devoted much time and attention to Tanzania, wrote that his government's most damaging economic policy errors had little to do with socialism *per se.* They were on the issue of exchange rate policy. In the early 1980s, most of the world's major economies adopted a floating exchange rate that depended on the supply and demand of the currency of any given country. Many low-income countries suffered from this system.

The power of Capitalism was already being challenged by serious thinkers who did not envisage its replacement but only its reform - people like the American lawyer Adolf A. Berle[6] whose passion for social justice kept him on the lookout for flaws in institutions. His 1932 critique of the profound changes wrought by the modern business corporation foresaw that corporations would become the dominant institution in society, becoming a force that would compete with the modern state for influence and power.

Decades of Debt

Nyerere had tried to influence the International Monetary Fund regarding the issue of the debt of former colonial countries, struggling to establish themselves as newly independent developing nations.

Back in 1975 when the first Lomé Convention was signed, it was hailed as a step on the road to a new international economic order. Named after the capital of Togo where it was signed, the then nine European Community states signed a cooperation agreement with forty-six African, Caribbean, and Pacific countries (ACP). It was designed to support the former colonies of Britain, France, Holland, and Belgium. It grew as

---

[6] Adolf A. Berle (1895-1971) was a lawyer whose thinking is explored today by the Berle Centre at the Seattle University School of Law.

the EU membership grew and became the biggest accord of its kind in the world.

But by October 1988 when negotiations began on the fourth Lomé Convention, negotiations were marked by a bitter battle among EU states over their contributions. The 1980s has been called 'the lost decade' for international development. Trade concessions were cut and ACP countries, for the first time, had to accept conditions on what they received.

If the underlying values of Lomé – poverty eradication and sustainable development – could be brought into discussions within the World Trade Organisation (WTO), then the peoples of Europe, in solidarity with the peoples of the global South, could make a big impact on the future shape of the world. But regrettably, the WTO agenda was more about the growth of trade than trading for development. This would cause much suffering for decades to come.

As enforced structural adjustment policies were introduced, 'partnership' became the new buzz word. It was a word that felt hollow in the countries of the global South. Whatever 'economic growth' meant, it did not mean the participation in the world economy of every nation, much less every person.

As the new millennium was approaching, the international debt crisis was staggering. Back in the early 1970s, when oil producing countries made a fortune, they put their money into mainly US and European banks. These in turn gave loans to poor countries, in many cases without checking where the money was going.

Then, at the end of the 1970s, interest rates soared, and the borrowing countries had huge interest to pay. At the same time, the prices they were getting for their exports dropped. The International Monetary Fund and the World Bank stepped in to give new loans to ensure that the indebted countries could meet their debt repayments. This had a devastating effect on health and education. In 1997 total debts in developing countries had risen to more than two trillion dollars. For every dollar sent in 'aid' by the rich nations, three dollars were being sent back by poor countries in debt repayments.

Julius Nyerere had asked: "Is human development a possibility when so much of Africa's wealth is channelled into debt servicing?"

Well-known journalist John Simpson wrote: "There is, after all, something truly absurd about sending aid to poor countries, when they are paying us back more in interest than they receive ... We have piled a mountain of debt on the poorest and most vulnerable countries in the world, countries which, on the other side of the ledger, we regard as being most in need of our assistance. It has become our modern equivalent of slavery."

Henry Northover, policy analyst with the Catholic Agency for Overseas Development (CAFOD) went further. He called the world debt crisis a 'silent holocaust', a situation which is silently and steadily killing men, women and children in the developing world.

In more than 40 countries, a movement known as Jubilee 2000 had been advocating a debt-free start to the new millennium for a billion people. Over 50 countries had debts that could never be paid back. Jubilee 2000 was inspired by the idea of the Jubilee Year which, in biblical times, was a season to apply self-righting mechanisms for restoring a balance to society. Every fifty years (seven times seven years actually), debts were forgiven, slaves set free, and liberty proclaimed throughout the land.

It was not only Jews and Christians who advocated this approach. The General Secretary of the Islamic Party of Britain, Sahib Mustaqim Bleher, explained:

> *The Qur'an encourages debt cancellation whenever a debtor is unable, due to his particular circumstances, to repay the debt." He explained that Islam is a religion which counts obligatory regular charity as one of the 'five pillars' on which it is built. Islam cannot be practised without due regard to its social dimension, nor without reference to economic justice.*

In their 1999 Lenten Message, the Irish Bishops wrote:

> *Where debts can only be repaid by denying basic services, they should be deemed unpayable. The original amount of these debts has long ago been repaid, but the global financial system is such that the countries are still paying the interest, which has increased over the years. We fully support the Jubilee 2000 signature Campaign.*

Pope John Paul II had already made his position clear:

> *Christians will have to raise their voice on behalf of the poor of all the world, proposing the Jubilee as an appropriate time to give thought, among other things, to reducing substantially, if not cancelling outright, the international debt which seriously threatens the future of many nations.*

Agenda for Sustainable Development

Debts were not cancelled but the focus shifted to goals for the new millennium that had been envisaged for some time. In September 2000 in New York, eight Millennium Development Goals were elaborated, with a view to reducing extreme poverty by 2015. The World Summit on Sustainable Development produced 'The Johannesburg Declaration on Sustainable Development and the Plan of Implementation", reaffirming the global community's commitments to poverty eradication and the environment, adding emphasis on multilateral partnerships.

In 2012, in Rio de Janeiro, UN member states produced 'The Future We Want', a new set of Sustainable Development Goals to build upon those that had been set for 2015. By the time 2015 arrived, the General Assembly had begun the negotiation process that culminated in the adoption of the 2030 Agenda for Sustainable Development with seventeen more goals at its core.

However, the very nature of capitalism was causing concern, heightened by the crash that reared its head in 2007. The crisis of capitalism has been occupying economists and other thinkers ever since. Some had been questioning it much earlier.

For more than 100 years, since Pope Leo XIII had published *Rerum Novarum* defending the rights of workers, the body of Catholic Social Teaching had been developing. Back in the 1980s the word 'solidarity' was on everyone's lips when workers at the Polish port of Gdansk, under the leadership of Lech Walesa, formed the Solidarity Movement, resisting the oppression that they were suffering from the communist regime of the time. With the Polish Pope, John Paul II, holding office, it is no surprise that the notion of solidarity would enter the vocabulary of the Vatican. Solidarity became a recurrent theme in Pope Benedict's 2009 encyclical *Caritas in Veritate.*

This encyclical rejected capitalism as we know it today. It proposed combining strict limits on state and market power with a civil economy centred on employee-owned businesses, cooperatives, credit unions and other community-based initiatives.

Although *Caritas in Veritate* did not receive a great deal of attention from ordinary Catholics 'in the pew', it was seen by economists as an important - some would even say a radical - intervention in the debate around the crisis of capitalism. Others would say the debate should not include a faith dimension at all. But it is obvious that the crisis of capitalism and the threat of violence from growing inequality affects believers and non-believers alike.

Pope Benedict pointed to the problem of food insecurity which needs to be addressed within a long-term perspective, eliminating the structural causes that give rise to it and promoting the agricultural development of poorer countries. This can be done by investing in rural infrastructures, irrigation systems, transport, organization of markets, and in the development and dissemination of agricultural technology that can make the best use of the human, natural and socio-economic resources that are more readily available at the local level, while guaranteeing their sustainability over the long term as well.

Economic activity cannot solve all social problems through the simple application of commercial logic. This needs to be directed towards the pursuit of the common good, for which the political community in particular must take responsibility. Grave imbalances are produced when economic action, conceived merely as an engine for wealth creation, is detached from political action, conceived as a means for pursuing justice through redistribution. The market is not, and must not become, the place where the strong subdue the weak.[7]

Pope Benedict also called for renewed solidarity in relationships between developing countries and those that are highly industrialized. What is needed is a redistribution of energy

---

[7] *Caritas in Veritate,* Par 36

resources, so that countries lacking those resources can have access to them. The fate of those countries cannot be left in the hands of whoever is first to claim the spoils, or whoever is able to prevail over the rest.[8]

Attention is also drawn to the phenomenon of migration as an aspect of integral human development. This requires bold, forward-looking policies of international cooperation if it is to be handled effectively. Migrant labourers cannot be considered as a commodity or a mere workforce. Every migrant is a human person who, as such, possesses fundamental, inalienable rights that must be respected by everyone and in every circumstance.[9]

Writing of 'economy and communion' Pope Benedict proposed a new composite reality embracing the private and public spheres. It views profit as a means for achieving human and social ends.[10] It is acknowledged that the Pope is drawing here on economic practices embraced by people and businesses associated with the *Focolare* movement.

For years, the ideas of its founder, Chiara Lubich[11], had drawn the attention of economists, sociologists, philosophers, and scholars from several disciplines. She spoke to politicians and business people in many countries and was warmly welcomed to address the leaders of all the main faiths. Members of the *Focolare* Movement can be found in 182 countries today. Many of them engaged in the business sector have applied these ideas about dividing profits so that a portion would be used to

---

[8] Ibid. Par 49

[9] Ibid. Par 64

[10] Ibid. Par 46

[11] Chiara Lubich (1920-2008) was born in the Italian city of Trent and founded the *Focolare* Movement following her experiences during World War II. See https://chiaralubich.org.

help the business grow but another portion to social development of those working in the business or the locality.

When invited to address the Parliamentary Assembly of the Council of Europe in Strasbourg in May 1999, Lubich cited examples of 654 businesses from a wide range of economic sectors in more than thirty countries where this approach was being profitably deployed.

Crisis of Global Capitalism

As soon as *Caritas in Veritate* was published, a group of economists and thinkers met at the University of Nottingham to study the new encyclical. They initiated a reflection on Pope Benedict's ideas. The papers they presented were published under the title 'The Crisis of Global Capitalism'.

John Milbank[12] observed that unrestricted movements of international finance now severely curtail the freedom of action of governments in a way that puts political democracy itself into crisis. The way in which excess capital from one part of the world can be so quicky transferred to another has in part generated the recent severe economic destabilization.

Mark & Louise Zweck who work on the border between USA and Mexico deploy the principles of Dorothy Day. They comment that the suggestion in *Caritas in Veritate* that businesses have a responsibility to all the stakeholders who contribute to the life of a business - the workers, the suppliers, the consumers, and the natural environment itself - would be a major change for firms on Wall Street.

---

[12] John Milbank, as Research Professor of Religion, Politics and Ethics at the University of Nottingham, has authored several volumes on theology and social theory.

Adrian Pabst observes that most essays in the collection propose a more radical programme in line with the Pope's encyclical: labour receives assets (in the form of stake-holdings) and hires capital (not vice-versa), while capital itself comes in part from worker and community-supported credit unions rather than exclusively from shareholder-driven retail banks.

For years, missionaries and volunteers working with community groups had seen on a small scale the benefits of different forms of micro credit. But *Caritas in Veritate* proposes that owners of big capital and those who influence the global economy be persuaded that providing credit that is community-supported is sustainable and is the way to avoid the social upheaval that is inevitable when the power of the 'haves' over the 'have nots' becomes unbearable.

Pile of Gunpowder

When Julius Nyerere visited Dublin back in 1996, he said: "Poverty without hope of relief is like a pile of gunpowder waiting to be ignited". Many thinking people were coming to the same conclusion.

The influential writer Anthony Atkinson published *Inequality: What Can Be Done?* He noted that rising inequality has been declared a priority both by Barack Obama and Christine LaGarde. Atkinson cites research carried out in 2014, in which respondents were asked about the greatest danger to the world. It found that in the United States and in Europe concerns about inequality took precedence above all other dangers.

Atkinson explores inequality from several angles. With an informative history of the problem, he examines the key dimensions of inequality, not just fiscal redistribution. He believes the reduction of inequality requires examination of all aspects of society, including the forces that are radically reshaping the labour markets of both rich and developing countries and leading to a widening gap in the distribution of wages.

Atkinson was a mentor of the French Economist Thomas Piketty, whose massive study *Capital in the 21st Century* became a best seller when the English translation appeared in 2014. He had already published the fruits of much research in *The Economics of Inequality*. In this later study, he focusses not only on the level of inequality as such but to an even greater extent on the structure of inequality. He is concerned about the origins of disparities in income and wealth between social groups and about the various systems of economic, social, moral and political justification that have been invoked to defend or condemn those disparities.

As expected, Piketty drew the criticism of other economists. They lost no time in publishing *Anti Piketty,* challenging his data, his theoretical framework and questioning his policy suggestions, especially what a progressive tax on capital adapted to twenty-first century conditions might look like.

Then, three years later, another bunch of economists published *After Piketty*. They presented a series of reflections and invited Piketty himself to write a response to their criticisms. Several scholars took up the challenge of identifying key issues that required further research on inequality and economic growth. In the same volume Piketty added some thoughts on a reconciliation between economics and social wellbeing.

This makes difficult reading for the ordinary citizen who has not specialized in economics. All the graphs, all the charts, all the equations, are incomprehensible to most of us. But one thing we can grasp is that the twenty-first century has provided the super-wealthy with new opportunities to manage political systems. They have abundant ways of using this power - influencing education, health services, charities, social campaigns, and use of the various media to promote their views. The problem does not end there, and I will discuss 'surveillance capitalism' in a later chapter.

The Good News

Economists aside, the ordinary person in the street knows that wealth inequality is not an accident but has been and still is an inherent feature of capitalism. The good news is that the focus on a new global economy, a new approach to capital, is on the agenda of groups of people in different walks of life and of all ages. The volume of writings on the subject shows that the issue of inequality is of great concern. In addition, the threat to democracy is evident. There appears to be an openness to something new.

In his 2013 Encyclical letter *Evangelii Gaudium,* Pope Francis wrote:

> *Just as the commandment 'Thou shalt not kill' sets a clear limit in order to safeguard the value of human life, today we also have to say 'thou shalt not' to an economy of exclusion and inequality. Such an economy kills.*

In February 2020, Francis called for 'new forms of solidarity' when he invited key figures in the global financial system to meet at the Pontifical Academy of Social Sciences. He asked them to address the problem of rising inequality through inclusion, integration and innovation.

Speaking to the gathered experts, Pope Francis explored some of the dangers that are lurking behind our current economic models. He pointed out that hundreds of millions of people are struggling in extreme poverty, lacking food, housing, healthcare, school, electricity and drinkable water. He lamented the fact that up to five million children die each year from causes related to poverty. Added to this, rising income inequality has left millions of people victims of forced labour, prostitution and organ trafficking. He said we should be concerned that the fifty richest people in the world, possessing the equivalent of US$2.2 trillion, could finance medical care and education for every poor child in the world, either through taxation or philanthropy. He condemned tax breaks for wealthy individuals as 'structural sin'.

As Pope Francis says, we are not condemned to global inequality. These are solvable problems. An economic system can be put in place that includes those left behind by society. If it can be accepted that economic rights form the basis of human solidarity, then disadvantaged peoples and developing nations would become a core concern for financial institutions. At the same time, proposals could address the question of the global climate and the associated displacement of peoples.

What Would It Look Like?

What would a global economy look like that puts people and the planet first? Pope Francis decided to put that question to young economists, young entrepreneurs and change makers. Invitations were widely circulated in universities around the world. Men and women under thirty-five years of age who had qualified or were taking advanced studies in economics and related subjects were asked to examine systemic inequality. They were invited to apply for a place at a Conference to be hosted by the Vatican in Assisi in March 2020. But by then Covid-19 had struck.

Six months later, in November 2020 the three-day event took place, live streamed around the world. It aimed at formulating a new economic vision, one that would take the emphasis away from growth and profit, and prioritise justice, equity, care of the poor, and care of the Earth. It drew upon the experience and vision of people like economist Muhammad Yunus from Bangladesh. His Nobel Prize in 2006 acknowledged his development of a global micro-credit movement.

Vandana Shiva, physicist and environmental activist from India was another of the specialists. Also involved was the French philosopher and professor of social ethics, Sister Cécile Renouard, who founded the *Campus de la Transition,* which aims at helping people move towards more sustainable ways of living and interacting. Professor Kate Raworth from the Environmental Change Institute at Oxford University, pointed out that what participants were about is a new journey, requiring a new vision, new ambition, and new policies.

A small group of young people led the online proceedings from inside the Basilica of St. Francis at Assisi, with participants on screens from all over the world. At the end of the three-day event, twelve action points were listed. These mirrored the twelve thematic hubs of the event, covering key topics. Top of the list was the need to slow down the economic pace globally to let the Earth breathe.

Another point was sharing advanced technologies to help low-income countries develop energy sources and economies in sustainable ways that do not contribute to global warming. Another hub stressed the need to place the stewardship of common goods, including the atmosphere and ecosystems, at the centre of government and academic agendas. The immediate abolition of tax havens worldwide was seen as another priority. The danger of returning to a pre-pandemic 'normal' was highlighted. Rather, the pandemic was seen as an opportunity to look at a changed and better future at the start of this critical decade.

The young participants accepted that many people would consider their vision utopian. But they preferred to see their position as prophetic. They said, "We can ask, ask, and ask again, because what seems impossible today will seem less so tomorrow thanks to our commitment and our insistence." By video on the concluding day, Pope Francis told them "Roll up your sleeves and take the lead".

As the live stream neared its end they declared: "This is just the beginning". And so, it was. They continued their work through regional hubs as well as through the 'village' hubs created around the twelve areas of concern. The website[13] developed around this carries informative contributions from some older, well-known economists.

The exchange of views continued and when they met again in Assisi in September 2022, the young people sent Pope Francis their "Pact for the Economy". It stated that, aware of the responsibility that rests upon their generation, they commit themselves to spend their lives so that the economy of today and tomorrow becomes an economy of peace not of war, that opposes the proliferation of arms, that cares for creation, that is at the service of the human person, family and life, respectful of every woman, man and child, the elderly and especially those most frail and vulnerable.

It will be an economy where finance is a friend and ally of the real economy and of labour, that values and safeguards the cultures and traditions of people, and of the natural resources of

---

[13] www.francescoeconomy.org

the Earth. Their encounters continue, indicating that this movement has an important future.
Concurrently with the above activities, economists of an older generation, highly qualified and experienced, were also putting their thoughts on paper. They express concern that democracy is under threat from the concentration of wealth in the hands of a minority.

In 2022 the Club of Rome published a detailed proposal towards a new economy. Entitled "Earth for All – A Survival Guide for Humanity". It outlines in detail the challenge of a 'Turn Around' on five fronts – poverty, inequality, gender equity, food and energy. It does not minimize the size of this challenge, but it shows that it can be done – though time is running out. Their website[14] keeps us informed of the urgency of the situation.

Among the many thinkers who have endorsed these proposals as brilliant and timely, Ban Ki-moon, former Secretary General of the United Nations and Deputy Chair of The Elders, wrote that "Earth for All" is an extraordinary book at an extraordinary time, and is a 'must-read':

> *This book offers a concrete, breakthrough vision on how to ensure well-being for all – in any country - on our finite planet. Together, we can build a world that is genuinely equitable by following the Five Turnarounds - a roadmap to accelerate the realization of the Sustainable Development Goals in the next decade. I hope it will inspire a new movement of minds and souls that are willing to save our precious humanity.*[15]

---

[14] www.Earth4all.life

[15] *Earth for All, a Survival Guide for Humanity,* Sandrine Dixson-Declève et al, New Society Publishers, 2022

CHAPTER 4

THE TEACHING METHOD OF PAULO FREIRE

MANUELA POURED ME A GLASS OF strong sweet coffee before she answered my question. It was darkish inside her little kitchen, the open door to the muddy yard, the only source of light. Across the table she propped her chin on her hands and thought a minute.

In silence, I marvelled yet again at the contrasts around me: her spotless home and her pretty and contemporary furniture, all matching in primrose yellow - the round kitchen table, the chairs, refrigerator, dresser, cooker, the row of plastic food containers, all so carefully chosen, all so neatly arranged. My eyes stopped at the tall plastic bin in the corner - her water supply for the day. The kitchen has neither sink nor tap.

In this three-roomed rented house, Manuela, now 29, and her husband Damiano, had lived since they married eight years earlier. They had two small daughters at this time. Eight years of hard work and sacrifice had furnished their home, but the street outside was still without asphalt. The area, like much of the rest of the periphery of São Paulo, was without piped sewerage.

Then she spoke: "So you want to know how I feel about learning to read and write? Well then, let's begin at the beginning.

Before I joined the group, I felt blind. I was a prisoner inside my own feelings. I couldn't escape. I felt like someone outside this world. Afterwards ...", she paused and sighed softly, "it was like being born into a new life. I am able to read a little now, some things at least, and I have faith in God to help me along the rest of the way."

"Manuela..." I asked hesitatingly, "can you say what the world looks like now you feel inside it? What is it like to experience this new life?"

> *The world looks beautiful", she replied, "even though it has so many problems. A person who can read can do something about the problems. Not being able to read, you do not know what is happening. Learning to read was like opening my eyes, not only to words but to the world, and even to life itself.*

She stood up. It was raining now, and big drops splashed onto the table through the precariously tiled roof. Patiently, she removed a dainty crochet centrepiece from the table and replaced it with a basin to catch the drops. As if there had been no interruption, she continued:

> *You know, when you cannot read, even your close relatives – maybe even your husband and children – think you are a fool. When someone writes a letter, you must ask another person to read it to you. When you are in the city, you cannot tell where a bus is going, and you always must ask someone in the queue. So now I feel much better about everything. When someone begins to read, that person is like a rosebud when it begins to open, and I feel like that now.*

At that time, I had known Manuela for just over four months. In that period, we had met three times each week for the two-hour sessions of our 'Cultural Circle'. During this time, skills in reading and writing were developed among a small group of women from our neighbourhood. They, in turn, shared their vision of life and together we tried to understand our world and its problems a little better, so that we could play our part in transforming it into a more human place.

Zélia was another member of our circle. Aged 37 years at the time and mother of six, she learned to read and write very quickly – after about 40 hours of our literacy programme.

> *Perhaps that's because I went to school for two years as a child", she felt. "Like most of the people who live around here now, we lived in the country then, and you had to work hard in order to eat. My parents needed my help on the land where they were hired. As soon as I was big enough to be useful, I got no more schooling. But when I grew up and came to live in the city, I realized how much I needed to read and write. I tried and tried by myself, but never managed to succeed alone.*

"I used to feel so sad", Zélia continued.

> *Often when I saw other people reading my eyes would fill up with tears. Until this last baby was born, I always worked for a family as a cook. When my employer first asked me if I could read, I was ashamed to admit that I couldn't. Well, you see, I did read a tiny little bit, so I said I could. Whenever she gave me a recipe to make and told me to buy the ingredients, I would spend such a long time worrying and trying to guess what was on it. Sometimes I had to ask a stranger in the supermarket to read it for me. I used to feel so ashamed, even though it wasn't my fault that I couldn't read properly.*

Before long Zélia was on the rota of readers at the Sunday liturgies in our local Christian community. She told me:

> *When you begin to read and write, you feel free, your embarrassment is gone, you take part in more activities, you can*

look for better work, you understand many things which you never knew before. It used to be so difficult when the children came home from school with a note, and you had to ask them to read it to you. Every piece of paper caused you a nightmare.

The teaching method we adopted in our 'Cultural Circle' was based on the belief of Paulo Freire[1] that adults can learn to read rapidly so long as reading is not part of a cultural imposition on them. The teaching must be rooted in the daily life of the community. Words represent ideas. The ideas represented by these words must be discussed before the words themselves are discovered in their graphic symbols.

It was customary in Brazil to equate 'culture' with 'formal education'. Our first step was to explore this and help the group to acknowledge that they had a culture that was valuable, even if they could not yet read and write. After discussing this one day, I asked the group 'so how would you explain culture – what is it?'. After a little thought, Zélia was the first to respond: "Ah, I suppose culture is everything a mother teaches her children".

That was an eye-opening moment in the group. They valued what they already knew. Even though they might not yet be able to read and write, they were worth something. This was mission critical. We had broken the culture of silence. These women were discovering that what they think is important. They were teaching me, and I thanked them for what I was learning.

The small teaching kit that we were using, provided to us by another group leader in our area, was a far cry from the

---

[1] Paulo Freire was born in Brazil in 1921 and died in 1997.

published thoughts of Paulo Freire in *Pedagogy of the Oppressed*.[2] Our photocopied kit contained a series of pictures to introduce the reading of different kinds of reality. It also contained a pack of cards, each measuring two inches square, on which were printed the essential basic syllables of commonly spoken Portuguese. These cards simplified the task of assembling words in the early days while the women were still learning the art of holding a pencil and forming their own syllables on paper.

A personal copy of the picture we would discuss as we began our work was handed around. The first question for reflection was 'What do you see in this picture'. We took time to name all the things - a tree, a cat, a road, a bus, a cloud, a boy on a bicycle, a supermarket ... whatever. Then we asked: 'What do you read in this picture? What is happening? What's the story? Everyone was interested to hear what the others felt was going on. We were also grasping the difference between seeing what is happening and reading what is happening.

Our third question was 'What do I hear? Is this picture saying something to me'. Now we were getting down to a bit of social analysis. Learning that their interpretation of their environment mattered to others was very valuable to each member of the group.

Our final question having read the picture was 'What do I feel?' If we felt disturbed in any way by what the picture was saying, or by what came up in the discussion of the picture, then maybe there was some action we could take - supportive action or action that could make a change for the better in our

---

[2] *Pedagogy of the Oppressed* was first published in Portuguese in 1968 and in English in 1970. It was later translated into a total of 20 languages. More than one million copies have been sold.

neighbourhood. We were not here only to learn to read written words. We were learning to 'read' reality - a key concept in the pedagogy of Paulo Freire.

The bus in our picture on the first day was going to Lapa. Everyone in the group knew Lapa, our nearest Metro terminal. Lapa has two parts - la and pa. We can call these parts syllables. On the flipchart we saw how 'la' is written. And then we saw 'pa'. Each member searched for these syllables among her set of cards and put the two together making 'lapa'. That's what was written on the front of the bus in our picture! We talked about big letters and small letters. Once you can read 'la' and 'pa', it is not difficult to learn to read 'ma' and 'da' and 'ca' and 'na' and 'va'.

'Oh, look here', said one in the group! This is 'na-da'. 'Nada' in Portuguese means 'nothing', a word we use every day.

Before going home after that very first session, everyone felt they were on an exciting journey. We had begun to awaken that self-confidence which Freire stresses is an essential step on the road to literacy and to so much more. Soon after that, I travelled a long distance by bus from São Paulo to attend a conference Freire was addressing at a University in the State of Mato Grosso. It was a great privilege to hear him speak and to meet the man himself. But the audience was an academic one. I did not meet anyone else there who was actually working at the coalface applying the principles he was advocating among people who so urgently needed the gift he was offering.

In 1963 Freire had been asked by the populist Brazilian government to coordinate a national literacy campaign. But that regime was quickly overturned with the coup d'etat of 1964. After 70 days in prison, he became exiled to Chile. Instead of his ideas being silenced, the leaders of the coup actually made it possible for his methodology to gain a wider international audience! After some time in Chile, he was invited to USA, and later to Geneva. He was not able to return to Brazil until 1979.

I had first become aware of Freire's methodology in Kenya back in 1977. At one of my Congregation's international meetings, several days were devoted to workshops given by Anne Hope and Sally Timmell. These two members of the Grail movement had met Freire in USA and later studied with him in Geneva.

Freire insisted that education is a form of politics and is never neutral. It always serves some interests and impedes others. But schooling can be used for liberation. He argues that education properly used will enable people to come to understand social systems of oppression and thus equip themselves to act to change that reality. Educators, Freire believed, should ask themselves for whom and on whose behalf, they are working.

In *Pedagogy of the Oppressed,* Freire introduced a radical distinction that has since become a feature of progressive educational thought: the difference between what he called "banking" and "problem-posing" education. Knowledge is something that is co-constructed, Freire would say.

While working in Brazil before his exile, Freire and his co-workers had been able to avail of active grassroots organizations to put his ideas into practice. In the farming and labour organisations, and in no small way, in the local Christian communities, the leadership that was essential could be tapped. Freire knew that the importance of forming trainers to carry out this work was one of the biggest challenges in pursuing his educational goals.

In 1970 Freire was invited to Boston by a group called *International Development and Social Change,* which was affiliated with the University at Harvard. Among those who signed up for Freire's course were the two members of the ecumenical Grail Movement whom I had first met in 1977, Anne Hope and Sally Timmel. They had already read *Pedagogy of the Oppressed.* They felt that these insights combined with group dynamics would greatly enhance the promotion of Freire's ideas in places where local leadership had to be developed. They later wrote:

> *Freire's critiques were compelling and enlightening. However, his philosophy and practical methodology needed to be incorporated into programmes that used insights about group processes, human relationships, and adult education principles and practice. Group leadership and group dynamics were tools to help a group move away from 'banking' education to participatory processes. This was essential if the work was to be effective.*[3]

When Anne and Sally took this work to Kenya in the 1970s, Anne was living in exile from her native South Africa where the apartheid system was still in place. Missionaries who were greatly inspired by the teaching of the Second Vatican Council Document on *The Church in the Modern World* expressed great interest in this new approach to organising development projects. The workshops we attended at our international meeting in Limuru, Kenya introduced us to Freire's thinking and methodology.

Sally and Anne had established a programme called DELTA – Development Education and Leadership Training in Action. They had been invited to work with the diocesan development programmes throughout Kenya. These were organized by an Irishman, Enda Byrne, who was Development Director for the

---

[3] *Training for Transformation in Practice,* Anne E. Hope and Sally J. Timmel, Eds., Practical Action Publishing Ltd, 2014

Catholic Bishops in Kenya. Guidelines for group activities were prepared in language and diagrams that were very accessible.

Freire's concept of 'generative themes' were explained. These are issues that are important to a local community. It is what the people are talking about. Even more than that, they are issues that people want to get up and do something about. The word 'generative', they explain, comes from 'to generate', to 'give life'. Another concept in Training for Transformation is that of 'codes'. These are tools, like pictures, stories, drama, or even a film which presents to the group a very familiar problem about which they have strong feelings.

By the 1980s, Anne and Sally saw that their growing collection of handouts, diagrams, and pictures should be collected in book form. This led to the publication in 1984 of the first edition of a 3-volume handbook for community workers entitled *Training for Transformation.* This publication from Mambo Press in Zimbabwe, proved to be an invaluable resource in countless small communities. Later a fourth volume was added.

Whether the goals included literacy or healthcare or income generation projects, once it involved a grassroots group of people with commitment, these handbooks provided precious tools. The language was simple, and the illustrations by Chris Hodzi were sources of productive reflection for groups of many cultures.

This work was never going to be easy. Evaluation of the process at various times showed just how difficult it is to stay with the process while grassroot leadership is developed and long-term commitment is assured. Not only were there difficulties from within the process, but some group members never embraced the process. Perhaps they had other development projects that were bearing fruit in different contexts, or they may have had negative feelings about the new and popular methodology.

To this day I meet missionaries who will recall 'there was a time in Kenya when I never wanted to hear the word DELTA again'. This can happen whenever a new idea becomes popular. In their enthusiasm, those who adopt the new thing can 'turn off' those who have not had the same experience. They feel the new idea is being rammed down their throats. They can feel threatened even though their own projects may be very satisfying and fruitful.

Within several Catholic dioceses in Kenya, the DELTA programme flourished until the pontificate of Pope John Paul II. During that period, the Church leadership became more closed to the idea that the message of Jesus Christ could be described as liberating people from what was experienced as oppressive. Despite this, much of the process had taken hold and became part of the technique most development workers used. Already, the ideas and methodology developed in Training for Transformation had spread to several other countries and had been embraced by people of different faith backgrounds and none.

As news of the work of DELTA in Kenya reached Nigeria, the roots of a new initiative began to shoot up. This happened in 1979, in Ajegunle, a densely populated suburb of Lagos. I had the opportunity of visiting Ajegunle that year and was introduced by a colleague[4] to the challenging work of promoting

---

[4] Felicity Cunningham (1915-1987) was born in Duns, Scotland. After searching for a spiritual home in Buddhism, The Quakers, and the Salvation Army, she eventually decided Catholicism was where she belonged and joined the Medical Missionaries of Mary in 1951, where her nursing skills were soon deployed in Nigeria.

healthcare under these difficult conditions. Walls of refuse six foot high lined the roadsides. Families crowded into three-storey housing blocks, one room to a family and no running water. I wondered just where anyone could begin to talk of health care! To me it felt like a hopeless case.

Yet it was here, in Ajegunle, that the initial steps of the Training for Transformation programme in Nigeria began. It was piloted by the leadership of the Cardoso Catholic Community Project. They drew together teams from identified groups, placing emphasis on holistic development. These people assumed responsibility to initiate the training of trainers and capacity building within existing initiatives.

Following a series of action-reflection-action events which explored concrete ways of empowering leaders, they decided to invite resource persons from DELTA in Kenya to assist the process. They flew over to Nigeria and provided workshops where ideas could be developed, and training and collaboration could be mapped out. This provided the background to the development of creative thinking around corporate social action.

In 1983, the name DELES was coined for the work in Nigeria: Development Education and Leadership Services. Development - integral human development - aimed to empower the individual. Purposeful educational intervention was aimed at the pursuit of social and political change locally. Leadership training for volunteers and professionals would further equip those who wanted to work for change in their communities. Many more people were drawn to participate in the ideas that had been developed in Ajegunle.

In 1985, the DELES Coordinating Committee employed its first full-time Coordinator, who was joined by two others a short time later. Then, at Easter in 1987, DELES experienced a wind of change and expansion, and concrete steps were needed to respond to the growing demands of the training programme. Instead of being managed by a small Committee based in the cities of Lagos and Ibadan, a new structure was created which established two operational Zones for decentralization of leadership and encouraged multiplier effects. Their website[5] tells us that DELES has since expanded to nearly all parts of Nigeria and has also helped other countries to develop their own educational programmes.

A close friend of mine[6] was a missionary in Nigeria in those years. She and other colleagues became very involved in the DELES adventure. The team travelled thousands of miles every year helping people to analyse their problems and empowering them to seek community-based solutions.

The Alma Ata Declaration

These theological and sociological insights were impacting missionary methodology. This was further challenged in 1978 when the World Health Organization and UNICEF held a ground-breaking International Conference on Primary Health Care, resulting in the famous Declaration of Alma Ata.[7] It reminded us that health is a fundamental human right requiring the action of many social and economic sectors in addition to the health sector.

In addition to hospital-based services we were challenged to increase our services in Primary Health Care. This is where the main health problems in the community are addressed. It

---

[5] https://deles.org

[6] Sister Maura Ramsbottom. See Postscript 4

[7] Alma Ata, is a city in Kazakhstan, now called Almaty.

includes education concerning prevailing health issues and methods of preventing and controlling them.

For some years before the Alma Ata Declaration, medical missionaries from the main Christian Churches had been discussing together these very issues. It was obvious to everyone that hospital-based care alone could make little change to the overall health status of the people. Yet the demands for curative care were so great that preventive care in many places had become a poor relation, undervalued and under resourced.

The coming to life of a community-based healthcare project is a gradual thing that requires a lot of patience. Different aspects of the project will develop at their own pace. These aspects include the whole area of the prevention of disease, nutrition, health education, raising awareness among the people in the villages about their need to become more responsible for their health and to do whatever they could to prevent sickness.

When I interviewed my colleagues in south-east Nigeria about their approach, they stressed the influence of the teaching of Freire on their methodology. They described to me in detail a project started in 1989 which became the model for others.

In the early days of the project, sixteen villages became involved, and this number grew as the years passed. Once the people had the initial awareness that they were not powerless to change their situation, they did their own survey of their health needs. Their leaders and some of their community were trained with the help of DELES to carry out the survey.

First, they looked at the incidence of disease and the prevalence of sickness within their communities. When they began to ask, 'what causes these sicknesses?' they discovered it was a lack of water, no sanitation, no access to immunization for their children, and no backup care for pregnant women resulting in a high incidence of maternal mortality.

Before long, the villagers and their leaders began to take steps to prevent sicknesses like malaria, polio, measles, TB, and to eliminate diseases that came from dirty water. Very early on, they requested the Core Team to organise immunizations in their villages on a regular monthly basis. These immunization clinics were carried out by a mobile team of nurses from the hospital in the nearest town.

After about five years of regular monthly immunizations, a marked drop in the incidence of polio, measles and TB could be observed. At that point, to enable on-going education in the villages, people were asked whether they would like to select one or two people from among them who would be trained as Village Health Workers. A six-week training course was organized, concentrating on how to prevent sicknesses in the villages and how to mobilize the community.

To sustain this activity, good leaders would be needed in the villages. The DELES team were invited to come and give their well-known four-phase Leadership Training to the people nominated by each village. This was very much appreciated. It gave the people who completed the Leadership Training some confidence and status. They would then be responsible to work in harmony with the immunization clinics.

The next major area to be addressed was the high mortality rate among pregnant women. All existing Traditional Birth Attendants were invited to come forward to update the training that had been passed on to them over generations in their villages. There was a very encouraging response to this invitation. These women, who play such a key role, underwent a three-month training course. They came in groups of about sixteen at a time.

The training course was given by the same nurse-midwives who worked on the immunization team, and who were well known in all the villages by this time. It was important that the people did not experience these developments as an imposition of Western culture, but rather a growth of their own cultural experience, allowing their own values to blend with effective measures for ensuring good health.

In rural areas, Traditional Birth Attendants are usually older women. During the courses these ladies were invited to share with us how they currently attended to their pregnant women. From that starting point, they were encouraged to see that they could improve their service by introducing better hygiene. Simple kits were provided. Safer methods of assessment were introduced, while emphasizing their important role in recognizing cases that needed to be referred to hospital.

Within a period of about five years from that time, yearly evaluations showed that no more women were dying in childbirth, children were not getting sick as much as before, and there were no new cases of polio. That encouraged everybody to keep going – for it is uphill work raising awareness about the fact that good community health is our own responsibility.

By this time the villagers and their leaders had begun to organise a safe, clean source of water. Before long, with help from Trócaire in Ireland and UK Catholic charity, CAFOD, six of the villages had sunk boreholes. The arrangement was that a borehole would not be completed until each village had contributed one-fifth of the total cost. In the slower communities, people were encouraged when they saw lovely clean water in the neighbouring villages. All this combined to reduce the mortality rate. It was a source of great pride for the villagers that they were now able to take care of their health.

Pre-natal care and hygiene are critical to community health. So also is nutrition. One of the health team began introducing sustainable agricultural methods into the villages. Before long, crops were yielding two harvests each year instead of one. As the workload grew, a retired teacher from one of the villages joined the team. In that way nutrition was greatly improved.

These gifted and highly committed women taught the people how to make the best use of the crops that were harvested. Soon families were enjoying more tasty meals that were very nutritious. At last malnutrition was noticeably decreasing. With the hardship of political turmoil this was a struggle to maintain. But the commitment of local people continued to bring about good results in their neighbourhoods.

Moving On

As missionaries we see our role as that of planting a seed, enabling the people to care for it, and then moving on elsewhere. Once we can see a project is quite sturdy, it is time for us to be thinking of moving on. In the above project, our daily involvement was gradually reduced to just weekly and then monthly visits.

The Village Health Workers, the Traditional Birth Attendants and the Immunization Team were well able to lead the project, maintaining the momentum of awareness and ongoing education. The Core Team of the project had regularly reflected on the future of the work, watching the little seed sown back in 1989 grow to a sapling, full of future potential. But the final step to complete self-reliance was important.

The DELES Team was once again invited to assist with this process to enable the project to function at its own momentum. They designed a three-phase process, each phase comprised of three days of workshops with the various groups involved. The DELES Team met with these groups in each of the villages to plan the workshops. There was a space of six months between each phase, and over that period of eighteen months the responsibilities of each group became clearer.

The Core Team became aware of changes that were necessary and inevitable. The Traditional Birth Attendants were affirmed in their ability to carry on their work. The Village Health Workers were given more confidence in their leadership abilities. The Immunization Team was animated to continue their regular monthly visits. The nutritional aspect was going well too.

The only area that needed attention now was the coordination of the groups. This need was very happily filled. The people could now move forward into the future development of their own new ideas and skills. The experience of this health-care model organized from the grassroots upwards, was put together and published[8] as a resource to help communities in other rural areas of Africa.

HIV and AIDS

In the early 1980s when HIV was first identified, our extraordinary adventure called for several new initiatives. Long-term commitment to this work involved supporting and enhancing people's own coping mechanisms while respecting their religious and cultural traditions. While treating the symptoms, empathy called for a diversity of responses, drawing on skills

---

[8] Aileen Doggett and Janet McVicar, *Handbook for Health Workers: An Introductory Training Course in Primary Health Care.*

in the fields of clinical, social, and pastoral care. For the next thirty years this would remain a major challenge.

In Lagos, a Nigerian colleague[9] was anxious to devise some response to the growing issue of AIDS. Freire stressed the importance of spending time among the people, listening carefully to find out what issues were important for them. My friend had already contacted other doctors in the densely populated city who – like herself – were anxious about the scale of the problem.

Nigeria at that time had a total population of more than 127 million people. An estimated 8% were living with HIV. It was thought that in one year close to half a million people may have died from AIDS. Some estimates for the number of children orphaned by the disease were as high as 2.6 million.

A number of agencies were involved, but my colleague suspected that more time was spent on collecting statistics than on providing a caring service to those who were suffering, and very little or none at all on education for prevention. She found the trends in HIV prevalence among women attending antenatal clinics ranged between 2.6% in low sero-positive areas, and up to 6.8% where it was high. She became convinced that raising awareness and education about the disease at all levels was essential, and where possible arranging Behaviour Change Workshops.

Within Catholic parishes, excellent volunteers were coming forward for training, to work in their communities. This called for engaging the services of experienced resource people for the training of trainers. The big question was 'where to start?'

---

[9] Dr. Felicia Muoneke is a Nigerian member of the Medical Missionaries of Mary.

My colleague told me:

> *I felt out of touch with the reality experienced by those who are most likely to be affected. I felt the best place to learn was in the market, where I could talk to the women. I would wander around, posing as a customer and pricing their goods. Sometimes I would buy things like peppers or tomatoes – anything to begin a conversation. On some occasions, when I came across a hairdresser, I would get a hairdo. That was a great way to introduce the subject of HIV and find out how much the people knew and what their attitudes were. At taxi parks, I would begin by enquiring about going to a distant part of the city and get bargaining about the price. After a while, I would get around to the topic I most wanted to hear them discuss.*
>
> *At all these places, I would try to find out how much the people knew, or if they had any information at all about HIV and AIDS. Generally, almost all had heard little bits here and there. Most of the time it was very inaccurate misinformation. Without telling them I was a doctor, I tried giving some basic information, and tried to raise a little awareness — all the time this was against the surrounding noisy, hassled environment.*
>
> *This gave me a background on which I could plan workshops. Eventually, we started running these workshops among church groups, health clinics and in schools. Families began to invite me to speak to them and to talk to relatives who they suspected needed to be encouraged to go for testing. These first steps helped to shape the plan for a more co-ordinated approach to the problem.*

A year later, she found herself deeply involved in the organisation of an important Conference on HIV/AIDS run by my

Congregation in the Nigerian capital, Abuja. The 75 participants included staff members from our hospitals and outreach services and members of other religious congregations who were working with the HIV pandemic. Everyone knew it was a problem which would affect Nigeria for a long time to come.

Even Bigger Questions

Another Sister[10] working in Uganda had to find a different kind of response. A mother who was dying of AIDS turned to her and asked: "What will happen to my children when I am gone? Will you take care of them?" Moments like this prompted her to think of ways in which she could help orphans who had been obliged to drop out of school to take care of their dying parents. As well as losing one or both parents, they find they have no money for school fees, uniform, and books, not even for basic food for themselves and the younger brothers and sisters left in their care.

Orphans like these are traumatised through witnessing the final illness of their parents. They are de-energized and suffer deeply from their grief and loss. Many of these boys and girls also suffer from depression and anxiety. Those who have been sent to live with relatives experience great difficulties in adapting in their new home, where they know they are an added burden. Some have been physically or sexually abused. Many of them find it very difficult to go back to school and keep up with the pace of studies when they have nursed one parent – or maybe both – through the last stages of AIDS. For many, the

---

[10] Ursula Sharpe, a native of Ireland, is a nurse-midwife and trained counsellor and is Congregational Leader of the Medical Missionaries of Mary at the time of writing.

only way forward that they can see is to beg on the streets or go into prostitution.

With our health team leaders, my colleagues in Uganda talked about this and tried to see what the positive elements in this dark situation were. First of all, there is the fact that the orphans have youth on their side. That means energy, ambition, young brains, and the ability to learn. And then there is land. Putting these positive elements together, they saw that as well as grief counselling, they needed to give them some activity that would harness their energy, nurture their ambition, and help them to acquire the skills that their parents would have given them if they had lived.

It was then that they came up with the idea of creating Farm Schools. They started first with one Farm School. This idea proved to be so popular and effective that it was not long until they had to find premises for a second, a third and so on. Before long they were running six Farm Schools in the vicinity of the townland of Masaka, each with about one hundred boys and girls with the gender fairly evenly balanced.

The boys and girls came to the residential Farm School for one week each month. It was obvious that they loved coming and really enjoyed managing school and home in this combination. You could tell this by their enthusiasm and eagerness to learn. They were proud to wear their school uniform. This seems to have helped them in their ongoing search for identity.

During the week at school, they learned to read and write if they had not already become literate, and to improve their literacy if they had already begun. They also learned basic mathematics, marketing, book-keeping and how to handle a bank account. There was also plenty of time for games, peer counselling and individual counselling. In this way, they got a sympathetic ear as they tried to work through their feelings of loss, anger, and fear. There was also ample opportunity to discuss HIV and AIDS and to grow in awareness of the virus that killed their parents and to try to avoid getting it themselves.

While they were at school, an adult would be available to care for their younger siblings. For the remaining three weeks of each month, they returned to their homestead and put into practice what they learnt during the week at the Farm School. The Agricultural Instructors on our team, two of whom were women, visited them on their land, to ensure that they were managing it well.

A small revolving Loan Fund was established, from which they could be granted money to implement any good ideas they had. The Supervisors also checked on how that small amount of money was being managed. Quickly, the Farm Schools showed encouraging results. With over two million children orphaned as a result of HIV and AIDS in Uganda at that time, the problem of orphan education was a huge challenge, not only to support the orphans themselves but also to look to the future economy of the country.

Nairobi Conference

In 2004, sixty-two members of the Congregation met in Nairobi for an important international Conference to take stock of the situation[11]. It was long before the days of Zoom. However, three months before we travelled to Nairobi, preparation was begun by eForum. For many of my colleagues living in remote parts of Africa or Latin America, this meant long journeys to the nearest Internet Café and then perhaps queueing for hours to get access to the Web. However, the eForum was felt to have

---

[11] The report of this Conference is available on CD.

been an indispensable tool, helping those in isolated missions to feel part of something much bigger than their own effort.

Over those three preparatory months, we debated a wide range of topics concerning the services we were providing. In this way, everyone became familiar with what was being done in other parts of the world. The topics included different kinds of experience and the many pitfalls encountered in setting up an AIDS programme.

There was discussion about newly developing anti-retroviral therapies; alternative therapies and relief of symptoms from herbal remedies; counselling; pastoral care; home based care; women in prostitution and victims of trafficking; care of carers; spiritual and ethical issues; orphans; prevention of infection; AIDS in the hospital; hospice and palliative care; poverty and AIDS.

When we met in Nairobi, we realised that we could no longer speak of HIV/AIDS as an epidemic, nor even as a pandemic. It was already endemic in our society all over the world. At that time, no adequate vaccine had been developed though much research was in progress. We looked on it as a condition that is not going to disappear in the foreseeable future. We saw that we needed a broad-based and multi-faceted approach to the services we were offering.

Eleven main papers were presented, sixteen participants from different medical disciplines were invited to talk about their personal experience and there were eight workshops – each of which was repeated so that everyone could attend all. The discussion which these evoked explored ways in which we could help one another to ensure best practice in the ongoing struggle to cope with this health problem.

In the evenings we relaxed and enjoyed some hilarious entertainment. But in general, it was a sombre event. Before we left, there was a passionate appeal to us all to remember that statistics do not cry; numbers do not tremble; graphs do not need a hug; data does not touch our hearts – but orphaned children should. We were told: 'If we do not cry, we should not be on mission. If we are not moved by what we are seeing, we should go home'.

Complementary Therapies

While in East Africa for that event, I took the opportunity to revisit my old home near Singida in Tanzania. Compiling the report of the AIDS Conference all that week in Nairobi, my hands had been overworked. Arthritis in the joint above my right thumb had flared and was quite painful. When travelling, I always packed in my hand-luggage an elasticated cotton 'tubi-grip' support in case this would happen. By the time I reached Singida it needed to be washed. It was when I asked for some soap flakes that I was introduced to Quantum Touch Therapy.

Sister Marian[12]told me: "I never say I can cure this way, but I may be able to help you. The healer is the one who is healed. The therapist provides the environment where healing can take place". She went on to explain this therapy which was new to me.

> *If we put ten grandfather clocks in a room, initially the pendulum of each of them will swing to its own rhythm. But if we go away and come back two days later, we will find they*

---

[12] Sister-doctor Marian Scena from Denver, USA, joined the Medical Missionaries of Mary in Boston and studied medicine in University College Dublin. She trained in Quantum Touch Therapy during a sabbatical in USA.

are all swinging to the same rhythm. They have been drawn to this by the waves in the universe, or an impelling energy force called resonance. Entrainment is the process by which things align their movement and energy together to match in rhythm and phase. This activity is known in quantum physics. In a similar way, a therapist can, through focussing and deep breathing, absorb the rhythm of the universe and then apply this rhythm to restore your injured joint to its original alignment, reducing the painful swelling." [13]

I was in no position to argue against ten grandfather clocks! I had just connected my phone to the Wi-Fi, and I was relying on radio waves that I could not see in order to get the news. Why would I disbelieve that there were other waves coming into the house too just because I knew nothing about them?

Half an hour later I was relaxing on the sofa in our community room with the footstool extended. Marian held the swollen painful joint as she breathed deeply. I was also listening deeply to the softly playing music she had asked me to select. After twenty minutes she said: "You may need another session when you get back to Ireland". But the pain was gone, and it never returned. Before then, it had been a frequent visitor in cold weather. However, I did locate a therapist in Dublin[14] and since then I always return to her for quantum touch therapy to top up my immune system before going abroad on various jobs. I have also availed of this therapy during times of great stress.

This treatment, and several other complementary therapies, have assisted in the work of healing, especially in communities where income levels are low. Reflexology, Tai Chi, exercises in

---

[13] Cf. Richard Gordon, *Quantum Touch, The Power to Heal.*

[14]Erica McKinney, *https://ericamckinney.com*

body, mind and spirit and expertise in locally produced herbal remedies have all greatly complemented the skills of medicine and nursing taught in the Universities.

Theories of Paulo Freire
In Traumatised Communities

The Spanish word *Capacitar* [15] meaning 'to empower' was adopted by a service begun in 1988 in response to the needs of grassroots communities in Central America. In many places, the trauma was collective and far-reaching. People were affected by violence, poverty, war and trauma. There could be no possibility of individual therapeutic services.

Using Freire's approach to popular education, the *Capacitar* methodology empowers participants to connect with their own deep wisdom in relation to body, mind, and spirit. The practices are simple, drawing from many ancient cultures as well as from current research in neurosciences and trauma healing. This educational and communal approach has enabled many people to benefit through group therapy. Participants in turn share the training with their families and communities multiplying the work to improve the lives of many.

Sister-doctor Geneviève van Waesberghe[16] told me:

> *Since 2006, I have given workshops in many African countries: Burundi, Cameroon, Central African Republic, Gabon, Kenya, Democratic Republic of Congo, Uganda, Senegal, South Sudan, and Tanzania. Participants included young people, university students, women's groups, teachers,*

---

[15] Capacitar was founded by Dr. Patricia Mathes Cane. *https://capacitar.org*

[16] Sister Geneviève van Waesberghe studied medicine at University College Dublin and has worked in East and Central Africa for most of her life since then. See also in Postscript 6 an account of her work in Rwanda.

artists, journalists, medical and mental health personnel, human rights defenders, lawyers, priests and religious, refugees, victims of conflict-related sexual abuses, prisoners, child soldiers both male and female, police, soldiers, UN personnel. It is in the most affected areas that Capacitar is most alive. As people heal, they discover their vocation to heal their society.

In Tanzania, when plans to establish the Arusha Mental Health Trust[17] were discussed early in 1996, empowerment of clients was a key concept. At that time, the city of Arusha was rapidly growing as an urban conglomerate. People had been moving in for work in tourism, mining of Tanzanite[18], and all kinds of petty business.

The population was very diverse with the dominant group being Tanzanian people of various tribes. There was a small but growing population from other African countries, as the Tribunal for the Genocide of Rwanda[19] was then setting up its Courts in the city. A large number of Indian and Pakistani businesspeople whose families had come to East Africa to build the railway were there as third and fourth generation folk. They were the backbone of the city's commerce. The residents who had come from overseas were largely made up of Lutheran missionaries from North America whose ancestry was Scandinavian. There was a smaller number of Catholic

---

[17] The Arusha Mental Health Trust, known as AMHT, is an NGO and close partner of the Government of Tanzania. With the support of the Medical Missionaries of Mary and the people of Arusha it was founded by clinical psychologist Dr. Sheila Devane MMM, assisted by the current director, Mr. Emmanuel Bujulu.

[18] Tanzanite is a gemstone of blue, violet and burgundy, found in a small mining area about 50 km south-east of Arusha. It has been marketed since the late 1960s.

[19] Commonly known as ICTR

missionaries who came from USA, Ireland, the United Kingdom or mainland Europe.

The needs of this community of mixed origins included various levels of mental illness. This included psychosis, epilepsy, trauma, alcoholism, cannabis addiction, depression, anxiety, as well as childhood disorders. In 2008 I was invited to spend some time in Arusha with a view to reporting on the strengths and successes of the programme, along with difficulties encountered and how these were addressed or could be avoided by others. It was one of the most privileged experiences I ever had to feel the warmth, witness the welcome, and sense the challenge of this endeavour. I wondered how did they ever get such a service up and running?

At the beginning, Sister Sheila Devane and her co-worker Emmanuel Bujulu held many public meetings. These took place wherever they could find a space — in any hall, church, hospital room, shed, or side street they could get. In conversations with the townspeople, they searched for ways in which they might address these needs and how best to use the skills of some nurses already trained in psychiatry in the government hospital. At that time there was no forum to practice skills that were so greatly needed. I was told:

> *What was important right from the beginning was that the people would own this programme, would be its co-creators and always have an active voice in every aspect of its service delivery. It was clear the Tanzanian government health service would have to be a partner as were many churches, mosques, and groups of any cadre willing to join in — even if it were only to say, 'we will send patients to you'. The collaboration, good will, and ideas of everyone were the*

foundation stones of the model of service delivery. This marked every level of development as the project grew.

The service now offers advocacy, training, psychotherapy, medication, rehabilitation, and recovery to the people of Arusha and far beyond. Prevention of mental illness is, of course, a high priority of the service. Among its accolades were the embedding of psychotherapy as a core aspect of mental health care; respect for and use of local knowledge and customs; collaboration with other service providers of state and faith; and efforts at all times to be client-led in any new directions and decisions.

Now located in a modern building situated close to a government hospital, the service closely partners with the Ministry of Health while retaining its considerable autonomy. As an organisational model and a partnership between government, mission, and people, it is greatly lauded and is thoroughly owned by the people of the town. On her visit to Tanzania in 2006, the then President of Ireland, Mary McAleese, made it clear that this was one programme she wanted to visit because of its model of care and strong grassroots partnership.

World-wide influence of Paulo Freire

Professor David Morley, of the London Institute of Child Health, gained wide experience as a paediatrician while working in Nigeria. The concept of older children passing on skills in health and hygiene to younger ones led him to found Child-to-Child[20]. He did this with Dr. Hugh Howes, an educationalist at the London-based Institute of Education. Dr. Morley also

---

[20] *www.childtochild.org.uk*

founded *Teaching Aids at Low Cost* (TALC) which has distributed more than 10 million books, slides, and accessories including *Where There is No Doctor*. He said: "Just as Paulo Freire used words that were important to people in order to teach literacy, so we can use child growth to teach numeracy."

Mothers can be shown what plotting a graph involves. They are accustomed to observing the amount of water being poured into a bucket hanging over a spring. They know how much they need and how long the bucket takes to fill.

Once it is explained to a mother that the vertical line in her child's health chart indicates months, she can easily come to understand the other sections of the chart, e.g. immunisations. Just as the water fills in her bucket at the well, once she can read her child's chart, and watch the lines in relation to what is normal growth, she can maintain her role in the 'driving seat' of her child's primary health care.

In 2013, Anne Hope and Sally Timmel[21] decided to evaluate the work of Training for Transformation in the sixty countries where it had been implemented. Everyone involved in community development knows that this process is neither quick nor easy. Thirty-seven practitioners from twenty-six countries were invited to come together to reflect on the ways in which they had adapted the approach to training for transformation in different social and cultural settings.

A 'Think Well' was created for them to write about how they had adapted the work. This resulted in the publication of *Training for Transformation in Practice*[22]. As the Preface states: 'This

---

[21] After Anne died on 26 December 2014, Sally wrote her autobiography *You Can Never Go Back*, Darton, Longman & Todd.

[22] Hope, Anne; Timmel, Sally. *Training for Transformation in Practice*. Practical Action Publishing, Rugby, Warwickshire, 2014

book is a down-to-Earth account of the trials and errors, traumas and triumphs of the journey'.

In an Appendix, this book includes tools to assess the impact of the process of Training for Transformation. No difficulty is left to the imagination! When I reached the final page, in response to the invitation from Amazon to write a review, without hesitation I gave it the maximum 5-stars, but I began my review with the words 'Do not buy this book unless you are open to be changed.'

CHAPTER 5

THEOLOGIES OF LIBERATION

'WHAT'S WRONG WITH THE TWINS?' The unuttered question nagged at the back of my mind all through that Sunday morning meeting. Each time my gaze wandered to the two pale, numb-looking faces across the circle from me, a fearful ache stabbed me deep inside. Could it be that they are on drugs?

I'd known Pedro and Paulo since they were ten. Now at thirteen they were handsome boys, almost identical, tall for their age, both exceptionally gifted at drawing and painting. They were the kind of boys, I had always thought, upon whom you could absolutely depend. Parents who have 'problem teenagers' might well be tempted to envy Pedro and Paulo's mum and dad for their fine sons.

Sadly however, their mother suffered from a serious mental illness, and lived in a state of constant depression. Their dad, at 46, looked like a man in his 70s, his body wasted from years of diabetes and alcoholism. At this time, he didn't drink any longer, but his health was permanently ruined, and he was unable to work.

It was not surprising then, that Pedro and Paulo were serious for their age. Their life had known little or no play. But they went everywhere together, accompanied by their eleven-year-old brother, who adored the twins, and by their sister, aged fifteen, who was dumb though not deaf. Her speech blockage, the specialists said, came from trauma due to the home situation. In a normal environment she still could, with therapy, overcome her problem.

The financial burden of this family fell on the two eldest – Cristina, aged eighteen, and seventeen-year-old Eduardo. Both intelligent and delightful young people, their appearance hardly betrayed the responsibility which life had placed upon their young shoulders. They worked by day and went to school at night from seven till eleven.

Cristina, on a scholarship, was due to finish her secondary education that year. She worked as a secretary, and a highly efficient person she was. She earned less than $50 a month. Eduardo's monthly income, as an office boy with a small firm, was less than $40. The father's pension brought in about $30 a month.

Cristina gave the little free time she had to the local community where she was a catechist. She was also on the co-ordinating team for our work among the physically handicapped of the parish. The boys and their handicapped sister always came with her to the weekend meetings. Despite their problems they were normally a lively bunch.

But on this particular day, the twins were dopey. They slouched in the chairs, their eyelids heavy. Although they rarely speak until they are spoken to, today they seemed not even to notice what was going on. We only realised what wrong with the twins when Cristina told us:

> *Last night I wasn't able to call on the disabled people I promised to visit. I was very tired after the Saturday house-cleaning, washing all the clothes, and doing my study. And*

because Eduardo is on a youth retreat this weekend, I had to get the bus to the Shopping Centre to collect the twins after their work – because you couldn't let them come home on their own at that hour of the night!

"The twins – you mean they are working too", I said. "Does that explain why they look so tired today?"

'Yes', she said. 'As you can see they are totally exhausted. They are doing work that strong men would find tiring – pushing a train of trolleys up that steep ramp from the car park to the Supermarket. When I collected them last night, their arms and legs were aching. They slept in the bus on the way home, even though we were standing all the way. It was so crowded they didn't fall. Otherwise, they would have.'

It was nearly two months since the boys started this work. They had to because the family were hungry with food, clothes, and bus fares so costly. The group began to ask questions. Paulo, usually the more silent of the twins, became suddenly vocal, in a torrent of half-controlled revolt.

They don't let you talk to the other boys while you are working, and you can't eat anything while on the job. If there aren't enough trolleys to be collected, you have to sweep the car park and the ramp, and the brushes are very heavy. You're not allowed to stop at all. There's a supervisor who shouts orders all the time, and if you do anything wrong, you get sent away on the spot.

Pedro added: "From Monday to Friday we go in at one o'clock and work till six, with no break whatsoever." Someone asked whether they are provided with a meal at the Supermarket. On Saturdays they have their lunch there. On weekdays, they eat at home at 11.30 am, and leave at noon to catch the bus for work. When they come out at 6 o'clock, they stand on the bus all the way home, take a rushed shower, and go into school at 7.15 pm. Only when they get home from school at 11.30 pm can they sit down to their evening meal. The twins never see Cristina and Eduardo whose schools are in the city. These older siblings don't get home till well after midnight and leave again for work at 6 am.

People at the meeting wondered why they get lunch at the Supermarket on Saturdays, and not on other days. Paulo clarified it all, with Pedro occasionally chipping in.

> *On Saturdays you have to go in at 10 am and you don't get out till 11 pm or even later. And they don't give you lunch, you have to pay for it in the Supermarket's restaurant. You're not allowed to go out to a cheaper place or bring your lunch in from home. You only get half an hour's break for lunch, around noon, whenever the Supervisor says you can go. That's the only time you're allowed inside the Supermarket. After that you have to work with no break and nothing to eat till you leave at 11 or 11.30 that night. We often get the last bus home. Some boys have no bus to their home at that hour and have to sleep on the street outside.*

Could it be worth it financially, I wondered – such risk to their health, and such a marked change in their outlook on life in two short months. Each earns a basic salary of about $20 a month, from which $15 each was deducted for uniform in their first month. Arriving late, or missing a day meant another deduction. The rest of their earnings came from the voluntary tips of customers, amounting to a maximum of about $5 per week. A joint income for the two, at best, came to about $65 a month. Their bus fare to work and Saturday lunch cost them jointly $20 per month.

"It's not enough, but it helps", said Pedro. "Some people are generous; others give you nothing. Hardly anyone ever smiles or talks to you. Yesterday, one of the boys wheeled out the trolley for a woman. It was full of cans of food and biscuits, and chocolate and lots of bottles of drink – like as if she was having a party. The boy put everything in the car for her, but instead of money she just gave him an orange. Oranges are no use to us because you can't eat at work and there's no place to keep anything till you're going home. So, he just threw it away, though he badly wanted to eat it. The woman got mad because she saw him throwing it away. When she went back to collect her child from the hobby horse, she reported the boy to the Supervisor. He was dismissed immediately because the customer was so cross.

The adults at the meeting fell into a stunned silence – all except Raimundo who spoke angrily about the powerful economic system that obliges boys like these to work under such conditions. Raimundo was the catechist who prepared the twins for First Communion, and he was particularly fond of them. Maybe, like me, he asked himself how long it will be before Pedro and Paulo are lured into the gangs of boys who grow weary of trying to earn an honest living and opt for a life of crime.

The boys, of course, were not employed by the Supermarket. The law that 'protects' minors would have prevented that. But a loophole in the law was easily discovered by the big money makers. A youth employment group was established who would tell you they are 'taking the poor kids off the streets' and 'giving them the chance to earn some pocket money'.

Raimundo's distress at the situation spread to the other adults present. 'As Christians we must do something to transform this situation', he said. But what? For a while, more feelings of helplessness and frustration were aired than bright ideas. Eventually, it was the physically handicapped co-ordinator of the group who hit on something concrete. He looked at me and suggested:

'You're on the Pastoral Commission for Human Rights, aren't you? Could we get orientation from them as to whether this group could be taken to court for exploiting child labour?' The adults thought it an excellent idea. But Pedro and Paulo looked terrified.

'We'd lose our jobs, and we can't afford that'. When we assured them their names would not be mentioned, they agreed. We warned them not to talk of our proposed action to anyone at all, in case somebody would reveal where the accusations came from.

Next day I was in the Curia and ran into the bishop on the stairs. 'How are human rights going?' he asked. I told him our latest problem. I could have bet a million dollars on his response. 'You should talk to the Pastoral Commission for Minors'. 'OK', I said, but we'll need legal help, so I think Human Rights should discuss it first. Besides, that is the group to which the people have asked me to take the case. Then we'll get together with the Pastoral Commission for Minors.'

Saturday came and, at the meeting of the Human Rights Commission, I read the written account which Raimundo had prepared. There were three lawyers present. 'We'd never win a case on juridical grounds' advised one. 'We'll have to try another line'.

An older lawyer suggested: 'I'd be prepared to join a small team to go and talk to the youth employment group. Let them give us their side of it and see if we can talk them into better terms for the boys before we propose any threats. They may well be sincere about wanting to help the children and may be open to suggestions. Either way, once they know the Church is taking action on behalf of the boys, they'll be afraid lest we stir up public opinion.'

'The bishop suggested we talk to the Pastoral Commission for Minors', I said. 'We could set up a joint group with them to go to talk to these people'. 'Good idea', said one of the priests, 'and we could get someone from the Workers' Pastoral Group on the Committee too – they should also be interested in the situation. Besides, if later on we should have to decide on any public action, we'll need as many of our groups as possible to back us up, so it is good to have them involved from the start.

Another lawyer broke in: 'We should get the Commission for Minors to send someone to the Supermarket and record testimonies from several boys. We'll need to have our evidence really well-mounted, because the other side will have a series of arguments to convince us that they are legally right. Our first line of action will have to be moral persuasion. Only if that doesn't work, will we try a public opinion offensive on the Supermarket.'

Various members of the Human Rights Commission were asked to talk to the Pastoral Commission for Minors and the personnel of the Workers' Pastoral Group. Another member was asked to see a sympathetic State Deputy about getting legislation introduced to cover the legal loophole. Another to check out who owns the Supermarket and whether there was any connection between them and the youth employers. I was to see the twins to get their approval of the proposed action.

The next Sunday, they turned up at our house with their sister for the meeting of the physically handicapped. They readily agreed to the proposal I explained to them. 'Know something?'

said Pedro. 'We're not afraid any more of losing our jobs. Cristina said a real Christian feels hungry and thirsty for justice and isn't afraid to fight for it. Besides, it is not so hard to fight when you know you are not alone'.

I was transferred from that area of the Archdiocese before the action discussed at the Human Rights Commission came to completion. I was never able to find out exactly what steps followed. But I met Cristina some months later and she told me things had improved considerably for the twins at the Supermarket. The twins gave me their approval to tell their story.

The above event which took place in the mid-1980s, is just one example of how local Christian communities put liberation theology into practice. It was barely ten years since Gustavo Gutiérrez had published *A Theology of Liberation: History, Politics and Salvation*. Soon other South American theologians including Jon Sobrino, Juan Luis Segundo, Leonardo Boff and others were teaching and writing on the same theme.

Already, during Vatican II in the early 1960s, the Council of Bishops of Latin America had been encouraging a more progressive stance to address the suffering of the poor and oppressed. Their 1968 Conference held at Medellin in Columbia had supported the development of ecclesial communities at the grassroots of society.

This was further affirmed in their 1979 conference held at Puebla in Mexico. In his opening address at Puebla, Pope John Paul II warned priests against direct participation in political parties and ideological movements. However, he stressed the importance of continuing the effort to alleviate social ills. Everyone was conscious of the role he had filled, while Cardinal Archbishop of Krakow, in supporting the solidarity movement of the workers in the port city of Gdansk.

As the Puebla Conference drew to a close, involvement in the struggle of the poor for justice was seen as crucial to the church's future. The bishops called upon the nations of Latin America to resolve their problems peacefully. They also appealed to the more affluent nations not to put obstacles in their way to progress.

The theologians who pioneered this emerging Theology of Liberation began to look at all aspects of faith from the perspective of the poor and oppressed. With them, the faithful reimagined their calling in the light of Jesus's proclamation that he had come 'to bring good news to the poor'. Sin is understood to be not just personal but also structural. The task of liberation theology is to help us integrate our faith in the context of this suffering, mostly caused by some form of oppression.

Mary, Mother of God, is seen as the first theologian. In her *Magnificat*,[1] she embodies the cry and the hope of the downtrodden who believe that God is on their side, a God who loves us and walks with us.

This theological reflection was accompanied with emphasis on developing small Christian communities among the densely packed populations of the cities. Likewise, among the rural communities – some of whom were threatened by drought, others by land grabbing, diversion of rivers, and felling of forests.

Two important branches of the Church served these needs. The *Pastoral da Terra* addressed the injustices related to farmers and the use of land. The *Pastoral Indígena* paid particular attention to the situation of Brazil's indigenous nations.

---

[1] Luke 1:46-55

In the urban area where I lived, the original parish had an estimated population of some 200,000 residents packed in fairly precarious homesteads up along the hillsides or down in the valleys of the expanding periphery of São Paulo. About 2,000 of those residents participated in various Catholic church groups and liturgies. They belonged to fourteen small communities located on the hillsides and valleys within the parish boundary, each community having a small chapel.

We religious sisters were known as *'irmãs inseridas'* (sisters inserted in the midst of the people). Along with other 'pastoral agents' who had a variety of skills – some in liturgy, some in catechesis, some in basic healthcare, home economics or literacy training – we joined together with the parish clergy in our service of the small communities.

Parishes were grouped in 'Sectors' and each Saturday morning, representatives of the thirty or so small communities in our Sector would meet with the priests, catechists, seminarians, and liturgical leaders for three hours. Scripture readings for that weekend were studied, and after a coffee-break preparations were made to address local events and issues.

The importance of the National Pastoral Plan, and its more detailed application in each Diocesan Plan, was crucial to the balance of activities where the message of Scripture was studied and applied. As could be expected, raising awareness of the injustices inflicted upon the poor and dispossessed led the Church authorities into tension, if not into conflict, with the political authorities.

And sadly, the development of a Theology of Liberation also led some of the Latin American theologians into tension and conflict with Church authorities in Rome. Some felt the church in Latin America was drawing on a Marxist analysis — no matter how much they pointed to the fact that Jesus came 'to bring good news to the poor'.

Feminist Liberation Theology

It is no surprise that during these decades as the writings of the Second Vatican Council were being studied and applied, women theologians were thinking along the lines of liberation.

On my bookshelf I find a small book in Portuguese edited by Delia Brunelli, the title of which translates as 'Liberation of Women – A Challenge for the Church and Religious Life in Latin America'. It was published in 1988 by the Conference of Religious of Brazil.

This collection of papers was the outcome of a two-year evaluation of religious life – looking back over the two decades since the Vatican Council and looking forward. A dozen theologians, men, and women from different religious congregations, were tasked with this review. The authors included Sister Lina Boff and her brother Fr. Clodovis Boff, siblings of Leonardo Boff.

The publication laments that Latin American Theology of Liberation had omitted to raise issues about the liberation of women, and that ecclesial practice continued to be discriminatory. It was seen that this presents a serious challenge. It calls for a pathway to be opened and followed but recognizes the numerous difficulties and conflicts this would imply. It saw that religious life, in its prophetic mission, is called to undertake this challenge. It concluded that this subject deals with a veritable socio-cultural revolution and a theological-ecclesial revolution, which without doubt would also be liberating for men.

The authors were well aware of the history of feminism from the late 19th century, and the emergence of a Feminist Theology in the second half of the 20th century. Far from the aim of treating women as a separate sector, what is envisaged is a theology that is preoccupied with the whole of the life of faith, taking up all the important theological questions from a feminist perspective.

These Brazilian theologians were aware that they were part of a world-wide movement to develop theology from this perspective. Such developments were also emerging in other religions. These include Buddhism, Hinduism, Sikhism, the Bahá'í Faith, Judaism, and Islam, as well as among the main Christian communities.

In the English-speaking world, Rosemary Radford Ruether was one of the most influential among women theologians writing from a feminist perspective. Her call to reassert the prophetic tradition that challenges the status quo is developed through some thirty-six books and hundreds of published articles. She acknowledges ideas from women theologians and feminists in Asia, Africa and Latin America.[2] Her critics are many, but they are respectful of her faith as she describes in her autobiography *My Quest for Hope and Meaning.* She makes the point that there can be no final synthesis regarding feminism.

This point is also made by the well-known Sri Lankan Jesuit theologian, Aloysius Pieris. He held that feminism needs to be a permanent ideological critique of religion. It is something that religions cannot do without. Our theological understanding from a feminist perspective must also be liberational for the

[2] Cf *Women Healing Earth: Third World Women on Ecology, Feminism and Religion*, Orbis Books, Maryknoll, NY, 1996

whole of society, inclusive of all social groups and races. Theology itself has to be liberated in order to serve, and feminist theology helps in this process.

Womanist Theology gained its name originally from Alice Walker, author of *The Color Purple,* which raised the awareness of many of us to the oppression endured by many African American women when it became a movie.

Lisa Allen, author of A *Womanist Theology of Worship: Liturgy, Justice, and Communal Righteousness* tells us that womanist theology has come a long way from its earliest beginnings. It seeks to find ways of proclaiming the Word and the Being of God in ways that heal, feed, nurture, inspire, and create community as part of our Sunday liturgies. She says womanist theological scholars have carved out an area of scholarship that is innovative, historically and theologically sound. These theologians work independently of feminists and scholars of womanist thought.

A major contribution to Feminist Theology comes from Africa where the historical context for women theologians is different from that of African American women. Among the latter, the issues of race, gender and class are major concerns. African women theologians have different priorities. They engage in open critique of patriarchy, but also address the impact of traditional societies, colonialism, and slavery on contemporary Africa. They are also concerned with the impact of globalization and economic structures. Their theological focus is that religion should liberate the human spirit for communication with God, and the building of community awareness.

This Feminist Theology has been growing over recent decades. In 1989 the inaugural meeting of the Circle of Concerned African Women Theologians drew more than seventy women theologians to a gathering in Accra. The movement has grown to more than six hundred members, who come from some twenty countries of Africa. Their multireligious and multiracial network aims at facilitating research and writing. Their desire is to reflect on what it means to be women of faith within their experiences of religion, culture, politics, and the social and economic structures of Africa. Their methodology uses a narrative theological approach of storytelling drawn from the rich African oral history and the Bible. They seek to collaborate with male theologians as equals in a complementary effort that puts emphasis on justice and participation.

Just as feminist movements differ in their focus according to different geographical locations, they also have a different focus from one discipline to another. Some call for increasing the role of women in ministry and in positions of authority in the churches. Others seek to reinterpret patriarchal imagery and language about God. Others study how images of women in sacred texts have been reproduced through the centuries. Some draw ideas from the study of religious beliefs in matriarchal societies. But the point is made by all that gender does not define human strengths and weaknesses. All agree that the structural injustice whereby men as a group have power over women challenges the development of theology.

Liberation Theology among the LGBTQI Community

Born in Argentina in 1952, Marcella Althaus Reid became the first woman professor of theology at St. Andrew's University in Scotland. An important influence on her early development came from Latin American theologians and feminist writers. She argues that sexuality must be at the core of feminist and liberation theologies. As she developed a theology of liberation for people in the LGBTQI communities, she set out to show that our sexuality and the influence that has on our lives informs our perspective. It shapes our understanding of God.

In her work *Indecent Theologies* she deals with the interplay of sexuality and the economic and political situation in Latin America's big cities. Women whose lives face a daily battle with poverty can be even more marginalized by their gender. Like Tissa Balasuriya in Sri Lanka, she calls for an understanding of Mary, Mother of God, from the feminist perspective of a woman trapped in poverty. She gives rise to the question: how can we present the woman who gave birth to her Son in a stable at Bethlehem as a source of strength for the women oppressed by poverty, for whom rape and incest are commonplace, bearing children as soon as their own childhood ends? These women are rarely virgins.

An earlier theologian who also seeks to shed light on the issue of sexuality in theology is James B. Nelson (1930-2015). He was Associate Professor of Christian Ethics at United Theological Seminary of the Twin Cities, Minnesota. During his forty-year career, he advocated for full support in Christianity for LGBT people. In his work *Body Theology* (1992) he says that dualism of body and spirit is one of the primary deficiencies in religion. He argues that this concept is neither Jewish nor Christian but was adopted through exposure to the Hellenistic culture and the later Greco Roman culture. It has continued to be a conflict in the doctrine and practice of faith from that time to the present.

In his study of Judaism and Christianity, Nelson finds a more authentic approach. In Hebrew scripture, the belief is that all of creation is innately good, having been created by God. Embodiment and sexuality are not alienated from spirit. Likewise, in Christianity the Earthbound experience of the body is important. The Christian message is not about the abstract faith of a disembodied spirit. Our embodied experience is crucial to our experience of God. However, patriarchal dualism has created polarities. The teachings of the Church often promote denial of body and the sinfulness of pleasure. And the resistance to equality of men and women leads to the lack of female leadership and direct ministry of women in religious settings. Nelson shows that these concepts in Christianity are at odds with one another. This puts us at risk of diluting or confusing the liberative message of Jesus Christ.

These writers invite us all to become responsibly aware that people in the LGBTQI community long for God but suffer from ecclesiastical rejection. Althaus Reid asks us to consider: must they be forced to live in a dualism of their sexual identity and their spiritual identity? Or can they – and we – see a God who embraces them in their sexuality, where all sexual orientation is recognized as a reflection of God's love?

African Liberative Theologies and Black Liberation Theology

On the continent of Africa, the term 'Liberative Theologies' is used to describe different genres of theological development in different contexts. In the 1950s and '60s, alongside the demand for independence from colonialism, a cultural rebirth also began to emerge. This extended to the field of theology.

The desire for an African theology was first put in print in 1956 by a number of African priests studying abroad. Their book in French entitled *Des Prêtres noirs s'interrogent* is translated *Some black priests wonder.* As the nations of Africa moved towards the formation of the Organization of African Union [3], so also

---

[3] Now the African Union. https://au.int

preparatory gatherings were held towards the formation of the All-African Conference of Churches (AFCC). This is where the development of African liberative theologies found a home and an inspiration. African leaders at the time, including Kenneth Kaunda of Zambia, who was Presbyterian, and Julius Nyerere of Tanzania, a Catholic, were asking why the church in Africa was not more African.

The emerging theologies focussed on several different strands with different nuances. Some theologians focussed on specific cultural issues. Their ideas can be grouped into 'Inculturation Theology'. This invoked a dialogue between faith and culture, enabling both to mutually enrich each other, while at the same time becoming freed from non-essential elements that were felt to be foreign. In August 1969, when Pope Paul VI spoke at the episcopal ordination of twelve Bishops at Kololo in Uganda, he encouraged the new bishops in the development of the native character of the church – what he called its 'African-ness'.

Another strand in the work of theologians was 'Reconciliation Theology', seeking to inspire the reconciliation of peoples for mutual coexistence after political instability, violence, and war. Then, there is the large movement of women theologians mentioned above in the context of Feminist Theology. Liberative theologies all sought to free the people from burdens laid upon them through cultural, economic, and political oppression. At the same time, in South Africa and Namibia during the struggle to end apartheid, Black Liberation Theology – closer to the Liberation Theology of Latin America – played an important role.

Black Liberation Theology was also a key development associated with communities in North America who are descendants of former slaves. The social system that discriminates against people because of their racial background has fed its growth.

Racism added new suffering for people whose forefathers had already endured incredible burdens when kidnapped from their homes and sold, like animals, in the markets of Africa both before and during the colonial era.

The Civil Rights Movement in the US, of which Rev. Martin Luther King, a Baptist minister, was a notable leader, focussed on integration, on putting an end to segregation. In 1964, he was awarded the Nobel Peace Prize for combating racial inequality through nonviolent resistance. But some who struggled for the rights of black people also believed in claiming their distinctiveness, not being assimilated into white culture. Malcolm X, a Muslim minister, opposed the efforts of Martin Luther King. His turbulent youth led him to more radical options in promoting black nationalism. The political scene during the lives of these two leaders was extremely fraught.

The assassination of Malcolm X in 1965 and that of Martin Luther King in 1968 challenged all Christian theologians of the era to think seriously about their task. They saw that Black Liberation Theology had to take on board the experience of black people, their history, their suffering, their pain, and their joy. Revelation was not just a past event, but in the present context it is a black event, it is what black people are doing about their liberation.

The revelation of Scripture was examined. How does God relate with human beings, with the world? How do we respect the language, art, and music of the black community in our worship? God's presence in the world and redemption through God's love is experienced as happening today. This revelation is an ongoing experience, and Scripture is an important source. It reveals God's solidarity with the oppressed. Jesus is the one who suffered unjustly, was arrested by an unjust political power. But these theologians remind us, this theology needs to be filled with hope, it is not all about pain and suffering.

In 1969, the Rev. James Hal Cone launched a more radical spiritual conversation. That year, he became a minister in an African Methodist Episcopal church. He had experienced the intense racial segregation of the 1940s and '50s. He spent decades teaching at New York's Union Theological Seminary, working on black liberation theology and studying the liberation theologies of Africa, Asia, and Latin America.

His book *Black Theology & Black Power* was fiercely critical of what he called "white theology", as he argued for God's radical identification with black people in the United States. He felt white people and white theologians just could not understand what their theology did to black people. Despite his dedication, it appears that this did not receive great acceptance among the communities who were striving for equal treatment. Neither did the theology he was developing receive the support of most other theologians of the time, who came from both black and white communities. Yet, we read that many of his ideas remain influential.

In 2020, the Archbishop of Washington DC, Wilton Gregory, became the first Black American to be elevated to the rank of Cardinal in the Catholic Church. This was welcomed as a powerful message of hope and inclusion. It came just a few months after the brutal killing of George Floyd by police in Minneapolis. Cardinal Gregory's appointment was welcomed as an important step in a longstanding Black Catholic freedom struggle against racism, slavery, segregation, and exclusion within the US church.

Reynold Verret, President of Xavier University of Louisiana, the country's only historically Black and Catholic university, said that racial discrimination is our great sin and he added, "The Vatican is leading us in a new direction, and I think Pope Francis is showing a new opening for us as a church, that we are one church."

Dalit Liberation Theology

From far away in India, a well-known Jesuit, Fr. AXJ Bosco, whose life is dedicated to the Dalit people, wrote of how the news of Cardinal Gregory's elevation encouraged their dreams. Dalits form more than sixty-five per cent of the Catholic Community of India and are dispersed all over the country. At the time of writing only four per cent of the 30,300 priests in India are Dalits. There are only twelve Dalits among the one hundred and ninety-four bishops. Fr. Bosco feels "the practices of discrimination based on caste continue in the Church and in society and Dalits continue their struggle to reclaim their dignity and affirm their equality."

In May 2022 Archbishop Anthony Poola, a member of the Dalit community, was called by Pope Francis to the College of Cardinals. This is a great encouragement to the Dalit Catholic community in India.

The deeply rooted caste system still holds the mainline Churches in its trawl. Fr. Bosco encourages the Dalit communities to appeal to the Universal Church to bring justice to Dalit Catholics in India who face discrimination in society as well as in the Church.

A similar call comes from Sister Robancy Amal Helen of the Religious Institute of Christ the Redeemer. She campaigns for equality and justice for Dalits. As part of her campaign, she coordinated Dalit programmes for the community when she worked for the New Delhi-based Catholic Bishops' Conference of India from 2014 to 2019. She is currently executive editor of the Dalit Christian Digest news portal launched in 2020. She also edits and writes for *Urimai* (which means "Right" in Tamil) a monthly magazine for Dalit Christians published by the Tamil Nadu Bishops' Council.

Interviewed in 2021 for the Global Sisters' Report published by the Washington-based National Catholic Reporter, she confirmed that, although Dalits are the majority in the Catholic Church, they are not treated equally. Dalit Christian children are not allowed to serve at the altar or to become lectors. Most so-called upper-caste priests do not visit the houses of Dalit Christians. Separate cemeteries and churches for Dalit and other Catholics still exist among followers of Christ. During parish feasts, religious processions are not made on streets passing through Dalit settlements. Dalit people cannot take the bodies of their deceased members for burial through the common street. Some Dalit Christian villages are still mission stations and their faithful remain unattended by clergy.

However, change is happening, most noticeably under the Bishops' Council of Tamil Nadu in southern India. A system of Dalit Christian Peoples' Cells trains women in entrepreneurship and leadership skills. There are 350 such cells in the 18 Catholic dioceses of Tamil Nadu, 50 of which are managed by Dalit women. Steps are also being taken to train women to become members of decision-making bodies of the Catholic church through the Tamil Nadu Regional Chapter.

Dalit liberation theology which has been developing since the 1980s has the same objectives and seeks to put a theological framework on the rise of movements in the political sphere to free Dalits from caste oppression. It was influenced by the emergence of Liberation Theology in Latin America two decades earlier. It shares its emphasis on self-identity as an oppressed people on an Exodus journey. The objectives of Dalit Theology are clear: liberation, conversion, empowerment, and solidarity with other oppressed people. They also criticise Western imperialism, and binary thinking – 'I am a non-Dalit, you are a Dalit'.

In Sanskrit 'dal' is the word for broken, crushed. In their Biblical studies, Dalit theologians find liberating energy. The Suffering Servant of Isaiah and the Exodus story, all give hope that they too are on a journey to freedom. Looking at the life of Jesus through the lens of Dalit experience there is much with which they can identify – his concern for the outcast, the people on the periphery of society. Most especially, they can identify with Jesus' brokenness on the Cross, the God-man who shares their brokenness.

As in Latin America, the intellectuals of Dalit theology come from, or have chosen to journey close to the Dalit communities. Theirs is an ecumenical theology. Several Dalit communities have been supported by impressive commitments from evangelical churches abroad.

The book *Why Not Now?* details the ongoing commitment of the Friends Church in Yorba Linda, California, particularly through investment in education. It also describes the brave, tireless work of the evangelical Bishop Joseph D'Souza, Primate of the Good Shepherd Church of India. Here we witness what belief means in practice, addressing both spiritual and social needs. The programme is noted for its ministries in the fields of education, health, job development, and literature.

In May 2022 Pope Francis canonised an Indian layman, St. Devasahayam. Born to an affluent Hindu family in 1712 in what is now Tamil Nadu, Nilakandan Pillai encountered the Christian faith from a captured Dutch prisoner. At baptism, he took the name "Lazarus" – Devasahayam in the local Tamil language. Despite the high offices he held, he fought caste discrimination. He was accused of corruption by political leaders and suffered immensely while a prisoner. Local priests believe it was his advocacy for social equality that led to his torture and murder. His canonization gives courage to those who are suffering today.

Challenges from Sri Lanka

In the theologies of liberation developed in Asia, the role of Europe and the association between Christian missionaries and colonial regimes has been deeply critiqued.

Most prominent among these critics was Fr. Tissa Balasuriya of Sri Lanka. A member of the Oblates of Mary Immaculate, he had graduated in economics at the University of Ceylon before his ordination in 1952. He also spent time at Oxford studying agricultural economics. Later, he abandoned academic life to work in the slum areas of Colombo. He went on to establish the Centre for Society and Religion with the aim of organising inter-ethnic dialogue and encounters with Hindus, Buddhists, and Muslims. He also helped to found the Ecumenical Association of Third World Theologians.

When the name of Fr. Balasuriya is mentioned nowadays people will say 'isn't he the only theologian that was excommunicated by Pope John Paul II?' They seem not to have noticed that the excommunication was revoked a year later, in 1998. He ran into trouble with the Vatican at the time when Cardinal Josef Ratzinger, later Pope Benedict XVI, headed the Congregation of the Doctrine of the Faith.

It was mainly the ideas developed in his book entitled *Mary and Human Liberation* that led to the excommunication. He saw in Mary, the mother of Jesus, 'a strong, mature, working-class woman'. It was to her that he attributed Jesus' understanding of his mission to save those who were downtrodden. He pointed out that after the arrest of Jesus, when many of the disciples fled, it was Mary and the women close to her who remained with him to the end.

Observers of his excommunication say that it was not so much his writing about Mary, attributing to her revolutionary ideas, but his position on the ordination of women that was the nub of the problem at the Vatican. As soon as his excommunication was announced, an intense international campaign began in his support, which led to severe embarrassment for the Catholic Church. After ongoing negotiations, he agreed to sign a document acceptable to Rome, though he continued to hold that it was wrong to claim that the Church could never ordain women.

Tissa Balasuriya had already published *Jesus and Human Liberation.* But perhaps – for a church on a synodal journey – the most challenging of all his ideas comes in his writing in 1977 on *The Eucharist and Human Liberation.* Bishop Leo Nanayakkara OSB, Bishop of Badulla, Sri Lanka, wrote in the foreword:

> *It is with a certain sense of pride that I introduce this second book of Fr. Balasuriya to the general public ... The author tries to make articulate this experience out of a sheer loyalty to the Universal Church. He tries to portray to us what the Eucharist should be in the light of Scripture and tradition. He therefore takes a long and close look at what it has been until now and argues that this most liberative act has been so domesticated by a socio-economic system that it now enslaves and domesticates its participants. He is also extremely sensitive to the longings and searchings of committed priests to make the Eucharist meaningful to themselves and to society.*

Balasuriya knew that what he was writing would make difficult reading for many. He introduced it by saying:

> *This book is meant to stimulate further reflection. Many of its sections need much further study and investigation ... This is an effort to contribute in some small way to the ongoing reflection on the Eucharist in relation to the life of human beings today. I hope it will help towards a better understanding of the spiritual life itself. I will be glad to receive any comments. I would not be surprised if there are strong reactions to it ... Perhaps it is through the agony of living these tensions and articulating them together that we can go towards a theology more true to Jesus and more close to the griefs and sorrows and the hopes and aspirations of the men, women and children of our age.*

He draws on St. Paul's criticism of the community at Corinth for their slowness in sharing during their Eucharistic celebration. He also cites religious guides through the centuries. He quotes the fourth century St. Basil: "If everyone took only what he needed and gave the rest to those in need, there would be no such thing as rich or poor." It is his view that the institution of the Eucharist has profound political implications. That is the nub of his argument. For Balasuriya, faith in Jesus and social involvement for justice are two sides of the same coin. In his 1983 publication *Planetary Theology,* he asked:

> *Why is it that most of the Christians who attend Sunday worship in the city of Colombo, Sri Lanka, hardly ever reflect seriously on the utterly inhuman conditions of the one hundred fifty thousand shanty-owners ...? The roof of their hovel cannot prevent the rain from drenching their one-room dwelling. The floor on which they sleep is damp. They have no clean water. There is one toilet for about every hundred persons. No schooling for children; no jobs for adults. They*

live in filthy conditions. Infant mortality is high; malnutrition is standard. And this continues from generation to generation; if anything, the situation worsens. The rich prosper, and many of them are Christians and consider themselves good Christians.

Balasuriya never condoned violence. But neither did he elaborate a methodology for enabling believers to engage in social change, forming alliances between the 'haves' and 'have nots'.

He was also concerned about the issue of climate change long before most of us took the problem seriously. In *Planetary Theology* he called for a radical reform of the United Nations Organization. He felt this should work to redress the impact of colonialism globally from 1492 to 1945, arranging a redistribution of land and population in order to deal with the big gap between rich and poor on the planet. The radically reformed UNO would also work on the impact of climate warming since the industrial revolution.

Water Buffalo Theology

Another Asian theologian, Kosuke Koyama was born in Tokyo in 1929. On completion of his doctorate at Princeton Theological Seminary, he was missioned by the United Church of Christ in Japan to northern Thailand. Once there, his theological development was influenced by his pastoral ministry at grassroots level. The water buffalos grazing in the muddy paddy field inspired him to preach to the farmers in the simplest way, developing a theology from below.

His writing and lectures contributed to eco-theology and liberation and called for Christian-Buddhist dialogue. In 1974, the Catholic Maryknoll missionaries in New York published a collection of his work in *Water Buffalo Theology.* It shows how

Koyama sought to bridge the boundaries between East and West, between Christianity and Buddhist thought and between rich and poor. It acquired the reputation of being a classic of Asian theology.

In the opening chapter, Koyama invites the reader to a theological travelogue, providing an informative description of the issues in Singapore, Thailand, China, Hong Kong, the Philippines, Indonesia, Japan, Taiwan, and Myanmar (then *Burma*). The cultural beliefs and practices in each of these are different. They challenge the Christian mission differently. He is concerned with the idea of contextualization, particularly in his insertion in Thai Buddhist society. He insists that our Christian interaction is not with Buddhism but with Buddhists.

Koyama sees contextualization as a two-step process, first to announce the message given to us by Jesus Christ in a culturally appropriate way, and secondly to exercise appropriate criticism and reform of that culture where it is against what Jesus proclaims. In Latin America this would be called 'announcing' and 'denouncing'.

In the World Council of Churches at that time, contextualization of theology was seen as the overarching theological principle. This distinguished 'contextualization' from 'indigenization' which tends to be used in the sense of responding to the gospel in terms of a traditional culture.

Koyama explains that contextualization, while not ignoring this, takes into account the process of secularity, technology, and the struggle for human justice. Authentic contextualization is always prophetic, Koyama taught. It arises always out of a genuine encounter between God's Word and this world and moves toward the purpose of challenging and changing the situation. He reminds readers that theological differences expressed through different Christian denominations and even different faiths are minute in comparison to the core theological beliefs that are shared. What is to be communicated is more than an idea. It is life, history, hope and love, which is only possible through the medium of a living person.

Third Eye Theology

Choan-Seng Song was born in Taiwan (then Formosa) the same year that Koyama was born in Tokyo. He ministered in the Methodist tradition. Like Balasuriya and Koyama, Song is deeply critical of the Western-centric nature of Christian theology. He emphasised how the people of Asia were victimized by a history of Western imperialism, creating an identity crisis for Asian Christians. His goal was to move on from the legacy of colonialism and the humiliation it implied, while embracing the liberating and life-giving message of Jesus Christ.

He was attracted by and adopted the methodology of Latin American Liberation Theology. While he stressed that God's redemptive presence in Jesus Christ provides people with a chance to be in communion with God, he also saw that our human community and our divine communion are interdependent. This world is God's mission field. The Christian is called to suffer with the oppressed in struggling for justice and freedom.

In 1979 his *Third Eye Theology* was published. Song borrows the term "third eye" from Buddhism. He draws particularly on the Japanese Zen master Daisetz Suzuki, who recommended opening and focussing a third eye to the hitherto unheard-of region we cannot grasp from our own ignorance. If successful we will find that cloud of ignorance disappears as we see for the first time into the nature of our own being. In this tradition, Third Eye Theology seeks to enlighten that darkness that separates

Christian spirituality from other Asian spiritualities. Only then will we begin to comprehend the love and compassion of God for the world.

This will require a blending of traditional Scripture with Asian folklore and culture, thus making Christianity relevant to the peoples of Asia. But the Christian Churches need to work together with people of other faiths to create a spiritual force that can deal with the issues that threaten the moral fabric of the human community.

Minjung Theology

In South Korea, theologians were inspired by the theology being developed in Latin America. The development of Minjung Theology over the decades is very well set out by Andrew Eungi Kim.[4] He explains that 'Minjung' translates as 'the mass of people' but a more comprehensive definition is 'those who are oppressed politically, exploited economically, alienated socially, and kept uneducated in cultural and intellectual matters'.

During the drive for industrialization, low-paid workers were severely exploited and any attempt to fight against this exploitation received harsh punishment, including imprisonment. Kim tells us that many of the early theologians exploring the theme of 'Minjung' were removed from their positions at universities and seminaries because of their defence of the oppressed. Minjung shares the belief of other theologies of liberation by insisting that oppressed people are subjects of history, not mere objects.

---

[4] Dr. Andrew Eungi Kim is Professor in the College of International Studies, Korea University.

Kim notes that from the early 1960s to the late 1980s, the church's active involvement in socio-political issues was a hallmark of Korean Christianity. Along with labour unions and student unions, the church was a strong force for the democratization movement.

As the political situation changed over the decades, a second generation of Minjung theologians embraced the Justice, Peace, and Integrity of Creation (JPIC) movement promoted by the World Council of Churches, and also embraced by many Catholic leaders and religious congregations. But as Koreans came to experience greater economic success, Minjung turned to other causes, like the human rights of foreign migrant workers, the environment and gender inequality, with many religiously motivated NGOs, Christian or Buddhist, taking up various causes in the search for justice.

There followed a sense of waning of the impact of Minjung until 2014. On 16th April that year world news drew attention to the sinking of the Sewol Ferry and the loss of more than three hundred lives, most of whom were high school students. The tragedy became a renewed call for the greater involvement of the churches in societal affairs. When Pope Francis visited Korea in August that year, he wore a yellow-ribbon commemorative pin, in solidarity with those who had been drowned. Kim writes:

> *On his return flight to Rome, the pope reflected on the incident: "I took [the pin] out of solidarity with them, and after a day, somebody came up to me and said, 'You should take it off; you need to be neutral'. I answered this way: 'Listen, with human suffering you can't be neutral'.*

Kim says the pope's comments and actions in Korea and elsewhere at the time and thereafter have been interpreted by some as amounting to an advocacy of liberation theology.

The Role of Hope

Well-known in international circles of theology and dialogue today, Dr. Jude Lal Fernando says that, traditionally, theology was defined as faith seeking understanding. But if the God in whom we believe is a God who saves, then theology must be primarily about faith that seeks and hopes for liberation.

What does it mean to have faith in God for those billions of poor who are struggling for their survival? What does God mean for women who are oppressed? Who is Christ for those who face racial discrimination? What does it mean to believe in a God of Creation in the age of climate change? Is ours a faith that hopes for justice, that hopes for human dignity, that hopes for reconciliation, that hopes for peace, that hopes for healing?

Fernando says faith in the God who liberates must be interpreted from time to time, from place to place, and there can be different interpretations. To stand for a theology that liberates demands a commitment of one's life, a giving up of oneself. It is a political commitment drawing on a liberation theology where sin is not only personal but also structural.

Some of the theologians mentioned above explore ideas that may go a step too far for many of us, but their work serves to stretch our minds as theology and spirituality develop. Acknowledging the clear distinction between theology and ideology, theologians of liberation remind us that whatever cause is important to a society, ethical discourse must play a part in the development of our theological understanding.

The development of theology must continue to move hand in hand with the struggle for justice for those who are on the margins of society. Like all branches of knowledge, theology needs wriggle room in order to develop. Doctrine provides stability in matters of belief, but academic discussion and debate can lead to a deepening of faith.

The challenge of alleviating the suffering of the poor and marginalized was embraced by Jesus during his lifetime and by his earliest followers. When the Bishops' Conferences of Latin America jointly and publicly declared this a priority following the Second Vatican Council they were adhering to this long tradition. Whenever our belief leads us to help one another by sharing their burden, then it is a liberating act.

Across the globe we have witnessed amazing efforts to enable communities to develop education, healthcare and social progress. The support of agencies in *Caritas Internationalis*[5] for development and empowerment is very significant. The work of the Society of St. Vincent de Paul is paramount. To be authentic followers of Jesus, our faith communities will always be challenged to adopt the cause of those among us who are oppressed and pushed to the margins of society.

---

[5] See www.caritas.org.

CHAPTER 6

INTERFAITH COLLABORATION

JOURNALIST JOHN L. ALLEN JR., REPORTING for the Boston-based Catholic news agency *Crux now*, wrote that "Interfaith outreach has now become part of the job description for any pope.[6] His report covered the 2016 gathering of leaders of the Great Faiths at Assisi, which marked the 30th anniversary of Pope John Paul's historic 1986 inter-faith summit. That initiative was repeated in 1993 and again in 2002, and yet another in 2011 presided over by Pope Benedict XVI.

John Allen adds something important. He says that Pope Francis, who invited the leaders to Assisi in 2016

> *brings his own unique style to the encounter. It is less focused on healing the wounds of the past, as with John Paul, or exploring theological convergences and differences, as with Benedict, and more on radical action in the here-and-now on shared humanitarian and social objectives.*

This is surely good news. Back in 1986, Allen reminds us that

> *The inter-faith gathering under Pope John Paul II was both innovative and controversial. The setting in Assisi was deliberate. Rome is the pope's town, while Assisi belongs to St. Francis, a universally admired figure for his commitment to*

---

[6] See www.cruxnow.com, Sep 15, 2016

peace, dialogue and simplicity ... Choosing this venue made it clear that the pope came as a brother to other religions and not as a commander-in-chief ...

The group that day included rabbis wearing yarmulkes and Sikhs in turbans, Muslims praying on thick carpets and a Zoroastrian kindling a sacred fire. Robert Runcie, the Anglican Archbishop of Canterbury, exchanged pleasantries with the Dalai Lama. Orthodox bishops chatted with Alan Boesak, the South African anti-apartheid activist and president of the World Alliance of Reformed Churches.

Back in 1986 when the first of these Assisi encounters took place, I had the privilege of being a member of the Inter-faith Commission of the Archdiocese of São Paulo. Our Archbishop was Cardinal Paulo Evaristo Arns. He asked us to help organise an event to celebrate what would be happening in Assisi when Pope John Paul would meet the leaders of the other faiths. A large part of the preparatory work from the Catholic community came from members of the Focolare movement.

Back then I was the English language Editor at the country-wide Ecumenical News Agency based in São Paulo.[7] In those days Brazil still had a big problem with illiteracy, so radio was an important news channel. Most Catholic dioceses purchased time on their local radio stations. Every day after the Angelus at 6 am and 6 pm, important news items were reported and commented upon from the perspective of our religious faith. The Methodists, Lutherans, Presbyterians, and Episcopalians all had their own radio stations throughout the country.

Our hard-working team of eight journalists in São Paulo reported daily for these broadcasters. My job was to publish a

---

[7] Agência Ecumênica de Notícias known as AGEN.

weekly print summary of the news in English for the supporters of our Churches in USA and Europe. Here's how I reported our São Paulo collaboration with the Assisi event. It took place in the huge square in the city centre known as *Praça da Sé*[8]. The large gothic Catholic Cathedral overlooked the square:

A most spectacular and harmonious blend of faith, politics and culture was witnessed by more than 30,000 people in São Paulo on October 26, during celebrations for the National Day of Manifestation, Meditation and Prayer for Peace. The event was promoted by Brazil's National Council of Christian Churches (CONIC), as a means of identification with the celebrations in Assisi on October 27, when Pope John Paul II and the world's religious leaders participated in ceremonies marking the International Year of Peace.

The preparations, as well as drawing together the main Christian traditions, received impressive collaboration from the city's Jewish, Buddhist and Hindu communities, and more than a dozen groups of ecologists and pacifists, all of whom were represented on the day itself. The Vatican was represented by the Apostolic Nuncio to Brazil, Archbishop Carlo Furno, and many Catholic bishops also attended.

The joy of the celebration was significantly diminished by the absence of the Muslim community. In the early stages of our preparations, their leader, Sheik Mahmúd Ahmad Al Asfar, Director General of the Islamic Centre of Brazil, had participated in our meetings. The Muslim youth had been part of the group which designed the act of reconciliation. But in September, the Islamic community suffered a shock with the assassination in Lebanon of theologian Subhi Saleh, the second

---

[8] This translates as 'The Square of the See' referring to the Archdiocese of São Paulo.

highest leader of Islam in Lebanon. It is not yet known which terrorist group was behind this crime. The Muslims claimed that their leader was a man "who always worked for peace – hence our mourning".

Because of this death, their community in São Paulo did not find themselves able to take part in a public manifestation of this kind. However, the following day a spokesman for the Sheik told our news agency: "We share from the heart, the letter and the spirit of all the manifestations for peace made in São Paulo as well as those made at the Assisi encounter." Their absence from the liturgy, however, provoked a genuine sense of loss as it was announced that the readings from the Koran and the message of the Sheik indicated on the programme could not, after all, be delivered.

On October 26 an hour before the scheduled starting time, São Paulo's central square filled up with enthusiastic participants. Many groups brought colourful banners calling for peace – for land reform, for food and for social justice – all of which are seen as essential to peace. The 16-metre-wide stage, erected for the occasion, bore the slogan 'Justice Leads to Peace'.'

After a short welcome by the Catholic Bishop, Ivo Lorscheiter,[9] President of CONIC, the act of worship began with a mime of reconciliation, enacted by young people drawn from the Catholic, Episcopalian, Methodist, Jewish, Buddhist and Hindu communities. Three months earlier, these young people had gathered together to reflect upon the enemies of peace. They worked as a team, visiting in turn the community centres of

---

[9] Though he was born in Brazil in 1927 to the Lorscheider family, his surname was incorrectly registered on his birth certificate and never corrected. He was a cousin of Cardinal Aloísio Lorscheider.

their various faiths, in order to rehearse the liturgy of reconciliation which they themselves designed.

The vast crowd was silent as the drama of violence was enacted, in mime, music and dance. First came the elaboration and denunciation of the individual violence which lurks in each person; then the violence that is enshrined in the structures of society. This was followed by a choreography dramatizing violence related to the concentration of land in the hands of the minority, and finally the critically threatening violence related to the arms race.

Each phase of these denunciations involved participation by the spectators. At one moment, everyone was invited to discover their neighbour's name; at another pause, each exchanged their programme with the other. At another, a human chain was formed, as people expressed their opposition to arms as a solution to conflict and committed themselves to plant seeds of peace.

The first reading was from the Hindu text, the Bhagavad Gita. Its message was then elaborated in an exhortation by Professor Luciana Ferraz of São Paulo's Spiritual University of Brahma Kumaris. Clad in a white Indian sari, she said:

> *The Lord of the world is working to re-establish peace on Earth. It is understood that in this transformation we must expect dramatic changes. Our desires and sentiments are for the construction of a new and stable world order.*

She invited everyone to experience the power of silent meditation, calling on each person to allow their personal anger to flow out of them, so that each might become the bearer of seeds of peace in the world. Then she concluded:

> *Peace can only come from the Ocean of Peace, which is the Father, and it is in the awareness of brotherhood and sister-*

hood that the presence of peace comes to us. In the power of a moment of silence, we open our eyes and perceive the fountain of love and of light which offers us the strength and the power to change.

As applause for the Hindu peace message died down, strains of oriental music filled the air, and the stage was occupied by the youth from São Paulo's Buddhist community, Risho Kossei-Kai. Their delicate ritual dance of peace further drew everyone's concentration toward the hope of harmony.

The microphone was then taken by the leader of one of São Paulo's Jewish congregations, American-born Rabbi Henry Sobel, who read – first in Hebrew and then in Portuguese – verses containing the vision of peace of the Prophet Micah (Ch 4, 2-4). "There was a time", said the Rabbi,

> *when religions were isolated islands without any type of bridge between them ... it was through the work, dedication and inspiration of great men and women of diverse beliefs, that we learned to take the first steps towards one another, while remaining profoundly rooted in our respective traditions and without violating that which is sacred to each one of us, but at the same time recognizing the holiness of the beliefs and traditions of others... What unites us today is not tolerance, but a spirit of reverence – reverence for the diversity and for the beliefs of others. It is only this reverence, this profound and genuine spirit of mutual respect which can lead us to peace.*

The Rabbi cited Ghandi, Anwar Sadat, Mother Teresa of Calcutta, Martin Luther King, Pope John XXIII and the 1986 Nobel Prize Winner, Elie Weisel, as proofs that we can love and embrace one another, no matter what our differences may be.

The Rabbi's words were enthusiastically received, and with equal enthusiasm the crowd vibrated to the rhythm of the popular religious music which followed, animated by a folk-group of the Jewish community. The Portuguese-speaking crowd quickly learned the Hebrew refrain of the young Jews' peace message which caught on like fire among the vast throng.

Conspicuous by their absence were the civil leaders who had been invited to participate, but not to make speeches. On the third-last Sunday before the General Elections, they were all involved in political campaigns and their seats among the dignitaries remained vacant.

The first Christian message was delivered by the Vice-President of CONIC, the Reverend Augusto Kunert, who is also Vice-President of the Lutheran World Federation. Referring to the Psalmist's words he said:

> *Justice and Peace complete each other, inter-relate and form a harmonious unity for the wellbeing of mankind of the whole creation of God. Justice and peace are inseparable. Where justice is trampled down there cannot be peace.*

The Lutheran leader denounced the escalating armamentation among the great powers, which threaten each other in the incomparable arms race in order to conquer, each side for itself, the hegemony of power. He also condemned the economic powers which oppress nations and people to the point of destruction of their dignity and identity, throwing entire populations into despair and misery.

The Gospel message of peace according to St. John[10] was proclaimed by the leader of the Episcopal Church of Anglican

[10] John 14: 27-31

Communion in São Paulo, Bishop Sumio Takatsu[11]. Following this, the Pastor of the Catholic community of São Paulo, Cardinal Arns, affirmed that all Catholics would identify with each of the messages which had been delivered during this celebration. The Cardinal led the crowd in prayer for peace in the home, in schools and on the street.

> *We ask the Lord of history and all those, who, from him, have received the power to decide, to ensure just and sufficient salaries, the distribution of wealth, land reform without delay and with justice.*

The Cardinal also denounced the arms race, discrimination and the destruction of natural resources.

The social and political content of the Jewish and Christian messages was then situated within the perennial conflict between good and evil by a school of ballet linked to the ecological movement and to the Hare Krishna faith. They explained:

> *The devotees of Krishna, in commemoration of the National Day of Peace, of such great importance, have brought their message of peace in the form of a dance which represents the eternal victory of good over evil. The dance represents the Supreme Being at the centre of all our interests, in such a way that violence can never be allowed to reign. In the name of the same Supreme Being, whether this name be Krishna, or Buddha, or Allah or Yahweh, we share the same sentiments of peace: Hare Krishna, Hare Christ, Hare Buddha, Hare Allah, Hare Eternal Peace.*

When the dance had ended, the moment of offering had come. In this act of worship five representative groups of society

[11] Bishop Sumio was President of the Ecumenical News Agency where I worked.

offered symbols of their struggle for peace. First came the ecologists and pacifists, then the nation's labour force, the third symbol came from the Afro-Brazilian people's struggle for an end to discrimination, the fourth was from the rural community's plea for land reform. Most moving was the fifth, the representatives of São Paulo's half-million abandoned children. They mounted a painter's ladder to hoist their roughly made flag appealing for peace.

After the crowd had sung the hymn of St. Francis – *Make me an instrument of your peace* – the final blessing was administered by a group of twelve children, representing Brazil's four main ethnic groups: the original Indians, descendants of the European colonizers, descendants of the African slaves and descendants of Oriental immigrants. Then the twelve children were joined by one hundred and fifty others. Colourful balloons were launched while the Cathedral bells rang out in celebration.

Bishops and Rabbis began to leave their places, cameramen and journalists went back to their studios, but the people would not go home. It was the first Sunday of summertime, daylight would linger a little longer. This carnival-loving people joined hands and danced to a new rhythm till long after the sun went down.

Invitation to India

A few years after this, while I was on sabbatical leave in the United States, I received an invitation to join the facilitation team of an inter-faith event in India. It bore the Sanskrit title *Sarva Dharma Sammelana,* meaning 'Religious People Meeting Together'. This encounter in Bangalore was scheduled for August 18-22, 1993, ahead of a bigger gathering, called the

'Parliament of World Religions', held in Chicago, August 28-September 5.

Both events were convoked to mark the centenary of the 'Parliament of World Religions' held in Chicago in 1893. On that occasion, a famous young Hindu called Swami Vivekananda[12], travelled from India and addressed the assembly with a story that has become legendary in the inter-faith movement:

> *A frog who had been born in a well grew up there and became sleek and fat. One day another frog that lived in the sea came to the well and fell in. 'Where do you come from?' asked the well-frog. 'From the sea", answered the other. 'The sea! How big is that? Is it as big as my well?" asked the first, as he took a leap from one side of the well to the other. "My friend", said the sea-frog, "how can you compare the sea with your little well?" The well-frog took another leap. "Is your sea as big as this?" he asked. "What nonsense you talk" said the sea-frog, "comparing the sea with your well". Furious, the well-frog retorted: "Nothing can be bigger than this!" and looking around he shouted, "This fellow is a liar, turn him out."*

"That has been the difficulty all the while', Vivekenanda told the Chicago gathering on 15th September 1893.

> *I am a Hindu. I am sitting in my own little well and thinking that my little well is the whole world. The Christian sits in his little well and thinks his well is the whole world. The Mohammedan sits in his little well and thinks that this is the whole world.*

While all others at the 1893 Parliament spoke on behalf of their own religion, Vivekenanda spoke of the *religion beyond religions.*

[12] Swami Vivekananda was born 1863 and lived until 1902

On his way back to India, Vivekananda stopped in Europe. It so happened that when he was speaking in London, the audience included a young teacher from Dungannon in Northern Ireland, Margaret Noble (1867-1911). She was so impressed that she moved to India and became his devoted disciple. There she was called *Sister Nivedita,* meaning 'the dedicated one'.

As an educator among poor Hindu girls, she played quite a role in India's struggle for independence. She also travelled with Vivekananda on his subsequent voyages and is acknowledged as being the person responsible for committing much of his teaching to paper.

Where Three Seas Meet

I had come to know an Indian Carmelite priest, Fr. Albert Nambiaparambil. He was a member of the Vatican Secretariat for Dialogue and the lead person on inter-religious cooperation on behalf of the Catholic Bishops' Conference of India. When he heard that I would be coming to India for the Bangalore event, he encouraged me to come earlier and be present for the gathering of the World Federation of Inter-Faith Councils called the 'World Celebration of Unity and Life'.

It was held in the little town of Kanyakumari, at the southernmost tip of India where three seas meet – the Indian Ocean, the Bay of Bengal, and the Arabian Sea. The spot is a sacred one where, every weekend, Hindu families come to bathe. Just half a kilometer off the coast lies Vivekananda Rock. On it a Hindu Temple dedicated to the memory of the famous Swami has become a place of pilgrimage for people of dialogue from all faiths. In the bookshop there, I found many items commemorating the Irish woman who had served so faithfully the renowned Vivekananda and the women and girls of India.

There were about three hundred and fifty of us in Kanyakumari – the majority either Hindus or Muslims or Christians, but also Jews, Sikhs, Zoroastrians, Taoists, Bahá'ís, Jains, and Buddhists. In Kanyakumari, a few hundred meters along the dust road from the shore, there was the large Catholic Seminary of St. Thomas, and a little further on a large Muslim centre. Most participants lodged in one or other of these, and the conferences were also held in these venues. Meals were served out of doors.

Lining up for lunch on the first day, an experienced English cleric whispered to me that it would be advisable to always select the vegetarian menu. He was unaware of the amount of goat and other creatures I had consumed on life's journeys. (I recalled to myself a very happy Sunday lunch in the lower ground floor home of a family in Brazil. My hostess got up from the table and stirred the pot on the cooker asking, 'would anyone like another piece of ear?') As I was a newcomer to Kanyakumari, I took the Englishman's advice and became vegetarian for the length of my visit.

For five days we took part in our chosen workshops. In the mornings they were held under magnificent flowering trees. In the evenings, when the mosquitoes had come out, we were indoors in the big auditorium of whichever venue was selected.

The Vatican representative was Bishop Michael Fitzgerald from the Pontifical Council for Inter-religious Dialogue. His sister, Dr. Christine, had been a colleague of mine in Tanzania years earlier. On the closing night in Kanyakumari, Bishop Michael was one of the leaders of our sunset pilgrimage to the seashore. During the hour-long procession, over the loudspeaker we would be invited to stop. In turn, a member of each of the different faiths would be called upon to come and offer a prayer. Then we would move on.

We had reached the sandy beach where the three seas meet when the loudspeaker called for the delegate from Ireland to come and pray. There was silence while I made my way through the crowd to the microphone wondering 'what prayer will I pray'? There was no time to prepare, so I sang the verse in my native language *'Glór agus moladh dhuit, Íosa, a Íosa'* – 'glory and praise to you, Jesus'. The sun was just slipping under the horizon to the west.

Meeting Soul Mates

On the walk home that night, I was joined by a Sikh who thanked me for my hymn. He said "all who seek truth, love and purity are my co-religionists. These values must be translated into acts of humanity.' For this reason, he had renounced his career as an Indian diplomat in Paris to devote all his energies to working with people living with leprosy.

I met Catholic women from Bangladesh and Indian women of other faiths. All of them were true soul mates. One of them who was Catholic lived in Bombay.[13] She begged me to come and stay in her home when the event in Bangalore would be over. I told her I planned to go for retreat at an ashram in Tamil Nadu in the country's east – a long way from Bombay on the western coast.

I had asked Swami Amal Raj if I could spend a week at his ashram. 'Sure', he replied, writing in my diary the directions to Aanmodhaya Ashram, de Mazenod Nagar, Enathur, Vedal PO, Kancheepuram. PIN 631552. He explained carefully how to get there: Take a train from Madras[14] to Chengalpattu, then

---

[13] Two years later the city was renamed Mumbai, in a nationwide effort to move away from Anglicised names associated with the colonial era.
[14] Now Chennai since 1996.

the bus to Kancheepuram bus stop and then get a rickshaw. Tell the driver you want to go to the Ashram beside Sandara College. 'See you there', he said as he turned to the next person in the long queue waiting to talk to him. I was sure that somehow, my very experienced Guardian Angel could manage those directions ok. I'd get an overnight bus from Bangalore to Madras. He gave me a phone number in case I got lost.

My new Catholic friend was insisting there would be no difficulty getting from the Ashram to her home in Bombay. "There is a train from Madras to our city", she insisted. "You can easily change your ticket home and we will drive you to the airport to get your flight." Sounded lovely, and indeed it was. I felt so much at home with her family and met many of her friends of different faiths. They enjoyed dressing me in a sari. We talked about everything under the sun, but mainly about women's issues, our role, what we have to offer, and our place in society. But before that there was Bangalore!

The previous year in December, the world was shocked at the violent destruction by Hindu fanatics of a 16th century mosque in the north Indian town of Ayodhya. More than 2,000 people are believed to have died in the Hindu-Muslim riots that followed.

Hindus make up about 80% of India's population of more than 800 million people. Muslims make up about 12%. India's Hindu-Muslim tension is more political than religious – and needs our prayers. But India is also the cradle of inter-faith cooperation and understanding. That is why it was chosen for these events marking the centenary of the 1893 Parliament of Religions.

Sarva Dharma Sammelana

There were about 600 delegates at the *Sarva Dharma Sammelana*[15] in Bangalore. It took place in a luxurious 5-star hotel, quite different to our surroundings in Kanyakumari. Representation of the different faith communities was unbalanced, but it was felt that in the organization of the event the inter-faith movement had renewed its purpose.

There were three streams to the conference. Participants had registered for the one of their choice. As I was involved with only one of these groups, to recount this event I will rely on the report written by Rev. Canon Alan Race, editor of *World Faith Encounter* in the November 1993 edition. He recorded how the groups dealt with the paradox of religious commitment in global times.

The first group faced head-on the knotty problem of the theological and philosophical interpretation of religious plurality. Most were clear that fundamentalist and exclusivist attitudes could not serve us well in the future.

Two different approaches were canvassed. The first was 'committed pluralism'. This suggested a unity of the religions at the ultimate level: a relationship of complementarity without mixing up beliefs and without saying all religions were the same really. The second group felt happier with a process of encounter, whereby traditions subjected themselves to mutual transformation as a result of critical dialogue.

The conference did not choose between these options. But there was a passionate plea from the Indian Christian theologian and former Director of the Unit on Dialogue of the World Council of Churches, Dr. Stanley Samartha. He felt that

---

[15] 'Religious people meeting together'.

without the grounding of inter-faith practical work in theology and philosophy we shall be failing at a profound level.

Alan Race wrote: "I wondered whether the stress on *process* alone was sufficient to help us avoid this failure. I was also aware that while the poor cannot afford the luxury of theological/philosophical problem-solving, the issue nevertheless has a rightful claim on us – so long as we remember that it is not an *alternative* to practical cooperation for the sake of a better world."

This group also wrestled with the proposed *Declaration of a Global Ethic*. This was modified some weeks later at the Chicago 'Parliament of Religions' where it was renamed *Declaration Toward a Global Ethic* and adopted, as will be described soon.

A second group explored the paradox of religious commitment in global times by going on pilgrimage to various religious temples and centres. Alan Race wrote: "They reminded us that the religious quest is deeply rooted in experience and spirituality, and that our pirouetting round the ideas of a global ethic and theories of religious plurality is an inadequate abstraction if the particular identities of different faith-communities are not taken seriously."

The experience demonstrated that the dialogue which is going to last and bear real fruit is going to have to be the product of long and patient listening at the temples of the other. In the balance between the head and the heart we need both to know and to feel the universe as others do. If the dream of inter-faith understanding and co-operation is to become more than the interest of a few, it will have to communicate both the urgency of the global problems confronting humanity and the deep possibilities of shared vision and ethical values that the world religions have to offer.

Prospective in Practice

The facilitating team for which I had been invited to Bangalore was charged with leading the participants in the third group. Our task was to envision a future where inter-faith cooperation could be maximized for the service of the global community. Our methodology was based on the future-oriented philosophy of Gaston Berger, founder of the French school of *Prospective.*[16]

In Bangalore our task was to share our inter-faith vision of how the future could be. We tried to imagine a world some decades hence, and then travel together back along the path that took us there, marking milestones. Reviewing the work of our group, Alan Race wrote:

> *Such unashamed dreaming might help local inter-faith groups in their shared project work to identify the obstacles to building trust and community. At another level, it could help us to imagine a role for a Council of Religions, perhaps a little on the analogy of the UN, a non-governmental organization for monitoring potential areas of conflict in the world. This is an intriguing suggestion, especially as bodies like the UN are now taking seriously the role of religion in their work of mediation and conflict resolution. Given the fact that many of the world's conflicts have religious antagonism at their roots, a Council of Religions could be a first step towards the religions making amends.*

---

[16] See Postscript 2

Back in 1993, the events I had witnessed in India were replicated in several other parts of the world. The Chicago event, the second 'Parliament of Religions,' gathered 7,000 people from 125 faiths for the 9-day event.

They included Archbishop Francesco Gioia of the Pontifical Council for Inter-religious Dialogue. He repeated the Catholic church's commitment to inter-religious dialogue. Cardinal Bernardin of Chicago was a prominent figure. So was the Dalai Lama. The secretary general of the World Muslim League, Adbullah Omar Nasseef, was there from Saudi Arabia.

With over 700 workshops and panel discussions by experts from different faiths, it was described by some as 'a supermarket of religions'. Undoubtedly, some were there to 'sell' their beliefs. But the majority had come to pray together, to listen and to try to understand.

An event on that scale inevitably had its moments of tension. But on balance the quest for harmony is thought to have far outweighed the discord. Many of the religious leaders signed the Declaration Towards a Global Ethic, the first draft of which had come from the German Catholic theologian, Hans Kung, and had been further developed at our Bangalore gathering.

In a world where two-thirds of armed conflicts invoke the name of religion, Hans Kung had been urging the adoption of a common global ethic which would condemn inequality, intolerance, ecological destruction and economic injustice. It was his view that if there is not peace between the followers of the Great Faiths, we cannot expect to have peace on Earth. More than that, the Declaration was a commitment by the leaders of these religions not just to be at peace with one another, but to work together for world peace.

Declaration Towards a Global Ethic

The document signed at Chicago in August 1993 was an invitation to further dialogue:

> *The world is in agony. The agony is so pervasive and urgent that we are compelled to name its manifestations so that the depth of this pain may be made clear.*
>
> *Peace eludes us ... the planet is being destroyed ... neighbours live in fear ... women and men are estranged from each other ... children die. This is abhorrent!*
>
> *We condemn the poverty that stifles life's potential; the hunger that weakens the human body; the economic disparities that threaten so many families with ruin.*
>
> *We condemn the social disarray of the nations; the disregard for justice which pushes citizens to the margin; and the insane death of children from violence and hatred in the name of religion. But this agony need not be.*
>
> *It need not be because the basis for an ethic already exists. This ethic offers the possibility of a better individual and global order, and leads individuals away from despair and societies away from chaos.*
>
> *We are women and men who have embraced the precepts and practices of the world's religions.*
>
> *We affirm that a common set of core values is found in the teachings of the religions, and that these form the basis of a global ethic.*
>
> *We affirm that the truth is already known, but yet to be lived in heart and action.*
>
> *We affirm that there is an irrevocable, unconditional norm for all areas of life, for families and communities, for races,*

nations, and religions. There already exist ancient guidelines for human behaviour which are found in the teachings of the religions of the world, and which are the condition for a sustainable world order.

We declare:

We are interdependent. Each of us depends on the well-being of the whole, and so we have respect for the community of living beings, for people, animals, and plants, and for the preservation of Earth, the air, water and soil.

We take individual responsibility for all we do. All our decisions, actions, and failures to act have consequences.

We must treat others as we wish others to treat us. We make a commitment to respect life and dignity, individuality and diversity, so that every person is treated humanely, without exception. We must have patience and acceptance. We must be able to forgive, learning from the past but never allowing ourselves to be enslaved by memories of hate. Opening our hearts to one another, we must sink narrow differences for the cause of the world community, practising a culture of solidarity and relatedness.

We consider humankind our family. We must strive to be kind and generous. We must not live for ourselves alone, but should also serve others, never forgetting the children, the aged, the poor, the suffering, the disabled, the refugees, and the lonely. No person should ever be considered or treated as a second-class citizen, or be exploited in any way whatsoever. There should be equal partnership between men and women, we must not commit any kind of sexual immorality. We must put behind us all forms of domination or abuse.

We commit ourselves to a culture of non-violence, respect, justice, and peace. We shall not oppress, injure, torture, or kill other human beings, forsaking violence as a means of settling differences.

We must strive for a just social and economic order, in which everyone has an equal chance to reach full potential as a human being. We must speak and act truthfully and with compassion, dealing fairly with all, and avoiding prejudice and hatred. We must not steal. We must move beyond the dominance of greed for power, prestige, money, and consumption to make a just and peaceful world.

Earth cannot be changed for the better unless the consciousness of individuals is changed first. We pledge to increase our awareness by disciplining our minds, by meditation, by prayer, or by positive thinking. Without risk and a readiness to sacrifice there can be no fundamental change in our situation. Therefore, we commit ourselves to this global ethic, to understanding one another, and to socially beneficial, peace-fostering and nature-friendly ways of life.

We invite all people, whether religious or not, to do the same.

Written thirty years ago, this Declaration is a bit wordy. But we can imagine how difficult it must have been to include the proposals that 7000 delegates from 125 different faiths wanted to include. It was, and is, regarded as a draft text to help us move towards an agreed global ethic one day. These are important principles to guide us and encourage us in our joint work for world peace.

What was confirmed is that each of the Great Faiths proposes and defends principles of social justice. Grounded in the origins of these faiths, the praxis of living our belief is updated by faith leaders as society changes with the passage of time. The Catholic theologian, Dermot Lane, provides a most helpful study of the steps taken to deepen understanding between faith leaders. He says:

> *The drive behind inter-religious dialogue is a drive to understand the other. There is a growing awareness that in the twenty-first century, to be religious will require that one be inter-religious and that to be authentically Christian will necessitate that one enter into respectful dialogue with other religions.*[17]

He shows that most religions have come into being through engagement with other religions. But now we are 'at the beginning of a new beginning' of dialogue, and this will be a defining feature of the first century of the third millennium. Interfaith dialogue and collaboration is not an optional extra but an essential part of the definition of what our faith means to us. Fr. Lane introduces us to the amount of scholarly work that has taken place to draw believers to a deeper understanding of one another. Against the backdrop of a rapidly changing world, he develops a theology of the role of the Holy Spirit as the foundation for dialogue with other religions.

World Congress of Faiths

Inspired by the 1893 Parliament of Religions, and with signs of a second world war looming, in 1936 The World Congress of Faiths[18] was established. Since then, in the face of the unjust and unfair experiences in which the majority of the world's population have to live, pathways to encourage collaboration between the followers of the ancient faiths were developed.

Since then, the problems of inequity between social classes has been exacerbated by the urgency which climate change

---

[17] Dermot Lane, *Stepping Stones to Other Religions*, Veritas Publications, 2011

[18] https://worldfaiths.org

brought to the plight of the Earth, everybody's home. It is recognised that dialogue between religious leaders, important as it is, does not automatically trickle down to ordinary members of faith-based communities. The task of finding ways of collaboration between people of different faiths in confronting our social problems remains urgent. What is hopeful is that the vision of committed leaders working at grassroots level has created networks which continue to expand.

Today, members of the World Congress of Faiths are drawn from all major faith traditions across the world. These are people who believe that by coming closer to each other, respecting the integrity of the world faith traditions, members of different religions could deepen their own faith and strengthen their concept of God.

The organization, while based in the UK, draws on an international breadth of knowledge. Today it works with other interfaith bodies to promote peace, justice, and ecology concerns. Its archive of publications is a rich source for anyone interested in interfaith relations. Collaborating with higher education and theological training, the World Congress of Faiths recognises the importance of spiritual life in society, as well as working for mutual trust and understanding among faith communities.

Interfaith Center of New York

Respect for one another's religious beliefs can grow when people come together to respond to local social needs. This is well modelled in the work of the Interfaith Center of New York (ICNY)[19] which was founded in 1997, just four years after the second Chicago Parliament of Religions.

---

[19] https://interfaithcenter.org

Across the five boroughs of New York, members of Muslim, Sikh, Hindu, Buddhist, Christian, Jewish, Afro-Caribbean and Native American religions have come together for social justice retreats and have collaborated in combatting real social problems. The terrible events of 9/11 put the emphasis on working together — as members of different faith traditions — to condemn terrorism and violence in the name of religion. Members work with the civil authorities in responding to the different crises the city faces. The multi-faceted work of ICNY has become an internationally recognized model of education, commitment and cooperation among faith traditions.

Since 2017 their Civic Leadership Academy has been providing training on diverse models of civic engagement and religious leadership. In this way they resource leaders with the tools they need to make a difference in their communities. This provides opportunities to benefit from expert trainers at evening workshops for faith-based activists, along with clergy and lay leaders. Participants are introduced to the benefits of civic engagement, policy advocacy and organizing strategies at grassroots community level. They also learn the approaches to interfaith dialogue and building personal relationships across faith lines.

Canada

The Canadian Scarboro Missions[20] drew on their experience of a century of Catholic global involvement to develop a service to the interfaith movement. Their outline of Principles and Guidelines for Interfaith Dialogue and their series of resources can be valuable to people on any continent. They speak of the interfaith movement as "a treasure chest of wisdom and learning opportunities." Through their website and social media,

---

[20] https://scarboromissions.ca

Scarboro offers guidance and techniques on the skills of dialogue and issues such as listening, interfaith etiquette, peacebuilding, the stages of dialogue and the difference between dialogue and debate. Like the New York initiative, they help communities to become engaged in collaborative civic action.

The Scarboro website provides valuable information on the shared values of the Abrahamic faiths. It explores the concept of mercy from the Jewish, Christian, and Muslim traditions. It also offers Christian and Jewish responses to the 2015 Vatican document on Catholic and Jewish relations.

Scarboro also provides links to international interfaith groups, including those dedicated to engaging young people in ending religious prejudice that can lead to violence. The Scarboro Mission sees its role in witnessing to the Gospel of Jesus Christ as safeguarding the rights of every person in a world community that is not limited by boundaries of race, geography, culture, or religion. The task is one of working together to secure human rights, to overcome the problems of hunger and poverty, and to pursue peace.

Another Canadian venture is called *Encounter World Religions.*[21] Established in the 1980s by an American Southerner, J.W. Windland, its Executive Director today is Brian Carwana. He gave up his career as a strategy consultant and venture capitalist when he met Windland. He has devoted the past twenty years to researching and educating others about world religions and now has an extensive following online.

In a 2022 interview he told CBC news "I don't belong to any of the religious traditions. I grew up Catholic and I was a committed Catholic into my 20s, but now I find something valuable in all of them. I'm inspired by the Sikhs and their commitment

---

[21] https://www.worldreligions.ca.

to service. I love going to the Synagogue. There's a Jewish rabbi who I just love listening to all the time. I'm deep friends with an Imam whose basic humility and kindness inspired me. But none of them is quite fully home. And yet at some time, at some level, they're all a little bit home."

Encounter World Religions sees the importance of forging connections across differences. It promotes religious pluralism, where people of diverse religious, spiritual and secular identities live and thrive in harmony with one another. Brian Carwana believes that promoting religious literacy is an important part of the work to achieve understanding and sensitivity. This organization invests in providing experiential learning for people in workplaces, schools, and community groups. It also engages in a serious way with business corporations to promote care of the environment and social justice.

Starting in Japan

In 1990 when Japanese Buddhist leader, Rev. Takeyasu Miyamoto (1918-2015), established the Arigatou Foundation, his motivation was to link prayer with action to secure the welfare of children. This work led him to realise how much greater the result would be if people of many faiths could be brought together for this cause.

In the year 2000 the Global Network of Religions for Children (GNRC)[22] was inaugurated. They worked with UNICEF, UNHCR and other international bodies. In 2002, when Miyamoto was invited to address a special session on Children at the UN General Assembly, he could report that some 300 religious leaders and grassroots workers from every major world religion in 33 countries had attended the first forum of the GNRC.

---

[22] https://gnrc.net.

He quoted Rabindranath Tagore – "Every child born comes with a message that God has not yet despaired of humankind."

Volunteers from different faith groups in dozens of countries soon became involved in collaborative work to improve the rights of children. They have established an Interfaith Programme for Ethics Education. There are now sixty-five country committees, with an extensive global outreach. Their website carries impressive testimonials from young people of diverse nationalities on how their worldview and commitment has been formed through the work of GNRC. The Secretariat is now located in Nairobi, from where its twelve-member team provides technical assistance to the networks and seeks to implement its strategic plan.

Interfaith Network for the United Kingdom

Founded in 1987, the Inter Faith Network for the United Kingdom[23] embraces the Northern Ireland Inter-Faith Forum, Interfaith Scotland and the Inter-faith Council for Wales. It also has membership of academic institutions and bodies concerned with multi faith education. At its foundation it acknowledged the many traditions and the shared wisdom that has been inherited as well as the tragic misunderstandings that have occurred. Today the network counts on some 200 member organizations including the Bahá'í, Buddhist, Christian, Hindu, Jain, Jewish, Muslim, Sikh and Zoroastrian communities.

Its range of activities and its local networks provide information and advice to many groups including chaplaincies, youth organizations, and Government departments. It provides opportunities to put interfaith engagement at the heart of local communities. It promotes mutual understanding of the

[23] https://interfaith.org.uk.

teaching, traditions and practices of the different faith communities in Britain. As well as promoting social action, it encourages celebration of the important festivals of member faiths. It provides training to equip people to be peacemakers, helps churches to become centres of reconciliation, and celebrates difference.

Drawing on the diverse background of the population of Britain today, the Inter Faith Network has a membership of fifteen educational and academic institutions, thirty-one national networks and a hundred local interfaith groups. It is also committed to collaboration with interfaith work overseas.

In Ireland

Through a simple initiative in Dublin called *Sisters of Faith for Peace*, women of different faiths are invited to befriend one another. This small group was founded in 2015 when two Christian women[24] visited the Islamic and Jewish communities in Dublin and talked about their idea that women working alongside men, regardless of religious background, race, or culture, could help the world to heal some of its differences. They support the principles of the international Charter for Compassion.[25] Founding member, Doris McCann, says:

> *The Sisters of Faith for Peace (SFP) are a women's interfaith group based on the shared spiritual source of the Abrahamic faiths. Whilst open to women of all faiths, the main foundation of the group are women of Jewish, Christian, and Islamic backgrounds. SFP aims to build bridges and human connections based on our shared common values. We believe that we*

---

[24] Doris McCann, German-born and raised in the Lutheran faith, now living in Ireland, and Nigerian-born Sister Sabina Anokwu of the Missionary Sisters of the Holy Rosary working in Dublin.

[25] https://charterforcompassion.org

are all one Human family under God, and peace begins with us breaking down barriers and stereotypes through friendships whilst respecting each other's faiths.

Our focus lies on projects that facilitate shared bonding and action, often in the Mosques, Churches, and Synagogues, where we visit together, getting to know one another simply as sisters of the same Human family under God. We also hold conferences and have worked together for different charity projects. With this process, we also seek to empower women of faith as we believe that women have a crucial role to offer in the peace-building process. We are proud to call Sabina Higgins, the current First Lady of Ireland, our Patron.

Abrahamic Faiths in Europe

A more recent development has come from the leaders of the Jewish faith in Europe. Recognising that people of the Abrahamic faiths share much in common, they set up the Institute for Freedom of Faith and Security in Europe (IFFSE).[26] Based in Munich and Brussels, this is a multidisciplinary think-tank which aims to bring together leading thinkers and policymakers to discuss ways of combating religious extremism and incitement to terrorism both online and offline.

This group works to create efforts in the field of integration so that religion is not politicised and used as a tool of hate and prejudice. While calling on government authorities to guarantee the freedom of religion, it also calls upon the various faiths to exercise leadership and engage in interfaith dialogue across religious boundaries.

---

[26] www.iffse.eu

The group sees the need for comprehensive programmes that involve cooperation between religions and society. They are greatly concerned about deadly attacks on the public and on places of worship. The connection between the rise of hate speech on social networks and physical violence requires a global solution. IFFSE seeks to mobilise faith leaders from across the world, in partnership with governments and NGOS to make digital services more responsible. Likewise, it seeks to mobilise religious leaders to use their places of worship to counter religious extremism and to protect ethnic minorities and refugees.

G20 Interfaith Forum[27]

The global agenda is the concern of the G20 Interfaith Forum established in 2008. It offers an annual platform where a network of religiously linked institutions and initiatives engage on global agendas. They are particularly focussed on the UN Sustainable Development Goals. They seek to contribute meaningful insight and recommendations that respond to and help shape the G20 and thus global policy agendas.

The G20 Interfaith Forum builds on the vital roles that religious institutions and beliefs play in world affairs, reflecting their rich diversity of institutions, ideas, and values. These include interfaith and intercultural organizations, religious leaders, scholars, development and humanitarian entities, and business and civil society actors.

Beginning in Australia in 2014, the G20 Interfaith Forum has convened annually in the G20 host country. Each Forum has considered wide-ranging agendas, including economic models and systems, the environment, women, families, children,

[27] https://www.g20interfaith.org.

work, humanitarian aid, health, education, freedom of religion or belief, global security, governance, human rights, and the rule of law. The agenda for each Forum is framed taking into account the annual G20 priorities outlined each year by the host government, together with topics that the various networks of religious actors recommend that the G20 leaders address.

They have established several Working Groups of experts to facilitate consideration of ways in which faith communities can contribute to progress on anti-racism, poverty and inequality, religion, health and wellbeing, education, the environment, gender equality and human trafficking, refugees, displacement, migration, humanitarian aid and – most importantly – youth. Their efforts draw on the collective wisdom of widely diverse religious and cultural communities and encourage robust dialogue.

Uniting to save our Planet

The crisis of climate change has galvanized interfaith activity in a number of countries through the GreenFaith International Network. Founders include groups in Australia, Brazil, Canada, Chile, India, Indonesia, Kenya, Nigeria, South Africa, Uganda, UK, USA, Zambia and Zimbabwe. They remind us that people of faith make up 80% of the world's population.

Members of GreenFaith recognise that religious and spiritual communities everywhere generate a moral awakening to the sacredness of our planet Earth and the dignity of all people. They seek to build resilient, caring communities and economies that meet everyone's needs and protect the planet. They hope to see the era of conquest, extraction, and exploitation give way to cooperation and community. They want to see despair replaced with joy, scarcity replaced with shared abundance, and privilege replaced with justly distributed power.

To achieve these goals, they formed a global multi-faith network of grassroots faith communities called "Faiths 4 Climate Justice". This has been co-sponsored by more than 100 organizations, with members from Jewish, Muslim, Hindu, Buddhist, Sikh, Jain, Bahá'í, Indigenous, Christian, and many more faith and spiritual backgrounds. They draw energy from their faiths and cultural values with a deep desire to end suffering and oppression.

They encourage members to value their religious feast days, as well as special days like Equinox, Earth Day, and World Water Day, to become engaged in addressing the climate crisis. They encourage people to form local GreenFaith Circles drawing on faith-based groups and neighbours. As heat waves, wildfires and floods damage our planet and kill thousands of people, they remind us that "these impacts are the opposite of what our religions call for: peace, well-being for all, security for children and families and respect for our precious planet."

In August 2023, another convening of the Parliament of World Religions in Chicago marked the 30th anniversary of the 1993 event. Like the GreenFaith Network, it was dedicated to achieving a just, peaceful, and sustainable world. It was attended by more than seven thousand delegates from ninety-five countries and representing two hundred and ten different faith traditions.

One cause motivated them all: the call to conscience in the face of the threats facing our communities and the world. It was considered a flashing emergency light affirming to the world that faith and spiritual communities are vital partners and first responders in the fight for justice, for freedom, for a healthy environment, for human rights and for democracy.

The event celebrated the 30th anniversary of what is now considered the Parliament's foundational document *Towards a Global Ethic.* Dr. Myriam Renaud, Director of the Global Ethic Project felt it was impressive to see how, thirty years on, the Parliament's 1993 document generated a lot of buzz. She said: "although most of us don't share the same beliefs, we agree on the basic values and principles expressed in the document." The input of prestigious speakers can be replayed from the Parliament's website.[28]

Pope Francis included many of the above concerns in his 2015 encyclical letter *Laudato Si'*. He concludes this document with a prayer he wrote that could be shared by all who believe in a God who is the Earth's creator.[29] Five years later writing in *Fratelli Tutti* he repeated the need for people of all beliefs to work together, declaring the adoption of a culture of dialogue as the path; mutual cooperation as the code of conduct; reciprocal understanding as the method and standard.[30]

When he conceived the idea of publishing the film on the plight of our planet *The Letter,*[31] he made it clear that our calling is to understand how the climate crisis deeply affects people in different parts of the world and that it is by working together that we must respond. In 2023 he followed this with a further development of the theme in *Laudate Deum.* He reminded us:

Everything is connected.
No one is saved alone.[32]

---

[28] https://parliamentofreligions.org
[29] *Laudato Si'*, par 246
[30] *Fratelli Tutti,* par. 285
[31] https://www.youtube.com/watch?v=Rps9bs85BII
[32] *Laudate Deum,* par 19

CHAPTER 7

THE GOD 'E'

AT A TRAM STOP ON MY WAY TO KOWLOON I saw a mobile phone for the first time. I was the only person in the queue who did not have one. Everyone was talking to someone somewhere else. When not in use, the large plastic brick was carried in the back pocket of the owner's jeans.

It was October 1989. I was heading to the Philippines to attend the first World Congress on Christian Communication[1]. I broke my outward journey in Hong Kong because one of the Columban Missionary Sisters had kindly offered to be my guide on a brief visit to China.

On return to Ireland, it was not long before I had a mobile phone too. With the antenna extended, it was about the size of a lady's high heeled shoe. To carry it around, my local shoemaker made me a soft leather pouch with a shoulder strap – an ancestor of the wearable technology that is now with us in the form of Fitbits and all kinds of gadgets that will be on the way quite soon.

In Manila, it was exhilarating to join 500 participants who had come from 80 different countries, all concerned about the

[1] The Congress was organized by the World Association for Christian Communication, which was linked to, though not part of the World Council of Churches – www.waccglobal.org.

future of communications as a tool of the Gospel mission. One of the preparatory papers for the Congress had noted general agreement that the human race was standing at an important crossroads in regard to the possibilities for communication.

Modern technologies offer opportunities to human beings to interact with each other, to share their thoughts, experiences, and cultures and to develop mutual understanding to a degree that would have been unimaginable some decades earlier. And yet, these same technologies can also cause societies to fragment, break down cultures and isolate people in an unprecedented way. That document said: "the principal impediments to community today are not modern communication technologies themselves, but the unjust structures through which they are used and controlled."

A well-known French priest, Pierre Babin OMI[2], was among the keynote speakers. He drew from his long experience at the ecumenical communication centre he had founded in Lyons – CREC-AVEX.[3] He was known to many of the participants who had come from countries of Africa and Asia where his teaching on catechetical communications had made a big impact.

Listening to Fr. Babin, I became aware that everything is being changed under the influence of this god 'E': our culture, our way of managing politics, our education, the running of our churches and of participation in society. This god is omnipresent and surreptitiously at work. "What peculiar and unique capacities does this mini-god possess?" he asked. They can be summarized in a single word: stimulation.

Using a small word processor, I took copious notes so that when I got home, I could publish the fruits of this Congress in

---

[2] A native of France, Pierre Babin was born in 1925 and died in 2012.

[3] www.crecinternational.org

the monthly publication of the Irish Missionary Union where I was working at the Communications Desk.

The electronic factor, or the 'coefficient E', as Babin also referred to it, is a super-drug. It affects our senses, our brains, our world. By means of light it lengthens our active day; by means of computers it creates endless interconnections; it abolishes the natural categories of time and space.

Like most of us gathered in Manila, Babin was born into a generation and a culture in which ideas dominated the world. It was the ideas of Marshal McLuhan that jolted him. He told us it took him 15 years of reflecting before he fully grasped how radically the scenario had changed. "I was focussed on ideas, on doctrine. McLuhan was pointing to technologies, and more particularly to the electronic medium. I thought: ideas govern the world. He was saying: technologies govern the world, especially when they are media."

Babin combined the insights of McLuhan with a Catholic educational and sacramental approach. In his view, communications media were environments that could reveal God's beauty, as well as being tools for teaching the Christian message. I later learned that Babin had collaborated with McLuhan on a prophetic book *'Autre homme, autre chrétien à l'âge électronique'*. Discussions with Babin also form the backbone of *'The Medium and the Light'*, a publication on McLuhan's religious views, co-authored with his son, Eric McLuhan.

A New Type of Culture

In Babin's understanding, technology is not a neutral instrument which can be mastered with the head. It is grafted on to our body, which it extends and modifies. It dictates a new type of culture. We have to change our definition of communication and participation, since the definitions that applied in a world which we might call classical and literary are no longer valid in the world of electronic media. In the era dominated by the print medium – the 'Gutenberg culture' – communication meant effecting a transfer of knowledge. In the electronic audiovisual world, communication means mutual stimulation. It involves modulation, i.e. a certain quality of physical vibration, using vision and sound, producing psychological effects.[4]

Babin called on us to acknowledge the value of the audiovisual culture and the language of modulation. By doing so, he suggested, we shall be doing revolutionary work in the direct line of the Gospel. As well as being the predominant language of our times, he said, modulation was the language most often favoured by Jesus Christ.

He went further, saying: "We would be less than faithful to the Incarnation of Christ if we were to reject this language and the culture deriving from it. I am not saying this language is the best: I am saying that it is there, and that because of the Incarnation we have to make it our body."

While it may feel new to those of us who grew up in the Western, so-called 'developed' nations, Babin went on to point out that modulation, i.e. stimulating vibrations, is the traditional language of the majority of cultures on Earth. Africans and Indians and the peoples of the Orient all speak first through gesture, signs, rhythms, music, and dance. They follow the singer rather than the song. More important still, it is the predominant language of the poor.

---

[4] Today, participants expect audiovisual stimulation in PowerPoint presentations, at Zoom meetings or Webinars. The conductor of a magnificent choir, or an orchestra can also create modulation similar to Babin's idea.

However, giving priority to modulation does not mean using it exclusively, much less uncritically. Communications in terms of modulation need to be complemented, extended and critically assessed by the intellect, reflection and science. We need our theologians and our thinkers.

Our corrective principle, Babin told us, is the Spirit of God in the Gospel and the Christian community. The age of electronics, which favours communication based on modulation, opens the way for communication from one being to another, that kind of deep communication which Christians call "communion".

Another speaker was the respected Indian journalist and author, BG Verghese[5], who was noted for his concern for marginalized peoples. He addressed the gathering about the communications revolution. Of the new vistas of opportunity that are opening up through the de-massification of communications he said:

> *While centralisation has been the hallmark of a great deal of modernisation since the industrial revolution, the micro-chip revolution has also had a diametrically opposite effect. The new communications technology is divisible, highly compact and easily portable, enabling individuals and small groups to use it personally or locally.*

In this, Verghese saw a transformation: the rejuvenation of small communities, members of which can be one despite living apart. He felt the mini-community could now better co-exist with the mega-community. For Verghese, fighting off alienation and rootlessness is a major challenge in a fast-changing milieu. He saw communication (in the sense of education, awareness-building, and information) as a key process in

[5] BG Verghese was born in India in 1927 and died in 2014.

creating the conditions for participative development. But he was highly critical of the consumerist advertising used by the media.

Communication and Liberation

The line of thought expressed by Verghese was echoed by the Argentinian theologian of the Methodist community, Dr. José Miguez-Bonino.[6] A pioneer of liberation theology, he described how communications can be seen both as a system of oppression and a struggle for liberation. To use communications to liberate, we must

> *let ourselves be involved in God's project with the poor ... It can only be born when the communicator becomes organic to the life of the poor, when he/she develops and maintains a close, deeply felt tie with the poor and a physical presence and involvement with them and their organisations.*

Bonino pointed out that it is not we who take God to the poor, it is the poor who take us to God, and God who takes us to the poor. It is this blessed reversal of grace which moves us to conversion.

Professor Herbert Schiller[7] of the University of California at San Diego also directed our attention to the issue of communication and liberation. Alongside Noam Chomsky, he had long been noted as a critic of media practice and policy, especially of what he called 'mind management'.

He painted a worrying scenario:

> *A vast technologically sophisticated infrastructure has been constructed in the last ten years. Privately-owned communi-*

[6] José Miguez Bonino was born in Rosario, Santa Fe in 1924 and died in 2012.

[7] Herbert Schiller was born in New York in 1919 and died in 2000

> *cation satellites orbit the Earth transmitting messages to all continents. Computer networks link the biggest banks, the largest transnational corporations, and the major intelligence agencies in the Western world ... The consumerist message – trumpeted by international advertisers on behalf of the giant consumer goods and services companies – blankets the Earth. No community is regarded as outside the market. Weakened national broadcasting structures are no longer capable of protecting national cultural space.*

The only hope in this bleak panorama was Schiller's belief that what people are experiencing may not be fully subject to the processing of the communication apparatus and its managers. The course of events proceeds whatever its representation, exclusion, or distortion. And it is the course of events that are in command, not communication about them. He concluded: "liberation for those who are today the global voiceless will produce its own communication."

The Lutheran World Federation sent their Executive Secretary for Women in Church and Society to address the Manila congress. Dr. Musimbi Kanyoro, born in a small village in Migori County in western Kenya, was a scholar of Hebrew and the Old Testament, as well as being an activist in social and political affairs.

She had just returned from a gathering in Mexico City where 80 women from 51 countries had met to discuss their prophetic mission in the face of problems like militarism, poverty, the debt crisis, violence, the integrity of creation, theology, and church structures. Fired by that experience, she brought to the Manila gathering the conviction that "our stories are not an endless litany of individual disasters and unimportant gossip.

In the process of collective storytelling, we began to see patterns, networks of suffering, pain and hope. We began to identify not with the privileged whom we have always been taught to emulate, but with the underprivileged, with the common people, with the Earth and with the endangered creation. This coming together was in itself an event of communication."

Dr. Kanyoro's gifted use of storytelling described realities of world significance from a woman's perspective. Speaking on Communication and Prophecy, she asked: "is it not time for the churches to recognize the women's movements as a prophetic sign?" The stories of ordinary mothers, she felt, must become part of the text and context for interpreting biblical prophecy and its challenges to communication. The experience of women's faith and struggle and commitment to change can become ingredients of a theology for the churches and for Christian communication bodies.

While listening in Manila from my own experience in Africa and Latin America, I could feel the impact of these stories acutely. As I embarked on my westward journey home, I was much more aware of the challenge presented by corporate ownership of the media. I was also aware of the importance of micro media in local communities. And I felt somewhat more ready to embrace the next developments technology would bring my way.

Bits and Bytes

About a year later, on a damp Saturday morning, I was sitting in the back row of a small, steeply tiered auditorium in Dublin's city centre. I had felt this was a "must go to" thing. The lights were dimmed as the screen illustrated the subject. Looking back now, I cannot remember anything the speaker said. It was during the interval that all my learning came from the person who was sitting next to me. "This is how we will communicate very soon", he told me. And he went on to describe the wondrous attributes of a new method of communication he called 'e-mail'. He had all my attention. What he described was exactly what I wanted because it was exactly what I needed.

In the weeks that followed my new friend lent me a black plastic box, measuring about six inches by eight inches. He explained that it was called a 'modem' because it could modulate and demodulate signals, making it possible for the telephone's analogue landline to carry communications to and from the digital world.

I learned that any alphabet character, any numeral, any picture or sound could be digitised, i.e. expressed in groups of ones and zeros called binary digits. Each one or zero was called a 'bit'[8] and eight of them grouped together made a 'byte'. I had known already about the Englishman, George Boole[9], who held the Chair of mathematics at University College Cork from 1849 and gave the name Boolean to this logic.

The speed at which this digitised data could be transmitted by the modem was called the 'baud rate'. The black box of 'magic' that now sat on my desk performed at a baud rate of 7bps, that is to say it could transmit 7000 bits per second. But soon much faster modems would be coming. I learned that 1024 bytes[10] was called a kilobyte. Multiplying that by 1024 gave us megabytes, which multiplied by 1024 gave us gigabytes and so on to greater storage capacity and transmission speeds in terabytes, petabytes, exabytes and zettabytes.

---

[8] Shorthand for 'bi(nary digi)t'

[9] George Boole was born in Lincoln, UK in 1815 and died in Cork, Ireland in 1864.

[10] 2x8x8x8 = 1024

My friend showed me how a cable from the modem could be connected to my PC through its serial port, which all the desktops and laptops had back in those days. Another cable connected the modem to the telephone's wall socket.[11] From my keyboard I could dial a number. As soon as it answered my computer was 'online'. It was connecting with a Bulletin Board Service (BBS) where information could be accessed. New words were entering my vocabulary at a great rate.

From a 'bulletin board' somewhere far away, I could 'download' information, or indeed 'upload' news if I had any. That would take seventeen concentrated keyboard steps, but I will never forget the feeling! The information I was downloading was contained in 'files'. They bore little relationship to the cardboard things hanging in my filing cabinet.

My digital files were stored in things called 'folders' which hung on the branches of a digitally constructed 'tree' which appeared on the screen as a vertical line with horizontal lines shooting out to the right. I could call my folders by any name I found convenient, and I could create as many sub-folders as I wanted. They would appear on new horizontal lines below the original one, making my tree grow many branches.

In those days you had to be your own search tool. I was told that when I was searching the tree in order to open a folder to retrieve a file, I was to behave like a mouse not a monkey — I must run back to the trunk and go up or down and out another branch to another folder. I could not swing from branch to branch like a monkey might. All this mouse-like running up and down the tree was done with the up and down and left and right arrows on the keyboard. When it came to trees, I

[11] Back then we had no 'wireless fidelity' — Wi-Fi — carrying data up and down the garden and all around the house.

thought Adam and Eve had it easy, but from that moment on my e-life never looked back.

Defying Death

In 1992 the Bishops of Malawi wrote a pastoral letter entitled *Living our Faith*. They thanked the government of President Hastings Kamuzu Banda for providing an atmosphere where peace and stability prevailed in the one-party State. But they said it would be a failure on their part if they kept silent on matters which affected the day-to-day lives of the people. They spoke about the rule of law, called for democracy, participatory government, transparency, accountability, and the fight against corruption. They deplored the poverty many people were experiencing.

For their trouble, the seven native Bishops were publicly vilified and threatened with a death sentence. The Irish missionary, Monsignor John Roche, who was Apostolic Administrator of Mzuzu Diocese, was expelled from the country and given twenty-four hours to leave. He fled by night into Zambia.

The Christian world, Catholic and Protestant, connected electronically in defence of the bishops. Through the Irish Missionary Union, we belonged to the Africa Faith and Justice Network – which was now able to connect globally thanks to the emerging technology[12]. Before dawn in Washington DC, in the small apartment where I was a guest, I watched the missionary sister who was my host put a three-and-a-half-inch floppy disc into the A drive of her computer.

---

[12] In 1983, the Congregation of the Holy Spirit (Spiritans), the Missionaries of Africa, and the Society of African Missions, founded AFJN. See www.afjn.org.

While she brewed the coffee, and lit a candle for morning prayer, the diskette moaned a little as it received data files from two journalists in New York. They were retained by the Africa Faith & Justice Network. Overnight they would have scanned the major news agencies for reports of interest on crises and emergencies around the world.

I accompanied my host as she took the diskette to her downtown office to upload the data to the Bulletin Board Service we all used. She would send the news to the Communications Desk of the Missionaries of Africa in Canada. They would forward it to the Dublin ground station set up by Fr. Michael Browne, a priest of St. Patrick's Missionary Society.[13] A few minutes later it would be on the screens of Protestant and Catholic missionaries in Belfast and London, in Rome and Geneva and in the other capital cities of Europe.

In Malawi, the authorities became aware that their actions were being observed internationally. They could no longer act as if they were an island. They needed to demonstrate some acknowledgement of universal standards of decency and respect. The lives of the bishops were spared.

In 2022 the Bishops of Malawi issued another challenging Pastoral Letter which marked the thirtieth anniversary of the 1992 letter 'Living our Faith'. The new letter said:

> *It is sad that a generation later, we are grappling with the same vices, in actual fact, it is regrettable that these vices which the Catholic Bishops condemned three decades ago, have become even more deeply engrained and are tearing our*

---

[13] My growing understanding of the digital world was facilitated by Fr. Michael Browne, who spent many Saturday mornings in my office giving me practical demonstrations about how the whole thing worked. I feel greatly indebted to him for the digital skills I have today.

society and our nation apart while keeping the vast majority in grinding poverty.

This time there was a gracious Government response. The Minister for Information and Government spokesperson told local media that President Lazarus Chakwera's government was "thankful to the Catholic Bishops for being open in pointing out governance issues." He said the government would consider the issues raised by the bishops.[14] But people are asking for more than this. Action to address the issues that are keeping the majority in poverty is urgently needed.

The Internet

When I began to learn about the Internet, I realised it could do much more than the Bulletin Board Services. I was told that it had been available for a long time in the military world and later in the Universities. But somehow, I felt 'at last it is mine'. It felt like mine because I needed it so much. From my desk at the Irish Missionary Union, I wanted to communicate with more than 8,000 Irish missionaries who were working in 83 countries on every continent.

When I saw a two-day course about the Internet advertised in one of Dublin's five-star hotels, my conscience struggled over the expense. It was not a residential course, but it cost more than a full term's tuition had been back in my university days twenty years earlier. After much thought I registered for it, and it was worth it. Soon I began to visit the Internet cafés that were beginning to emerge in Dublin's downtown shopping areas.

On my office wall I mounted a large map of the global growth of the backbone of the Internet. I could see that not many

---

[14] Cf Vatican News, 8 March 2022 and www.voanews.com, 7 March 2022

African countries appeared among those that were connected to this marvellous electronic world. The main growth was in the Western world. Asia and Oceania were quickly catching up. Africa was lagging behind, except for some of the bigger cities, mostly in South Africa.

By 1991 when I landed in New York at the start of a sabbatical year, I had acquired a laptop. It was more luggable than portable, and I still had to be my own mouse. My first task was to purchase a modem. Not far from the Port Authority Bus Terminal on West 42nd St, I entered a small store laden with gadgets. The modem I bought had a baud rate of 14 bps. It would be a collector's item now. Lugging my laptop, I boarded a coach to Boston.

On arrival that evening for the first time I connected to the Internet from my own PC and listened to music online from a local radio channel. I then connected to the Bulletin Board Service for news from Africa. A programme on my laptop called Bluewave enabled me to select the countries from which I wanted today's news. I downloaded the latest activities of the SPLA in their ongoing struggles in the southern area of Sudan[15].

It so happened that one of my community in Boston, Sister Nina Underwood, was leaving for Juba the next morning. We knew each other well from our East African days twenty years earlier. Nina was the pilot who flew our small Cessna between the far-flung missions in the Turkana desert. She was astonished when I handed her sheets of tractor-fed pages with news of the war zone she would soon re-enter.[16]

---

[15] This was many years before the country of South Sudan was formed, and where MMM now staffs a Health Centre in the Diocese of Wau. See also Postscript 6

Back to School

During that year in Massachusetts my devotion to the god 'E' was growing all the time. Back in Dublin after my sabbatical, I took up my assignment as Director of the Communications Department of the Medical Missionaries of Mary. We were still using dial-up telephone connections. It was a cold dark evening in November 1993 when I received my first email from Africa. It came from a colleague in Harare, Sister Cecily Bourdillon. What excitement! I wanted to share it with other friends, but since they were not yet connected to the Internet, I had to print the message and resort to a fax machine to share it.

In the early 1990s it was mainly university students who had access to training in computers. Elsewhere it was pretty sparse, and where available was very expensive. I felt nobody should have to struggle the way I did to master what is basically quite simple if properly explained step by step. So, in 1994 I furnished a small room in our Communications Department with four workstations and I invited missionaries who were on leave in Ireland to take a 40-hour course over two weeks in groups of four. In the following eight years, more than 300 missionaries availed of this, and it proved to be great fun!

With each group, on the Wednesday evening of the second week I would organize a Graduation Dinner – a student was eligible to graduate once he or she could electronically design and print their Graduation Certificate! They all managed that. At a pizzeria in Dun Laoghaire, I would book the window table overlooking Dublin Bay. These graduation dinners were hilarious.

But in class on Thursday morning, I would notice a big change. These missionaries were students no longer. They now acted like masters of a set of tools that would facilitate their work when they returned to their far-flung destinations. The task of designing and printing their Certificates, my signing and presenting them, was a sample of that positive form of communication which Babin called 'modulation' – the use of audio and/or visual media that involves mutual stimulation producing psychological effects.

The last steps of our 40-hour course included hitching a laptop to jump leads to enable charging from a car or truck battery. On two occasions the Irish overseas development agency, APSO, funded me to visit my former students in their locations in Africa. On those visits I learned a great deal more about the challenge and potential of this great new e-world. Solar power was becoming available – so we wouldn't need the jump leads for much longer.

I went back to school myself on Saturday mornings and graduated with my City & Guilds in HTML,[17] the computer language in which a website's content is written. That was before programmes like *Dreamweaver* and *Front Page* and later web authoring tools were available. When Ireland Online arrived, I registered a couple of web and e-mail addresses. By 1995 I was ready to launch the first version of my Congregation's website[18].

Back in those days I did not stop to ask, 'is this new e-stuff really mine?' I felt it was, but it did not occur to me to ask 'in what way does it belong to me? Would it be more accurate to say that I belong to it?' Those questions would be asked much, much later. I had forgotten that Babin had used the word 'surreptitious' about the god 'E'.

---

[17] Hypertext markup language

[18] www.mmmworldwide.org

The TRINET Project

Hope of a solution to our communications problems was greatly boosted when I was invited to link with a team of experts working at Trinity College Dublin to supply 'last mile connectivity'. They were joined by a team from the Dublin Institute of Technology[19] who built an aerial to enable communication with a low Earth orbit satellite. It was called the TRINET project.

Leading the group was Professor Gordon Foster who had set up a simple ground station in his office at the rear of the Trinity College campus. He spoke softly, but with enormous commitment about bringing the information superhighway 'up some muddy lanes' as he put it to me.

One of the aerials was fixed to the chimney above his office. Five times each 24 hours for 11-14 minutes every part of the Earth's surface would fall under the footprint of our little satellite. It had been bought second-hand after it was no longer useful to its previous owners. When it was passing, the aerial on the chimney over Professor Foster's office would become active – downloading any files destined for this ground station and uploading any that were waiting to go.

Whenever I found myself in Nassau Street, I would gaze up at the aerial to see if by any chance the satellite happened to be passing. If it was, the antennae would move up and down. I would feel great excitement knowing any files I had sent were going up, and I would wonder if a report I was waiting for from the other side of our world might be coming down!

Gordon Foster's interest in Africa was an inspiration. He was passionate in his belief that the socio-economic development

---

[19] Now the Technological University Dublin, located at Grangegorman.

of countries depended upon information technology. At Trinity College he had established an M.Sc. course in systems development for students from the global south. He was engaged with the international aid and development communities in a range of research projects. He brought to this challenge a lifetime of experience and knowledge.

As a young graduate in 1942, he was one of the mathematicians engaged at Bletchley Park in England on the task of solving the code used by the German army and navy. A decade later he was the person who devised the ISBN code for the book publishing profession. He later became a consultant with the United Nations International Development Organisation. Training in informatics was shared between Trinity College and the United Nations University in Japan. His job was to facilitate scientists, researchers and administrators in the global south.

Together with the Dublin Institute of Technology, he had established educational outreach links with partners in Ghana, Nigeria, Uganda, Zambia and Zimbabwe. The difficulty of maintaining frequent communication with these partners stimulated the need to develop the TRINET project. We were still living in the days when half of the world's population lived more than seven days' walk from the nearest telephone line.

Some of my colleagues in Tanzania, living among the Maasai people in a remote area called Loolera, availed of different technology. It was provided with assistance from the Flying Medical Service based in the city of Arusha. Fr. Pat Patten, who was involved in running the service and was one of its pilots, explained to me:

> *Our Bushlink e-mail system works by way of a special high frequency radio modem and radio call connection. Instead of*

a telephone line, high frequency radio signals can follow the curvature of the Earth. They do this by being reflected off the ionosphere – a charged layer in the atmosphere which varies greatly in density and height above the Earth, according to solar activity. This can be done with relatively inexpensive radio equipment. It can also be done with relatively little power. The remote hospital uses a computer to send and receive e-mail as usual. However, instead of the link from the computer to the Internet being by telephone line, it uses a radio call. Mail is sent and received in this way. It is totally automated and operates 24 hours a day.

On a visit to Tanzania in 2008 in a remote village I watched women collecting water at a well while speaking on tiny mobile phones as they did so. The cellular networks had arrived!

On a long journey I'd notice a companion in the jeep opening what looked like a pillbox, and then replacing the sim-card in her phone. That told me we had passed from the reach of one cellular network to another. When I got to Makiungu, a tall mast in the centre of the hospital compound provided Internet access, enabling the pharmacist to order all her supplies online. When I was hospital administrator there thirty-five years earlier, we could speak by radio-tel to the Africa Medical & Research Foundation in Nairobi once each day for quick messages, but our post came by bus from Singida only twice a week.

It was great to see how things had developed in my much-loved Makiungu. There was an Internet café in the village. Before sundown people who owned mobile phones headed to a spot near the airstrip where the anthills were exceptionally tall, reaching four or five feet in height. People would climb up the base of the anthill to get the best possible signal for their messaging. I wondered, did the ants know something we don't know about communications? Pat Patten said no – it is just the height of the anthill that helps. But there were higher locations like flat rooftops and the people didn't choose any of these. I'm still wondering about those ants.

The Cellular Information Highway

In November 2020 an urgent job landed on my desk when the Chancellor of the Diocese of Ogoja in Nigeria requested an account of the work of the Medical Missionaries of Mary in that diocese. They were preparing to celebrate the centenary of the celebration of the first Mass in Ogoja, which took place on Pentecost Sunday in 1921. Their request was urgent with just about three months to gather the information they required.

It was a mammoth challenge! Our earliest Sisters departed Ireland for Ogoja in 1945. They sailed in convoy through mine-strewn seas before the second world war ended. The work grew rapidly. Between then and 2003 when developments had made it possible for us to hand back the administration of five hospitals and two health centres to the Diocese, 129 of our Sisters had staffed these facilities.

In the early 1940s leprosy – renamed Hansen's Disease by the UN in 1948 – was rampant in the area. When Bishop Tom McGettrick first begged us to help, no census of the infected population had been carried out. But the government estimated there could be as many as 75,000 people with this highly infectious disease in Ogoja province, which was roughly one quarter the size of Ireland.

In January 1945, the Irish leprologist, Dr. Joe Barnes, was warmly welcomed by the local Clan Chiefs who worked with him to devise a scheme to tackle the huge problem. In other countries large segregation settlements had been created. But this scheme would be sensitive not just to the need to contain the disease but to the needs and rights and cultural values of those who contracted it. Each Clan would develop its own special village in their local area under the supervision of the local Clan Council. The infected people and their relatives built the houses, each family having its own house and plot of land.

Everyone knew this would be a long-term project, as it would be many years before the discovery of effective drug therapy. Those infected supported themselves in the villages by their own industry, thus combatting the depression which so often followed the dreaded diagnosis. In each village local health workers were trained to supervise discipline, sanitation and food supplies. Medical care was complemented by close attention to the social and cultural life of those who were infected.[20]

This was greatly facilitated from 1950 onwards with the arrival of professional social workers, a physiotherapist, occupational therapists and teachers - all of whom developed close friendship with the residents in each of the villages. Maternity care was an important part of the work as well as education of the children. Participation of everyone in weddings and other celebrations was common, and the marching bands of the school children were always pressed into service. Despite the awfulness of the disease, life was made as comfortable and happy as was possible, even through the extremely difficult years of the country's civil war, 1967-70.

In November 2020, the task of tracing all this effort seemed impossible since we were in lock-down due to the Covid pandemic while the rush to produce a vaccine was still under way.

---

[20] Cf Manton, John, (1996) *The Roman Catholic Mission and Leprosy Control in Colonial Ogoja Province, Nigeria, 1936-1960,* doctoral thesis presented at the University of Oxford.

Our archives were closed to researchers. Our archivist was working from her home in Northern Ireland with access only to finger-tip searches of the limited amount of digital material available to her.

Luckily, I had on my bookshelves the bound volumes of our missionary magazine from January 1940 to the present time. These contained many records of the work and our appeals for funding. I also had ten other works that told parts of the story in different ways. But the task could not have been completed without the involvement of a team of colleagues who had personally served in Ogoja over the years. In all, a team of fourteen of us – located across eight time zones – was able to connect electronically to piece the story together. Critical to this were the advanced cellular networks now available across Africa.

Three women who were born in Ogoja diocese had become Medical Missionaries of Mary. I call them the 'Daughters of Ogoja'. The eldest of them, Sister Alice, is a nurse tutor with decades of experience in different countries. The youngest, Sister Prisca, had recently graduated in nursing from the Atlantic Technological University in Galway She was now back in Africa and working in South Sudan. The third became my virtual personal assistant. That was Sister Elizabeth. She was leading the health care team in the village of Zaffé in the Republic of Benin where the quality of the cellular network is the best I have experienced anywhere.

Zaffé was an hour ahead of Dublin. Many mornings before 5 am I would sit up in bed and call Elizabeth by WhatsApp before she headed out to the 6.30 am Mass in her parish church. I would give her a list of questions I had for colleagues in various countries of Africa, whom she could reach though I could not. Each morning over the following week she would give me the information I needed – from Kampala or perhaps further north in Uganda, from Eldoret in Kenya, from Lilongwe in Malawi, from Wau in South Sudan and from Luanda in Angola. Other colleagues now living in Boston, and of course at our Motherhouse in Ireland also responded with a waterfall of emails and photos as we pieced together our story for the team who were preparing the centenary celebrations in Ogoja.

It was a joy to record that at the 15th International Leprosy Conference in Beijing in 1998, Sister Margaret Anne Meyer who was the last MMM sister-doctor to work at Ogoja, was able to show how the estimated 40,000 persons with the disease in Ogoja Diocese in 1945 had been reduced to just 420. While it was worrying that 26% of these were children, drug therapies had advanced greatly, making segregation no longer necessary and the hope of a complete cure was high.

Thinking over the Ogoja story, I recall a day in 1993 when Dr. Joe Barnes and his wife, Betty, were retired near the foothills of the Dublin mountains. Their seven children had now fled the nest and were rearing their nineteen grandchildren and a growing family of great grandchildren. In his eighties, Joe still cycled a few times each week the five miles to Dublin's city centre to the Royal College of Surgeons, where he had become Emeritus Professor in Tropical Medicine. His experience as a world-renowned dermatologist was greatly valued.

I was writing the Ogoja story for our Yearbook and I phoned Joe to ask if I could talk to them. In their home, after checking a few facts, over a cup of tea I asked, 'how did you two meet?' Betty smiled. Joe glanced at her as he stroked his chin before replying: "We were both looking down the same microscope at the same bug." That was at the Royal Infirmary in Leeds in 1948 after Joe had completed studies of the leprosy bacillus at the Sorbonne, while working at St. Louis Hospital in Paris.

The young English woman, Dr. Betty Allday from Surrey, shared his research interests and agreed that after they married, she would be happy to leave immediately for Ogoja. They packed the lower tier of their wedding cake in a trunk to share with the community and sailed for Port Harcourt. Born in Belfast in 1914, Joe lived to be 102 years of age.

The Smartphone

Nowadays I rarely make a phone call but the instrument that is called a Smartphone has put my laptop into semi-retirement. It has also replaced my still-image camera and my video-camera. It has become the gateway to my Kindle library. It provides a raft of programmes – 'apps' – which offer me services for everything I need, with Bluetooth connecting a keyboard whenever text is required on the screen. Bluetooth can also send the music or news from the radio station I am listening to on the 'phone' straight into the buds in my ears.

But if I am not careful, this Smartphone could be smarter than I am. Being careful means scheduling dedicated weekly periods of digital detox. Each Saturday at 18h, I begin a 24-hour 'no-look-no-touch-do-not-disturb-me' sabbath.

Much as I depend upon it, there are few things that prick my conscience in the way my 'phone' does. Its journey from the Earth to my pocket has been filled with unfair practices. In addition to the eighteen million people who work in the electronics manufacturing industry, another one hundred million work in mining the materials used. They face various types of inhumane conditions.

My 'phone' contains tantalum, used in the battery's capacitors to store electrical energy. I read that 67% of the world's tantalum is found in Rwanda and in the northeast of the Democratic

Republic of Congo. Some 120 militant groups operate in this border area. From the respected Nigerian researcher, Oluwole Ojewale,[21] I learned that coltan is the metallic ore from which tantalum is extracted. Before artisanal miners can access the coltan mines, which can be quite dangerous, they have to pay taxes to the armed group controlling the area. This in turn funds the purchase of arms.

In 2017 I learned that child labour may have been used in the manufacture of my 'phone'. The cobalt on which the batteries depend is often mined by children from as young as six or seven years of age who come from extremely poor families.[22] Some of the children have been sold into the mining industry, becoming slaves through human trafficking. Younger children are normally involved in sorting or washing of the material extracted. Older children are tasked with digging and going down into the holes.

In Pursuit of Fair Play

Much of the above information came to me when I discovered Fairphone,[23] a manufacturing group based in The Netherlands. In their film *Behind the Screens,* I learn that there are now more mobile phones than there are people on our planet. More than 1.5 billion phones are sold each year.

Fairphone believes everyone should have sufficient income to enjoy a decent life, should have a safe workplace and the opportunity to have their opinions and concerns heard. They establish schools near the site of some of the small mines so the

---

[21]Dr. Oluwole Ojewale is Coordinator of the Regional Organized Crime Observatory for Central Africa at the Institute for Security Studies in Dakar, Senegal. See also www.theafricandream.net.

[22] See 'Global Report on Trafficking in Persons 2020' at www.unodc.org.

[23] www.fairphone.com.

children can spend part of their day at school, even if they have to be in the mines for some hours to help their families to survive. Fairphone is also aware that the materials used have an impact on our planet.

Fairphone has formed a partnership with a collective of European companies that are working together to create a more responsible and ethical way of operating in the technology sector. This is called FairTEC and comprises companies like Commown, TeleCoop, The Phone Coop and WeTELL. These are working together for fairer sustainable practices in the electronics industry.

If I felt ill-at-ease about my 'phone', I felt even worse when I discovered that the Internet, my friend of more than thirty years, was sick. Not a virus, nothing a vaccine can prevent. It was quite a shock when I came upon the work of the former Harvard Professor Shoshana Zuboff, economist and social psychologist. Since 1989 she had been writing about the future of technology and data in the workplace. Her ideas in *The Age of Surveillance Capitalism: The Fight for a Human Future at the New Frontier of Power* were first published as an essay in a German publication in 2014. In 2020, after ten years of research on this topic, the book was published.

Zuboff points out that the latest 'raw material' of production is our own behaviour. She goes further than many economists who write about technology-enabled globalization as drivers of inequality. She views the rise of 'machine intelligence' as the new frontier of power which marks 'the fight for a human future'. The interviews she has given to print journalists and on YouTube, go some way towards elucidating the ideas which, in her book, are too complex for me or many ordinary readers to grasp.

Some of her critics suggest that capitalism has always sought new markets and new ways of marketing, and that the concept of democracy also undergoes change. But most are grateful to her that the topic is now out there for discussion and that users of digital media are more aware than heretofore of what they ought to know.

Algorithms

Years ago, which of us didn't grasp with open arms the search tools the Internet offered? We searched the searchers until we found our favourite one. We made it part of the precious tools we use to negotiate our way through the world of knowledge. But we were outsmarted. What Zuboff calls 'surveillance capitalism' has found value in things I do that I don't even notice are happening. Long ago, the cached information I leave behind after an Internet search was considered trash – until people saw that there was monetary value in it.

Zuboff explains that it can be little things that are of interest to the algorithms observing my digital behaviour. Whether I used dashes or bullet points when I am writing up the minutes of a meeting may tell them a lot. My data, when analyzed, can go beyond commercial outcomes to political outcomes. It might give clues as to how I will vote.

How many times have I clicked 'I agree' or 'I accept' to pages and pages of legal stuff that I could never understand even if I took the time to read it? How many times have I downloaded an app without realising the amount of personal stuff I may be giving away – perhaps my photo albums and my contacts. I may also have given them my agreement to sell on the data they find to third parties, and I have no idea of the terms and conditions they agree between them. Most of all it is my behaviour that is valuable.

Zuboff warns that making unfettered use of such data defies fundamental human rights. The struggle is no longer between capital and the labour market. It is between capital and society. It is between capital and human behaviour. It is between computation and politics. It is between control and democracy.

She points to regulation as the key to a solution. She calls on giant corporations to come up with a way to correct this. She encourages citizens, journalists, scholars, and lawmakers to awaken to our shared future. Business needs consumers and consumers need to call for controls. We are at a crossroads. We can choose to allow technology to enrich the few and impoverish the many. On the other hand, technology can be harnessed in a way that its benefits are distributed fairly. How this choice is made, Zuboff says, will shape the rest of the twenty-first century.

Other scholars have responded with a critique of Zuboff's analysis of behaviourism. Again, it is pointed out that capitalism has always been developing new markets, bringing into play elements that were never considered saleable in a previous generation. Even her notion of democracy has been challenged.

But in general, her concerns have been affirmed by one of the Internet's key developers, Jaron Lanier[24] who is considered to be one of the world's most celebrated pioneers of digital innovation. His earlier books include several international bestsellers. Writing with urgency in 2019, his *Ten Arguments for Deleting Your Social Media Accounts Right Now* was acknowledged in the *Financial Times* to be "a short, snappy, impassioned takedown of the surveillance capitalism operated by the giant Silicon Valley corporations". Danny Fortson summed it up in

---

[24] It is worth viewing some of his interviews on Youtube.

the *Sunday Times* saying: "Every time you log on, you are adding to a fire that is burning your house down".

When Lanier dedicated his younger years among the experts who created the technology that underpins the Internet, he never envisaged this outcome. His criticism is not of the technological advances but of the business model that has developed around it. His disappointment at where the service has arrived is unconcealed. His first input in his new book is headed 'Welcome to the cage that goes everywhere with you'. He argues that social media today attack the user's free will, undermine truth, destroy the user's capacity for empathy, fight against economic dignity and make politics impossible.

> *Just in the last five or ten years, nearly everyone started to carry a little device called a smartphone on their person all the time that's suitable for algorithmic behaviour modification ... We're being tracked and measured constantly and receiving engineered feedback all the time. We're being hypnotized little by little by technicians we can't see, for purposes we don't know. We're all lab animals now.*

He affirms Zuboff's view: algorithms gorge on data about us, every second. It is the third-party pressure that is the problem. He contrasts this with our interactions with Netflix and eBay, where no third party is involved. When Netflix recommends a movie or eBay recommends something to buy, at this time neither of these is being paid by third parties to influence our decisions apart from the immediate business we do with each of these sites.

Both Lanier and Zuboff collaborated with a bunch of younger technologists, researchers, and activists in an effort to align technology with the interests of humanity. They produced a documentary film called *The Social Dilemma*[25] which can be viewed on Netflix. It invites us to reflect on *the Mental Health Dilemma, the Democracy Dilemma, and the Discrimination Dilemma.* These researchers point out that if we can't address our broken information ecosystem, we will never be able to address the challenges that plague humanity.

Augmented Reality

The digital world's impact on healthcare is of special interest to me. Among all the technological developments, the role of Augmented Reality (AR) is of great relevance. Some say it is a close cousin of Virtual Reality (VR), but from what I read it seems more like a very distant cousin. VR generates computer simulations of real-life activities. It is useful in facilitating some services I receive every day, unaware that it is lurking in the background. But I don't play computer games and neither do I feel a need to be entertained by walking virtually around the leaning tower of Pisa while I'm actually eating my lunch in Dublin.

Both VR and AR play an increasing role in medical training today. Long ago, when I returned to Dublin for holidays from my studies in Maynooth, our student house was always crammed to capacity. We were a lively bunch! The large room where I slept doubled by day as the library for my community who were preparing for exams in medicine, radiography, physiotherapy, pharmacy and nurse tutorship. At night, the last student to leave would put a cap and gown on the skeleton in the corner before the library became a dormitory again.

Today, students of these professions have more than a skeleton to help them. Using anatomy apps, they can see digital

---

[25] www.thesocialdilemma.com.

reproductions not only of the bony structure of the human body, but of the entire vascular network and all the human organs in their rightful place. The use of VR and AR tools in medical schools not only allows students to get internal anatomical views but can also provide hands-on practice. That is a lot better than reading diagrams in a textbook and poking around the skeleton in the corner.

Augmented Reality (AR) is quite different from VR. It adds to what a person can see with their eyes and understand with their brains by using multiple layers of technology with very useful data to augment the experience. In other words, it does not merely replicate lived reality in a virtual way. It combines the real world with computer generated content. Earliest efforts at this date back to the 1950s. I find it easier to think of this marvellous developing service as 'augmented experience', but for now I will stick with the term in wide use.

There seems to be unlimited potential for AR to assist in surgical planning and in augmenting the options for surgeons in their most delicate tasks. AR can visually map a person's body so nurses can more easily locate veins. It can present abnormalities in 3D. The range of information that can be supplied is very wide, as AR can replicate what is perceived in many modes – visual, auditory, somato-sensory, and olfactory. The computer-generated content is interwoven seamlessly with the physical world in a way that enables the user to perceive it as part of the real environment.

For companies developing AR, the healthcare professions are of great interest. Using holographic visualization, developers are working on ways of showing the anatomy floating directly over the client during the procedure, permitting less invasive surgery.

Researchers are doing a lot of work on wearable devices. Much is reported about 'smart eyewear' which will link what is really in front of us with augmented, digitally generated, information which could be useful to people engaged in many different activities. Cameras within the frame of the spectacles will intercept the real world and augment the view by overlaying AR imagery.

AR is also used in the business and industrial world. If I want to buy a new desk for my office, I don't need to take the bus to IKEA. I can visit their website, key in or dictate some information, then point my camera at my office space and view the desk I could buy as if it were there. The view of the real room is augmented with the digital image of the furniture I might buy. Today many people expect to have these services as part of their purchasing experience. We are beginning to take AR for granted.

This technology can also augment the facility of Quick Response (QR) Codes which have become part and parcel of our lives. A QR code can be read either electronically or from a printed paper. Rarely now can I pay with coins or even a card when parking.

Owners of the parking business want me to use my 'phone' to take a picture of the QR Code on the parking meter. When I book an airline ticket, I am offered a QR Code which will, after I have checked in online, give me access to the departure area at the airport. When our public health service sends me confirmation of my vaccination against Covid, it contains a printed QR Code giving me access to various places where I would not be admitted without it. In my local restaurant AR had already replaced the old plastic menus with an untouchable one I can read at the counter in the bar.

Artificial Intelligence

Several years ago, when the London Docklands Light Railway took me from City Airport to Canary Wharf, I felt safe even though there was no human driver at the front of the train. I presumed that someone, somewhere, was controlling the Artificial Intelligence (AI) that was getting me there. But when driverless cars and buses appear on our city roads I will probably want to stay at home. I am sometimes amused, but more often annoyed, when AI empowers predictive texting in my 'phone' to change what I have written because it thinks it knows what I want to say better than my fingers do.

It could be helpful to have a small robot driven by AI to cut the grass in my garden. However, it would make my present human gardener redundant. If I were living alone, needing assistance of some kind and my caregiver was a robot, then all kinds of AI would be invoked.

But as the universities are finding, each new development raises new questions for experts in ethics, psychology, sociology and law. How intrusive may the robot be? Who may have access to what the robot knows? What is the risk of this intelligence being hacked or spammed? If the robot became an Android or a Gynoid, how would my human friends feel if I became more emotionally attached to my new human-like helper than I am to them?

There are pluses and minuses at each step of this technological journey. The use of AI in the prediction of disasters like earthquakes, tsunamis, wildfires or other environmental disasters such as swarming locusts gives great hope.

AI is measured in comparison to the functions of the human mind. At this time, it falls into four categories two of which already exist. The third is here though still in its early days. The fourth category doesn't exist yet except in science fiction. It will be a while before it exists, but researchers are working on it. It is called 'self awareness'.

Some analysists add three more categories of AI – Artificial Narrow Intelligence (ANI), Artificial General Intelligence (AGI) and Artificial Superintelligence (ASI). Naveen Joshi writes that "ASI, in addition to replicating the multi-faceted intelligence of human beings, will be exceedingly better at everything they do because of overwhelmingly greater memory, faster data processing and analysis, and decision-making capabilities. The development of AGI and ASI will lead to a scenario most popularly referred to as 'the singularity'.

And while the potential of having such powerful machines at our disposal seems appealing, these machines may also threaten our existence or at the very least, our way of life."[26] Teachers tell me they are concerned about sources of artificial intelligence where teenage students seek data with ChatGPT[27].

The possibilities opened up by this technology for accessing and transferring information are immense. It was not long on the market before it had more than 100 million users. Top experts from academia and the tech industry expressed concern at the potential of this development which claimed great attention all through the year 2023. One thousand experts from academia and the tech industry wrote an open letter[28] to developers of advanced AI to halt what they call a 'dangerous' arms race. Signatories included the co-founders of Apple, Pinterest and Skype, top AI professors, and Elon Musk. Their letter said:

---

[26] See Naveen Joshi, www.forbes.com.

[27] An AI chatbot developed by OpenAI, launched November 30, 2022

[28] Published 29 March 2023 by the Future of Life Institute

Recent months have seen AI labs locked in an out-of-control race to develop and deploy ever more powerful digital minds that no-one – not even their creators – can understand, predict or reliably control.

Meanwhile the business community is concerned about the importance of upskilling the workforce to harness the potential of generative AI and take full advantage of emerging technology. It is a field where industry, government and academia need to work very closely together.

The Manhattan Manifesto

The thinkers and scientists who devised the UN Manhattan Manifesto for Digital Health in 2022[29] take a very positive view of digital advances in health care. The Indian-born venture capitalist, Vinod Khosla, claims that "in the next ten years Data Science will do more for medicine than all of the biological sciences combined". The Manhattan Manifesto, developed by fifty digital health leaders, drew up twelve guidelines for governments to adopt to drive the transition to a digital healthcare system.

In June 2023 at my Alma Mater, Maynooth, an International Digital Health Summer School took place. We were invited to learn how digital health is emerging as a completely new discipline, one which combines intersecting disciplines of health, technology, engineering, economics, demographics and more.

Over two days crammed with short, well-prepared inputs, we were shown how the potential for deploying robots to save

---

[29] https://redzinc.net/wp-content/uploads/2022/12/NYC-Manifesto_05Dec2022FINAL.pdf

time and cost could change the hospital experience for those providing care as well as for those receiving care.

Digitally enabled devices will speed up diagnostic procedures. A robot can change the air in an operating room twice as fast as conventional ventilation systems. The ability of AI to process and interpret data can also greatly speed up research initiatives. A new role for pharmacies in healthcare management is already emerging and there is a push to make this much more significant.

Hopefully, before too long, the dream of having a digital tool where each individual's entire health record can be safely stored and available where appropriate, will be realised. To global travellers that would be a huge gift.

The call of the Manhattan Manifesto is to shift the burden of care out of hospitals and back into the community. Medical missionaries of all denominations throughout the global south, have been doing this since the Declaration of Alma Ata back in 1978. How wonderful life would be if this happened now in the more technologically developed countries with much more sophisticated services!

Governments cannot implement this on their own initiative. Enormous advances in social planning, involving citizens through a range of agencies would be essential. That kind of advance does not happen at the same speed that digital technology advances.

The Metaverse

All these advances are part and parcel of the emerging so-called metaverse.[30] There seems to be little agreement about what this word means. Some say it refers to a network of interconnected virtual worlds where people can communicate, do business, buy and sell digital currency and play games with people who may be on different continents. Some see in it great potential to empower everybody. Others fear it may diminish the positive energy of human interaction.

Some say an early development of the metaverse is here already. It is where the Internet was when the 21st century was dawning — when all we were worrying about was the millennium bug! These thinkers believe the metaverse will become a successor to the Internet. Others say it is not so, at least not yet and not for a long time to come. The technology may be there or may be emerging, but agreed communication protocols don't yet exist. Industry-wide standards need to be set.

Critics point to the attempt to create the metaverse from the perspective of big business — from the top down — instead of waiting and letting it grow through the usage people will make of the new technologies as they become available. It is argued that the adoption of the name 'Meta' by Facebook, is part of this big business initiative, and some suggest that we should abandon the term metaverse altogether.

With the application of these technologies in the development of 'smart cities', the need for internationally agreed protocols covering a range of topics became obvious. A trawl of the

---

[30] The word is borrowed from the popular 1992 sci-fi book *Snow Crash* by Neal Stephenson

Internet shows how such concerns were occupying thinkers and politicians around the globe since at least the 1960s. Now, with each passing week, knowledgeable journalists attempt to update us about developments around these issues.

In the US, a framework for developing AI regulations was published for discussion in 2023. In the UK, Prime Minister Rishi Sunak convened a global summit on AI safety. Bletchley Park - which played such a key role in codebreaking during World War II - was the venue where Chinese experts sat down with other key players in a first step. But it was still a far cry from a global accord, and the deadline to implement controls was felt to be only twenty months away.

In the EU, before the end of 2023 after two years of work, the AI Act was agreed as an ongoing step towards regulating the development of technology. Contentious issues included real-time facial recognition, the issue of fundamental human rights and the interpretation of intellectual property law. While this legislation remains under review, citizen groups have raised several issues that are not adequately covered, including migration and border control and remote biometric identification.

Terms like 'algocratic governance' or 'algocracy' have entered our vocabulary. As the increasing speed and role of algorithms enters our world these terms have replaced concepts like 'cyberocracy'. As we begin to understand how the unfettered power of algorithms could over-ride important human judgements, we realise this could replace democracy.

The Italian Franciscan priest, Paulo Benanti, who studied engineering before he became a theologian, has coined the term "algor-ethics", a branch of ethics grappling with how human principles are implemented by machines. He is respected by several important leaders in Silicon Valley. His role in including ethics in the discussion is very influential as a member of the UN Advisory Body on Artificial Intelligence. He is also the head of an Italian government commission on safeguarding journalism from fake news, and a consultant to the Pontifical Academy for Life.

Pope Francis' New Year Message for 2024 was devoted entirely to the topic of AI. This was followed a few weeks later by further thoughts on the subject in his message for the World Day of Social Communications. His key concerns include fundamental human rights, discrimination, and the danger of remote weapons systems. At the same time, he calls on us to set aside catastrophic predictions and their numbing effects. Instead, he asks us to study how we can use this cultural transformation to serve a good purpose, recognising our distinctiveness and the future of the species *homo sapiens* in the age of artificial intelligence.

The 'Rome Call for an AI Ethics,[31] promoted by the Vatican's RenAIssance Foundation, has been embraced by the Chief Rabbinate of Israel's Commission for Interfaith Relations and also by the United Arab Emirates' Abu Dhabi Forum for Peace. There was never a more critical time for inter-faith collaboration.

---

[31] See www.romecall.org

CHAPTER 8

THE COSMIC CHRIST

THE SUN WAS JUST COMING UP over the Pico do Jaraguá as I left our house in São Paulo very early on a Wednesday morning. My first stop was at the scrapyard where Bruno bought and sold all kinds of things that other people had thrown out. Occasionally I had found something useful there, but mostly I stopped by just to greet Bruno and wish him well.

An elderly lady was there before me, weighing the black plastic bag of stuff she had scavenged on the streets of our neighbourhood. Everyone knew her. She never spoke, just applied herself to her task. She almost always wore the same azure-blue wool dress that was a size too small for her. She politely accepted the coins Bruno paid for her bagful of rubbish and went upon her way.

As she left the yard, two boys, aged about nine or ten, were coming in. They needed two tin cans around which they could wind the long twine for their home-made kites. Bruno told them to pick the ones they wanted from the huge pile of stacked cans in the corner. There would be no charge.

Now it was my turn. "How are you today, Bruno?" I asked. "I am feeling very good", he replied, "thanks to the grace of God".

"That's wonderful", I said. "Tell me, how would you explain the grace of God you speak about? What's grace?"

"Grace?". He was surprised at my question. "Grace? – you saw it there. You saw that elderly lady who comes here every day to weigh the bag of stuff she has collected along the streets. She has no wealth. She has no power. She works hard for the few coins I can pay her. But you saw that I treat her the very same as I treat you – that's grace! You saw those two small lads looking for a tin, each of them, to wind the twine to fly their kites. They have no wealth. They have no power. But if I treat them the very same as I treat you – that's grace!"

Bruno's scrapyard was a meticulously ordered collection of leftovers, things he valued as reusables producing a modest income for him. All this happened several decades before commercial recycling became part of our modern lives. It was there, as the sun rose in the blue morning sky, that I received a demonstration of one of the most profound precepts of my faith. Grace is how we are empowered to act. Grace is what we are empowered to do. Grace is how we relate in kindness, in benevolence, in generosity, even in the smallest of ways. Grace is given to us in order that we may give graciously.

"Where did you learn about grace"? I asked Bruno. He drew himself up to his full height, over six feet tall and gazed into the distance for a moment before he replied. "I grew up in Recife. I was an altar boy at the church were Dom Hélder Câmara was in charge. He taught me about grace, and about everything I needed to know."

Observing Bruno, it dawned on me that grace is a powerful energy, an inner force, a social exchange.

Teilhard de Chardin in his seminary days in Jersey recorded that "Matter, life and energy are the three pillars on which my inner vision and happiness rests."[1] In Bruno's scrapyard all three were evident. Matter – stacks of it, carefully sorted. Life in the buyers and sellers who came from that economically poor neighbourhood. And energy — in Bruno's response to his clients, generated by what he understood as grace.

Teilhard, while serving as a stretcher-bearer during World War I, was thinking about 'the call of grace'. In the trenches, in moments of lull between the fiercest of battles — at Marne and Ypres in 1915, Nieuport in 1916, Verdun in 1917 and Chateau Thierry in 1918 — he availed of an upturned crate for a table on which he wrote down his thoughts. Against this background, the young Jesuit priest who had become a stretcher-bearer described grace as a spiritual energy in which one person exercises an influence upon another.[2] This is exactly what I had witnessed in Bruno's scrapyard.

Cosmic Presence

Theologians through the centuries have worried over the question of human freedom in the face of this spiritual energy. In 1919, after he returned from the war, Teilhard wrote that grace does not force us to enter another universe; it introduces us "into an extension of our own universe".[3] The freely offered gift of grace invites and enables us to situate ourselves in a context bigger than our personal immediate preoccupations. For Teilhard, later on, this would lead to exploring a much bigger reality – the Cosmos into which we were born, and its evolution.

In the opening lines of the Gospel of John, we read words that describe the cosmic presence of the Logos, the Word, the

---

[1] *Pierre Teilhard de Chardin and the Cosmic Christ*, Alex Terego, Amazon Kindle Edition, 2013.

[2] *The Spirituality of Teilhard de Chardin*, Thomas Corbishley SJ.

[3] *Cosmic Life: Writings in Time of War*, p. 48.

person we have come to know as Jesus Christ. "Through him all things came to be, not one thing had its being but through him, all that came to be had life in him." [4]

In the early centuries of Christianity, this grasp of the presence of Christ in everything that exists seems to have been well understood. In the writings of St. Paul, the cosmic dimension of Christianity was explicit. To the people of Ephesus, he speaks of how God the Father's plan would bring everything in the heavens and everything on Earth together under Christ.[5] At the beginning of his letter to the people of Colossus he wrote

> *The Son is the image of the invisible God, the firstborn over all creation. For in him all things were created: things in heaven and on Earth, visible and invisible, whether thrones or powers or rulers or authorities; all things have been created through him and for him. He is before all things, and in him all things hold together.*[6]

For thousands of years the Messiah had been awaited. His lowly birth at Bethlehem accompanied by the strange, powerful events witnessed by the shepherds and the travelling astronomers seeking him, fulfilled that long-awaited hope in a way no one could have expected. That the infant born in Bethlehem was truly God, and at the same time continued his far wider role in the unfolding of creation is not easy for any of us to grasp. But John the Evangelist and Paul introduced their followers to this mystery with great assurance. And for hundreds of years, through various developments in society and in the

---

[4] Jn 1:3.

[5] Eph 1:10.

[6] Col: 1:15-16.

growing community of believers, this all-encompassing role of Jesus Christ was understood.

Origen (c. 185 – c. 254) is thought to be the first of the Church Fathers to teach explicitly about cosmic Christology. In reference to the text "I am the Alpha and the Omega, the First and the Last, the Beginning and the End"[7] he writes:

> *God the Logos is the Alpha, the beginning and the cause of all things, the one who is first not in time but in honour... Let it be said that since he provides an end for the thing created from him, he is the Omega at the consummation of the ages. He is first and then he is last, not in relation to time, but because he provides beginning and end.*[8]

St. Augustine felt it important to draw attention to the Incarnation of Jesus as redemption from human sin. This downplayed the more cosmic role, taking the emphasis away from the wider holiness of the natural world in which we live. But this did not extinguish the religious awareness of our human place in nature during the centuries that followed.

I Arise Today

In Ireland, St. Patrick (c. 385 – c. 432) has left a legacy that is greatly treasured among people of Christian faith to the present time:

> *I arise today through the strength of heaven, light of the sun, radiance of the moon, splendour of fire, speed of lightning, swiftness of wind, depth of the sea, stability of Earth,*

---

[7] Rev. 22:13.

[8] Cf Lyons, J.A. *The Cosmic Christ in Origen and Teilhard de Chardin*, Oxford University Press, 1982

firmness of rock ... Christ with me, Christ before me, Christ behind me, Christ in me, Christ beneath me, Christ above me, Christ on my right, Christ on my left ... Christ in the heart of everyone who thinks of me, Christ in the mouth of everyone who speaks of me, Christ in every eye that sees me, Christ in every ear that hears me. I arise today through a mighty strength, the invocation of the Trinity, through belief in the Threeness, through confession of the Oneness of the Creator of creation.

About 500 years before St. Patrick was born, the same awareness of the natural world is invoked in the Book of Daniel. When his three young companions are cast into the furnace because they refused to worship the golden statue made by King Nebuchadnezzar, we read that they experienced a coolness such as wind and dew bring, so that the fire did not even touch them or cause them any pain or distress. In unison, still inside the furnace, they called upon all of nature to join them in blessing God:

Sun and moon! Bless the Lord;
Stars of heaven! Bless the Lord;
Showers and dew! Bless the Lord;
Winds! All bless the Lord;
Fire and heat! Bless the Lord;
Cold and heat! Bless the Lord;
Dews and sleet! Bless the Lord;
Frost and cold! Bless the Lord;
Ice and snow! Bless the Lord;
Nights and days! Bless the Lord;
Light and darkness! Bless the Lord;
Lightning and clouds! Bless the Lord;
Let the Earth bless the Lord;

Mountains and hills! Bless the Lord;
Everything that grows on the Earth! Bless the Lord;
Springs of water! Bless the Lord;
Seas and rivers! Bless the Lord;
Sea beasts and everything that lives in water! Bless the Lord;
Birds of heaven! Bless the Lord;
Animals wild and tame! Bless the Lord;
... for he has saved us from the burning fiery furnace,
rescued us from the heart of the flame...[9]

The years passed and two kings later, King Darius found it useful to promote Daniel in charge of his henchmen. They were jealous of Daniel and, when they found him praying to his God against the prevailing edict, they forced the King to abide by what had been decreed – that anyone praying to any power other than the King should be thrown into the lions' den. The King wasn't happy about this, but he was weak.

He said to Daniel: "Your God himself, whom you have served so faithfully, will have to save you". Daniel was thrown into the lions' den. The King didn't sleep a wink that night. He got up at the first light of dawn and went to the lions' den and there was Daniel, fit as a fiddle. "My God sent his angel who sealed the lions' jaws, they did me no harm", Daniel reassured King Darius who was overjoyed.

I sometimes wonder about those lions and what they must have experienced. They must have felt something so powerful that they suspended their natural behaviour for a time.

Later mystics were inspired by an amazing awareness of creation. Hildegard of Bingen (1098-1179) wrote of the Earth as mother of all that is natural, mother of all that is human. The Divine is actively at work in all around.

---

[9] Daniel 3:62-88, Jerusalem Bible.

I, the fiery life of divine wisdom, I ignite the beauty of the plains. I sparkle the waters, I burn in the sun, and the moon and the stars. With wisdom I order all rightly. I adorn all the Earth. I am the breeze that nurtures all things green. I am the rain coming from the dew that causes the grasses to laugh with the joy of life. I call forth tears, the aroma of holy work. I am the yearning for good.[10]

Today, Francis of Assisi (d. 1226) is the best known and perhaps the most influential of all those who experienced the divine in our natural surroundings. His influence on contemporary theologians is very vibrant – especially on men and women scientists and theologians of the religious order he established.

Franciscan sister, Ilia Delio, who holds doctorates in science and theology, is regarded as a major thinker on the frontier between religion and science. She tells us that personal divine love is invested organically with all of creation, in the heart of matter, unifying the world.[11] She and theologian Richard Rohr insist that Franciscan mysticism is about an *intuition of Jesus as both the Incarnate Human One and the Eternal Cosmic Christ at the same time.*[12]

A Reflection in the Mirror of the Real

The Irish geologist, John Feehan, finds inspiration in Thomas Aquinas (1225-1274). For Aquinas, living creatures are incarnations of the divine, they present something of God to us. Feehan freely translates Aquinas thus: "He has therefore – in

---

[10] Reprinted in IDOC Bimestrale, Vol 21, No. 4.

[11] Cf. Ilia Delio, *The Unbearable Wholeness of Being: God, Evolution and the Power of Love*, Orbis Books, 2013.

[12] Cf. Richard Rohr, *The Universal Christ*, SPCK, Kindle Edition.

order to share his goodness – brought into physical being creatures; and through them he reproduces in material reality aspects of his own goodness."[13]

Feehan writes that each creature is a reflection in the mirror of the real, shaped by matter and energy, of an aspect of the beauty of the creator. Out of God's plan has unfolded the utterly amazing diversity of living things, each an embodiment of some facet of His goodness, so that what is lacking in one may be found in another. Goodness, which is God, is refracted into endless multiplicity in the beauty of the living creation.[14]

Acknowledgement of Divine presence in all of nature continued up to the time of the great plague that struck Western civilisation in 1347 – the Black Death. After the loss of life on such a scale, people felt a need to be saved from the natural world. Christians lost sight of the cosmic dimension understood by St. Paul and by the theologians and mystics who followed for hundreds of years.

By the time the Industrial Revolution arrived, the sense of the Divine presence in nature was lost. The understanding that human life came from and belongs to Earth's community of creatures was gone. Earth came to be regarded as a resource on which to draw without balance or limit. It was there to plunder without calculation of the consequences.

In the 20th century, the unease that people began to feel did little to slow down the plundering. As both science and technology developed, human needs drew more and more on Earth's

---

[13] *'Produxit enim res in esse propter suam bonitatem commicandam creaturas, et per eas repraesentandam.'*

[14] John Feehan, *Reflections on the presence of God in creation*, 2015. p. 16 – self-published in response to requests from many of those who had heard his talks.

resources, to the point of destruction of which we are now so acutely and so frighteningly aware.

Discoveries of physicists and cosmologists like Albert Einstein (1879-1955) and Edwin Hubble (1889-1953) taught us that our universe is much more extensive than was previously known. It is not finished at all but is expanding. The fact that cosmologists could date its development to more than 13 billion years ago led everyone – scientists, philosophers, theologians, and ordinary folk – to take another look at where we stand in relation to our universe. This new awareness, along with the eventual acceptance of Darwin's theory of evolution, changed our perception of life and history – both past and future.

The Pure Majesty of the Real Itself

Teilhard de Chardin was a contemporary of Einstein and Hubble. His scientific work in palaeontology revealed further secrets of the evolution which Darwin had described. The three pillars Teilhard had identified years earlier while in the seminary in Jersey – matter, life, and energy – now preoccupied him in his scientific research. As a priest, they raised for him profound questions about the Divine presence in this process. His writings to trusted friends reveal how much he struggled with these questions. When, during his sojourn in the remote Gobi Desert of China, he found himself without the bread and wine to celebrate Eucharist he saw that the world itself could provide all that was needed. The remarkable text of his "Mass on the World" marks a further step in awareness of the presence of the Divine in the material world. It is a text where poetry, mysticism and theology meet.

> *Since once again, Lord – though this time not in the forests of the Aisne but in the steppes of Asia – I have neither bread,*

nor wine, nor altar, I will raise myself beyond these symbols, up to the pure majesty of the real itself; I, your priest, will make the whole Earth my altar and on it will offer you all the labours and sufferings of the world.

Over there, on the horizon, the sun has just touched with light the outermost fringe of the eastern sky. Once again, beneath this moving sheet of fire, the living surface of the Earth wakes and trembles, and once again begins its fearful travail. I will place on my paten, O God, the harvest to be won by this renewal of labour. Into my chalice I shall pour all the sap which is to be pressed out this day from the Earth's fruits...

Do you now therefore, speaking through my lips, pronounce over this Earthly travail your twofold efficacious word: the word without which all that our wisdom and our experience have built up must totter and crumble – the word through which all our most far-reaching speculations and our encounter with the universe are come together into a unity. Over every living thing which is to spring up, to grow, to flower, to ripen during this day say again the words: This is my Body. And over every death-force which waits in readiness to corrode, to wither, to cut down, speak again your commanding words which express the supreme mystery of faith: This is my Blood.

This fifteen-page text has inspired people all over the world to this day. There are several videos on YouTube that witness to the ways different groups have felt spiritually enriched by it. But the spiritual awareness that Teilhard grasped through his study of science and evolution, was something the guardians of theology at the Vatican in the first half of the 20th century would fail to grasp. The repeated rejection of the various texts that were submitted was difficult for Teilhard. He worked on revisions, but even so the answer was No. This was still the situation when he died in New York, on Easter Sunday, 10 April 1955, just eight days before the death of Albert Einstein in Phoenix.

Second Vatican Council

One of today's enthusiastic scholars of Teilhard's work, John F. Haught, writes:

> *When I first explored his writings, Teilhard's bold ideas had already influenced some of the theological reflection that would make the Second Vatican Council such an important event in the history of the Church. Because of church censorship, however, Teilhard was never given the opportunity to expose his work to the critique of other experts. No doubt, there are deficiencies in his writings that could easily have been avoided and corrected had his beloved church allowed for the circulation of his ideas.*
>
> *After Teilhard's death in 1955, at any rate, his lay friends fed his manuscripts to hungry publishers who marketed them widely. Some of these were immediately devoured by theologians who helped shape the documents of the Second Vatican Council. Teilhard's hope for the future of humanity and of our need to take responsibility for 'building the Earth' greatly influenced one of modern Catholicism's main documents, Gaudium et Spes. This is ironic, because, in 1962, the same year the council met for its first session, the Holy Office of the Vatican issued an admonition advising seminary professors and heads of Catholic colleges and universities to "protect the minds, particularly of the youth, against the dangers presented by the works of Fr. Teilhard de Chardin and his followers."*[15]

---

[15] John F. Haught, The *Cosmic Vision of Teilhard de Chardin*, Introduction

This same hesitancy and fear continued to have influence for some years to come. But when I took up studies at the Pontifical University in Maynooth in 1966, Teilhard was spoken about as a writer who built on traditional foundations to present to us a faith fitted for the twentieth century. In philosophy courses we were encouraged to study *The Phenomenon of Man* and *The Divine Milieu.* Essays like *The Heart of Matter, Christianity and Evolution* and *Toward the Future* mingled comfortably with the Conciliar documents that were challenging us to build a changing church community. The specialized language Teilhard used made it difficult to grasp his message, and yet we students felt there was something there to be pursued. Scholars who followed in later years would make Teilhard's insights more accessible to those of us who lacked scientific training.

In New York in 1967, Bishop Fulton Sheen wrote: "It is very likely that within fifty years when all the trivial, verbal disputes about the meaning of Teilhard's 'unfortunate' vocabulary will have died away or have taken a secondary place, Teilhard will appear like John of the Cross and St. Teresa of Avila, as the spiritual genius of the twentieth century." [16]

In his *Introduction to Christianity* as early as 1968, the then Cardinal Ratzinger made no fewer than eight positive, even complimentary, references to the work of Teilhard, with several quotations. He later recalled Teilhard's influence on the Second Vatican Council:

> *The impetus given by Teilhard de Chardin exerted a wide influence. With daring vision, it incorporated the historical movements of Christianity into the great cosmic process of evolution from Alpha to Omega... The Council's 'Pastoral Constitution on the Church in the Modern World' took the*

---

[16] 'Footsteps in a Darkened Forest', New York: Meredith, 1967

cue; Teilhard's slogan 'Christianity means more progress, more technology', became a stimulus in which the Council Fathers from rich and poor countries alike found a concrete hope.[17]

Encountering the Work of Thomas Berry

In the summer of 1980, I was packing my bags to take up a new assignment in Brazil. An American friend who was a Passionist priest, handed me a sheaf of typed pages, saying "take those and study them, because they are going to be important". They were an early draft of the thoughts of his fellow Passionist priest, Thomas Berry. This latest writer to influence my missionary journey had retired from academia a year earlier. He had founded the Centre for Religious Research in Riverdale, New York – just a few kilometers south of the Jesuit Novitiate at St. Andrew-on-Hudson where Teilhard had been buried.

As the twentieth century moved into its final decades, people were grappling with what it means to be human in the midst of the growing knowledge about the Earth and our planet's place in the wider Cosmos. In the summer of 1990, the Rome-based international resource centre IDOC published a collection of articles on the emerging cosmic spirituality. It told readers that

Scientists, psychiatrists, economists, feminists, environmentalists and theologians all concur: there is a generalized discomfort being experienced by the human species as a whole: a yearning for a greater bondedness; a more coherent myth to

---

[17] 'Principles of Catholic Theology', Ignatius Press, 1987, p. 334.

give meaning to life, to energize us and make us once again leap with joy.[18]

It quoted Buddhist therapist Joanna Macy: "I have learned through my work that there is an immeasurable collective pain in our society over what is happening to our world, a common grief and fear for our common future."[19] Citing many thinkers, the editor concludes: "In agreeing with the pain, these ponderers are also coming to startlingly similar conclusions regarding the cause of our malaise: we have forgotten our oneness with the universe."[20]

Among the thinkers I read about in this issue of IDOC was Thomas Berry. It reprinted his twelve principles that underlie our existence as part of the Earth community. These were the fruit of decades of study and reflection. He went on to call for the development of a spirituality aware of the inter-connectedness of all life, and the cosmic presence of the Divine. He did not produce a 'way forward' or a blueprint for action, but a call for a new relationship. In the face of the destruction of our planet he observed: "We will not save what we do not love, and we will neither love nor save what we do not experience as sacred."[21]

Fr. Berry perceived that we have lost our sense of identity. The original Genesis account of our origin, he felt, leaves us without a sense of being connected to the universe's natural development. We need a new community story, one that will place us within the cosmic order, would tell us where we come from, who we are, and where we are headed as a species in the light

---

[18] IDOC, op cit, p 1.

[19] Ibid p 20.

[20] Ibid p 1.

[21] Quoted by Tim Flanders, *Thomas Berry's Sacred Surround*, Two Rock Publications, 2011, Kindle Edition.

of what science now reveals to us. It is the story of the universe, the story of the Earth, the story of human evolution and the story of the Christian faith, all part of the same story. This story will affirm the sacredness of nature, and our relationship with the Divine who is immanent in all that has evolved, to be found at the centre of the Cosmos and the natural world.

Riverdale on the Hudson

In the summer of 1992 when I was coming to the end of my sabbatical year, I had a few days free in New York. I boldly picked up the phone and rang Riverdale asking to speak to Fr. Thomas Berry. I told him simply that I would love to meet him. "Why don't you come over for coffee tomorrow?" was his reply. I was still using paper in those days, and I have kept all my Filofax diaries. On 1st July I had scribbled his directions:

> *5801 Palisade Ave, last street before Hudson River. Near Mt. St. Vincents ... On Broadway, W on 261st. Dead end. Left on Palisade Ave, 400 yards sign on rt to Retreat Hse. Next turn on R, Riverdale. 10.30 am for coffee.*

This was long before Sat Nav equipment existed for ordinary folk. I studied the map and planned my route. Our headquarters for the region of the Americas was located on the tiny City Island out beyond the Bronx. My diary notes: Pelham Parkway W, Fordham Rd on to 207th, I repeated: R. on Broadway to 261st.

I wrote my name in the community diary where everyone logged her need for a car. I didn't tell anyone that I'd never driven in New York before. On my 17th birthday, my Dad had put a driving licence inside my birthday card on the breakfast table, and I had my first driving lesson in Dublin's Phoenix

Park that evening.[22] He never considered that I was yet ready to graduate from the private school of motoring where all our family were tutored. Twenty-five years after that first lesson, when I came home from overseas, to my Dad I was still a teenager. As a responsible citizen, he would have to take me to Dublin Airport to show me the new road markings before he could risk lending me his car. He was very generous about the car but only God knows what bad habits I might have picked up in those strange faraway places! I didn't tell him that in Boston I'd mastered the automatic gearbox. I had managed a 4WD jeep alone across the desert in Tanzania on moonless nights when blood had to be collected from donors for an accident victim. I had clocked up 100,000k on a little Yamaha motorbike over and back the busy 6-lane *Marginal* each side of São Paulo's smog-bound Rio Tieté. A sunny summer morning in New York couldn't be all that difficult! This was no time to be acting like a novice.

Next morning after Mass I pretended to myself that I wasn't scared and took off towards Yonkers and along by the blue waters of the Hudson.

This learned historian – who had studied the Chinese language and culture, who had mastered Sanskrit, and taught Asian religions at several New York universities, who had published books which are considered classics on Buddhism and the Religions of India – was now serving me coffee. The room had open glass doors to a leafy garden. The sense of tranquillity and hospitality was palpable. When my host sat down and began to speak, I felt I was listening to an old friend. He was a fatherly figure. My memory of what he said is all about the importance of the story. I should not have been surprised, nor

[22] There was no such thing as a Driving Test back in those days.

was I, though perhaps I expected he would speak about creation, or cosmogenesis, or the legacy of Teilhard. But not so, it was all about the concept of story.

"We are our story", he said. "Every Institute is its story. The problem with Christianity is that we have only been taught the history of the human story. If we realised that we are part of the story of the Universe, we would be different."

The need for a new creation story was his main preoccupation. He referred to his recommendation that we would do well to leave the Bible on the shelf for a while and give ourselves the opportunity to set down the story of how life really began in the light of current scientific knowledge and of the Divine role in that. He was not at all suggesting that we should reject or abandon the Bible. The Genesis account of creation is itself a story. But Fr. Berry's view was that we need to understand the creation story and our human relationship to the rest of creation in the light of the scientific insights of today.

When I was leaving, he reached for a copy of a recent publication *Befriending the Earth.* This text was developed from a symposium at Riverdale in dialogue with the Jesuit, Thomas Clarke, on a Theology of Reconciliation between Humans and the Earth. Signing the book he said: "Remember that your message, whatever it is, is part of a larger story. Be sure to tell the larger story."

Followers and collaborators of Thomas Berry tell us that he knew his challenge to Christianity and to theologians was a big ask: the Genesis account of an historical creation has to be replaced by an understanding of cosmic evolution with its cycle of creation, dissolution and recreation – this as our primary revelation. Christianity is also challenged to rethink its understanding of the future – an understanding of a final redemption at the end of history.

He did not minimize the revolutionary nature of what he was proposing. He likened it to a new Exodus in which Christianity would leave behind these now unhelpful concepts and enter a new Holy Land. He coined the term 'Ecozoic' to name the new era we are now entering, 65 million years since the beginning of the Cenozoic era, the end of which we are now witnessing.

Divine Dimension

Those who have studied Berry's work explain that the principle of the Logos of John's Gospel, opened the way for an understanding of creation grounded in a cosmic, time-developmental context, infused from the beginning with a Divine dimension. This cosmological evolution as a continuing revelation of the Divine, Berry believed, accorded with the view of Thomas Aquinas concerning the cosmic community as the 'perfection of the universe', which participates in the Divine goodness and represents it better than any single creature whatever.

While presenting a radical change, Berry felt this was an established tradition of Catholic theological reform. "Just as Clement of Alexandria presented Christianity within the context of Hellenism, as Augustine worked within the Neoplatonic frame of reference, Thomas Aquinas within the Aristotelian perspective, and Ignatius Loyola within the context of Renaissance humanism, so now there is need for us to think and act and create within a new period of Western Christianity by working within the context of this new story of the universe." [23]

When Thomas Berry died on June 1st, 2009, the change of perspective that he saw as necessary in Christianity was also leading deep thinkers elsewhere to ponder. A bare two months later, at Vespers in Aosta in northwest Italy, Pope Benedict XVI expressed a view that:

> *The role of the priesthood is to consecrate the world so that it may become a living host, a liturgy: so that the liturgy may not be something alongside the reality of the world, but that the world itself shall become a living host, a liturgy. This is also the great vision of Teilhard de Chardin: in the end we shall achieve a true cosmic liturgy, where the Cosmos becomes a living host.*[24]

Insights from the East

The two priests, the French-born Jesuit Teilhard de Chardin and American-born Passionist Thomas Berry, had deep connections with China and the religions of Asia. The problem of our dis-ease arising from our loss of a true awareness of our human place in nature is largely a Western one. This was also understood by the English-born Benedictine priest, Bede Griffiths. (1906-1993) whose faith, mysticism and understanding of the Divine in the Cosmos developed greatly during the second half of his life which he spent in India.

As a young adult, having abandoned the Anglican faith in which he was raised, Alan Griffiths lived for some years

---

[23] 'Christian Cosmology' in *The Christian Future and the Fate of the Earth*, Tucker ME and Grim J, Eds, Orbis Books, Maryknoll, NY. cited in Tim Flanders 'Thomas Berry's Sacred Surround'.

[24] Flanders, ibid, location 840.

without any formal religion. His spiritual rootedness in nature was deep. Then, at the age of 25 and in continued contact with C.S. Lewis who had been one of his tutors at Oxford, he re-embraced the Christian calling. Thus began his road to becoming a monk in the Benedictine community at Prinknash Abbey, where he took the name Bede. When called in 1955 to establish a monastery in Kengeri, Bangalore, he adhered to the accepted Benedictine style. But during the following three years, as he observed the culture in which he was surrounded, he saw the need to move towards a more austere, Cistercian-like way of life. He moved to Kerala to establish an ashram at Kurisamala. His life now could be based on utter simplicity.

Fr. Bede saw that the Christian tradition of contemplation would be enriched with the Hindu understanding of *advaita.* This Sanskrit word is usually translated in English as 'non-dualism'. I wish someone could find a better translation, but this is the English term frequently used today by Christian theologians. At the personal level it is an invitation to focus on the inner self. With or without a religious connotation, there are few concepts that have enjoyed greater marketing success. We are surrounded with evidence of how this concept has invigorated a variety of disciplines to embark upon meditation or yoga as essential to a balanced way of life.

In 1968 Fr. Bede took over the Shantivanam Ashram in Tamil Nadu. This was a further step in his spirituality and a greater opportunity to grow in his understanding of the religions of the East, especially Hinduism. He was always seeking common meeting points. He drew upon several different disciplines in order to better understand and express his experience of reality as sacred and interconnected. He valued the concept of cosmic revelation evidenced in the Hindu scriptures generally. The Upanishads, in particular, held a great resonance with his cosmic Christology. Thus, he saw that Christ has a universal relevance for all religion, as well as particular relevance for Christianity. Many pilgrims from the West went to the ashram to listen to him and to deepen their personal spiritual lives. His influence has continued long after his death in India in 1993.

The South African Methodist Professor, Dion Forster, gives us a very readable account of the life, study, and insights of Bede Griffiths, this Western monk whose major influences came from living in the East.[25] Rev. Forster describes what exactly is meant by the term 'cosmic Christ':

> *It is used to explain the manner in which Christ is related to the whole of the created order. Christ's relationship with the created order stretches beyond human and earthly affairs. It stretches beyond one particular culture or religion or planet. It affirms that Christ has significance for the whole of the Cosmos or created order and not just for the Christian faith and those human persons who adhere to it. The cosmic Christ has significance for animals, for plants, and even for inanimate objects such as planets and stars. He reminds us that cosmic Christology has a long and rich history in the Christian tradition. It is certainly not new to mainstream Christology.*

In the thirty years since the death of Bede Griffiths, people of all faiths and none have been pursuing their search for an understanding of self, of community and of the spiritual dimensions of life in all sorts of ways, drawing on all sorts of traditions. Social media channels are full of methodologies in addition to the plethora of printed material.

---

[25] Cf. *Christ at the Centre – Discovering the cosmic Christ in the Spirituality of Bede Griffiths.*

This self-searching has been complemented by a worldwide awareness that saving our planet from destruction needs urgent action at both personal and political levels.

These two axes of awareness have drawn people in many parts of the world into a commitment that takes different forms, from the purely spiritual to political protest, some of which can be radical and even violent.

Praxis

It is challenging to observe how the ideas I have been exploring above are now taking the form of praxis. In many countries, innovative approaches have become part of a developing Christian spirituality that embraces the awareness of the Divine in the Cosmos and at the same time works seriously to establish a more harmonious relationship with our planet. Among these initiatives, one of the most exciting is the Songhai Centre, developed from 1985 at Porto Novo in the Republic of Benin by the Nigerian Dominican, Fr. Godfrey Nzamujo.[26]

It so happens that he and I shared a mutual close friend, Maura Ramsbottom, whom I mentioned in my Chapter on Paulo Freire. Maura devoted most of her life to teaching theology in Nigeria with a lot of grassroots involvement. She was steeped in St. Paul's theology of creation. On several occasions she had said to me "I wish you could meet Nzamujo". She died in Ireland on the feast of St. Paul in January 2007.

Some weeks later I was in Lagos where her community asked me to go through her personal papers and select what should be archived. When I completed that sad task, I crossed the border into the Republic of Benin where I met Nzamujo in Porto

---

[26] Pronounced 'En-sam-u-joe'

Novo. There was a poignancy to our encounter as we shared the same grief. We also shared the same passion – that nobody on the continent of Africa should experience hunger.

Nzamujo – as everyone calls him – was born in Kano, Nigeria, in 1950. After his profession of vows in the Dominican order, he had the opportunity to study widely. Following his bachelor's degree in modern philosophy and mathematics, he obtained a master's in theology and a doctorate in economic philosophy. Then followed another master's, this time in microelectronic systems engineering; then another doctorate in electrical engineering and computer science; and yet another in management sciences from the International Institute of Advanced Studies.

In the early 1980s he was teaching at the University of California, Irvine, when the devastating famine in Ethiopia was screened on news channels across the world. Nzamujo felt an urgent inner call to return to Africa and address the question of food production.

In mediaeval times there were several famous Empires in West Africa, the last of which was the Empire of Songhai, which flourished between 1492 and 1592. It was marked by the pivotal organisation of social life and the development of trade with the Arab world. Centres like Timbuktu and Jenne became famous centres of learning. Nzamujo chose the name 'Songhai' for his new project because he wanted to create a new spirit among Africans. The 'Timbuktu Effect' which Songhai seeks to emulate today is based on pride, progress and effective results. Songhai symbolises Nzamujo's belief that Africa's ecological characteristics are advantages rather than impediments. He develops these ideas in his book *Songhai: When Africa lifts up its head*.

No Waste is Wasted!

As we shook hands that morning in Porto Novo, his graciousness was reflected in all that I observed. It was twenty-two years since Nzamujo had returned to Africa. One of the best photos I have ever taken captures the intricate crafting of wood and bamboo in decorative screens. These line a veranda above the curved tiled steps leading up to the Centre's restaurant. Nearby, enthusiastic students were engaged in a plethora of workshops. A walking tour of the then 18-hectare site began with a demonstration of how all waste material is harvested – from kitchens, metal workshops, and toilets. The water is purified, and the waste materials are processed to produce the gas that powers the machinery.

In the metal workshops, grinders and other machinery adapted to local needs are manufactured to a highly professional standard. The same was evident as we toured the centre for development of appropriate technologies, then the fruit juice and jam-making workshops and the bakery. Nearby, motor mechanics were meticulously training their students in the repair and maintenance of a range of vehicles.

Nzamujo opened a heavy iron door to show me racks of chickens cooking on a dozen spits. The next door he opened showed joints of the hugely nutritious local wild boar. These and other larger game form part of the tasty menus at the restaurant. Likewise, the impressive poultry and fish farms revealed centres of development in themselves. But it is the seed nurseries that are central to the research and development activities of Songhai. Traditional and emerging methods and use of hybridization are all part of the effort.

Elsewhere I observed students taking courses in business management, marketing, credit management, group dynamics, office routine and office services – including document reproduction, laminating, and binding. Nzamujo told me: "Our aim is to show young people that their ancestors knew how to organize themselves productively and they too can do that – but knowledge has to be translated into skills and irrigated by the right value systems. We believe that the only effective way to fight poverty is to help the poor to become productive. The development of the human person is paramount. We must unleash new human capacities increasing the level of creativeness and inventiveness."

Nzamujo knew that information technology would enable Africa to leapfrog centuries of development and become a player in the modern world. But he stressed to me the importance of what he calls 'antenna-receiver logic'. It is not just a matter of being capable of accessing information anywhere in the world, but of the capacity to select and fine-tune information that is relevant to the development process of the community. He told me:

> *"We must avoid the pitfall of passive information consumerism which is a real danger in developing countries today. Songhai is not a 'how to do it' institution. We do not hand out recipes. This is first and foremost a 'how to be' organization — wanting to 'be more' is the source of creativity and inventiveness.*

It is not surprising that the Songhai concept has spread far beyond the Republic of Benin. Today there are Centres in no fewer than 18 countries of Africa and Asia[27] while Songhai

---

[27] Benin, Burkina Faso, Chad, China, Democratic Republic of the Congo, Equatorial Guinea, Gambia, Ghana, Guinea, Liberia, Malawi, Nigeria, Republic of the Congo, Senegal, Sierra Leone, Thailand, Togo, Viet Nam.

collaborates with supporting agencies on all continents. The list of Awards conferred on Fr. Nzamujo could not have been imagined when he accepted the vocation to leave his successful academic life and devote his priesthood to applying his knowledge at the grassroots of African society.

At Songhai, I did not observe religion explicitly mentioned. But I could see how this Dominican applied what Thomas Aquinas meant when he wrote of God: "He has therefore – in order to share his goodness – brought into physical being creatures; and through them he reproduces in material reality aspects of his own goodness."

Developments in Ireland

It was in Ireland, at the Dominican Centre in Wicklow, that I first became aware of this teaching of Aquinas. In the 1990's a small group of Dominican Sisters set about establishing an ecological project in Wicklow. The 70 acres of land they owned on a hillside overlooking the Irish Sea had been rented out to farmers for many years.

In 1998 they decided to reclaim the land and use it for an organic farm. They consulted the local community who contributed their expertise in farming, forestry, and other local knowledge. Alongside the farm they would offer opportunities, both residential and otherwise, for people to come and study on short or longer courses or engage in retreats while enjoying the organic farm produce.

The Sisters named the centre with an Irish word – *An Táirseach* – which means 'Threshold'. They tell us:

> *This was chosen as a reflection of our being 'in-between' understandings of our place in the world. As a human race, we had come to believe that the planet belonged to us. Our*

mission is to raise awareness of the place of the human as part of the web of life, through practice and education. At An Táirseach, through retreats and courses, we seek to convey a sense of the vastness of the time it took the Universe to create first the stars, then the planets including planet Earth, and finally, to burst forth into life itself. In contrast, we also invite people to enter into the inner world which is as mysterious and deep as the outer world is astonishing. The tranquil organic environment and teaching at An Táirseach provides an opportunity to reflect on the interconnectedness of all creation and our place within this.[28]

The followers of St. Brigid at Kildare are doing something similar. The Brigidine Sisters have called their centre "*Solas Bhríde*", the Irish language term meaning "The Light of Brigid". This Christian Spirituality Centre welcomes people of all faiths and none. The vision of the centre is to help all to know and be inspired by Saint Brigid, who died around the year 525. Her legacy is found to be more relevant than ever for our world today. The Centre's ecologically sustainable building is shaped like St. Brigid's Cross.

The hermitages and conference rooms attract individuals and groups who are seeking a spirituality that is closer to nature. A year-round programme of events focusses on important aspects of Celtic spirituality. The programme is particularly creative around the feast of St. Brigid on February 1, the first day of Springtime in Ireland.

Pilgrimage is seen as the core ministry. The cosmic walks may take pilgrims to the ruins of an ancient Christian monastery, or to wetlands where the Earth today is in need of help to

---

[28] See www.antairseach.ie/aboutus.

regenerate. Awareness of our culture is also a priority. The Brigidines tell us:

> *Knowing our story awakens in us a sense of beauty and the mystery of which we are a part, evoking a sense of awe, wonder, gratitude and compassion. It enables us to make sense of our own lives and our place on the planet.*[29]

Spirit of Fire

In 1996 the General Chapter of the congregation of the Presentation Sisters invited their communities to take up the care of the Earth as a priority in their spirituality and ministries. In response it was decided to start an organic farm at the birthplace of their founder, Nano Nagle, at Ballygriffin in County Cork. The aim was to integrate the three areas of heritage, spirituality, and ecology at this special location.[30]

Some years ago, I spent a memorable three days there at a programme conducted by Professor Ursula King, author of *Spirit of Fire*[31], one of the most widely read studies of the work of Teilhard de Chardin.

A two-kilometre walk around the property is laid out with Stations where pilgrims are invited to pause and reflect on the different stages of the 13.8 billion years during which scientists currently believe our Universe has been developing.[32] This meditative journey begins at a large silver globe. In it pilgrims

---

[29] See www.solasbhride.ie.

[30] See www.nanonaglebirthplace.ie.

[31] Ursula King: *Spirit of Fire: The Life and Vision of Teilhard De Chardin, Orbis* Books, 2015.

[32] Data coming back to Earth from the James Webb Space Telescope launched in 2021 may change this and no doubt future discoveries will reveal a lot more. But for the present, cosmic spirituality focusses on the 13.8-billion-year-old 'flaring forth' or 'big bang' theory.

can see their reflection. The very same elements which make up the human body today – hydrogen and oxygen – were those which emerged at that first moment. The different stations on this walk trace the length it took our Cosmic Story to evolve.

Reflecting on our evolution from the first 'flaring forth' to the present day, the Stations wind around the upper fields and hedges and then descend steps to the banks of the River Blackwater. This reflective journey ends at the Sundial where 40 linked hands, each representing 50 years, reflects back to the moment when Jesus was born.

With the long tradition in education which Nano Nagle initiated, the year-round range of activities at this Centre includes specially designed retreats and renewal days for those engaged in the education sector. Online and in-person events include discussions on justice and a right relationship with the universe, the UN sustainable development goals, and health-related inputs on body, mind, and spirit.

Laudato Si'

The above examples are part of the widespread praxis today that seeks to respond to the threat being experienced by our planet, a healing of human malaise and a recovery of the spirituality of our Christian forebears.

This praxis is most comprehensive in the call of Pope Francis to the Church and the world. In his 2015 Encyclical *Laudato Si'*, he spelled out the basic issues which we need to own and which we need to allow to challenge us in terms of our personal faith, our local communities and our societies.

> *St. Francis, faithful to Scripture, invites us to see nature as a magnificent book in which God speaks to us and grants us a glimpse of his infinite beauty and goodness.*[33]

> *The external deserts in the world are growing because the internal deserts have become so vast ... For this reason, the ecological crisis is also a summons to a profound interior conversion.*[34]

> *The entire material universe speaks of God's love, his boundless affection for us. Soil, mountains, everything is, as it were, a caress of God.*[35]

> *Living our vocation to be protectors of God's handiwork is essential to a life of virtue; it is not an optional or a secondary aspect of our Christian experience.*[36]

> *The universe unfolds in God, who fills it completely. Hence, there is a mystical meaning to be found in a leaf, in a mountain trail, in a dewdrop, in a poor person's face. The ideal is not only to pass from the exterior to the interior to discover the action of God in the soul, but also to discover God in all things. Saint Bonaventure teaches us that 'contemplation deepens the more we feel the working of God's grace within our hearts, and the better we learn to encounter God in creatures outside ourselves'.*[37]

Of the contribution of *Laudato Si'* to the Church's social teaching, Damien Howard SJ pointed out that:

---

[33] *Laudato Si'*, par 12.

[34] Ibid, par 17.

[35] Ibid, par 84.

[36] Ibid, par 217.

[37] Ibid, par 233.

> *In this encyclical, we see two great bodies of thought jolt palpably in each other's direction like tectonic plates, changing the landscape and opening up new perspectives. On the one hand, it brings the prophetic urgency of the ecological movement to a Church that hitherto has been at odds with itself as to how to respond to huge and undeniable (but oft denied!) global challenges.*
>
> *On the other, it proffers the fresh spirituality and theological vision of Catholicism to a campaigning agenda which all too often has resorted to fear-mongering to advance its arguments. The dialogue between the two, which has clearly been going on for some time in the Pope's heart and prayer (even informing the selection of 'Francis' as his papal name) now holds out the promise of an exciting new synthesis which may just help to change our civilisation.*[38]

Pope Francis followed up the Encyclical with the project he called 'The Letter'. This is a film, circulated widely on social media and through parish networks, which enables us to watch and listen to the size of the ecological challenge and its call. 'The Letter' shows advocates for change in different parts of the world receiving an invitation to meet Pope Francis at the Vatican. This introduces us to their story. We see for ourselves the realities that affect a climate refugee from Senegal, a young activist from India, two marine biologists from the United States and the leader of an indigenous community in Brazil.[39]

We are invited to reflect personally and discuss together what we are learning. Then, as part of the synodal process Pope

---

[38] *Blog by Damian Howard SJ, lecturer at Heythrop College, University of London and a member of the editorial board of Thinking Faith.*

[39] See also www.laudatosiactionplatform.org and www.laudatosimovement.org.

Francis invited communities everywhere to discern through the gift of the Holy Spirit what God is saying to us.

There is much to be done. Our journey to understanding the Cosmic Christ is far from over. St. Paul told the people of Corinth: 'If anyone is in Christ, the new creation has come'.[40] To grasp what this means for us on our synodal journey, we will need to draw abundantly upon that grace of which Bruno spoke at the beginning of this chapter. Sometimes this synodal journey can feel overwhelming.

The poem by the late Sister Raphael Considine of the Presentation Sisters, gives me courage. While the Dominican Sisters take the Irish word '*Táirseach*' – threshold – as their inspiration, this poem is called '*Trasna*', the Irish word for 'crossing':

> *The pilgrims paused on the ancient stones*
> *In the mountain gap.*
> *Behind them stretched the roadway they had travelled.*
> *Ahead, mist hid the track.*
>
> *Unspoken the question hovered:*
> *Why go on? Is life not short enough?*
> *Why seek to piece its mystery?*
> *Why venture further on strange paths, risking all?*
> *Surely that is a gamble for fools – or lovers.*
> *Why not return quietly to the known road?*
> *Why be a pilgrim still?*
>
> *A voice they knew called to them, saying:*
> *This is Trasna, the crossing place.*
> *Choose! Go back if you must.*

---

[40] 2 Cor 17.

You will find your way easily by yesterday's fires,
There may be life in the embers yet.

If that is not your deep desire,
Stand still. Lay down your load.
Take your life firmly in your two hands
(Gently… you are trusted with something precious)

While you search your heart's yearnings:
What am I seeking? What is my quest?
When your star rises deep within,
Trust yourself to its leading.
You will have the light for first steps.

This is Trasna, the crossing place.
Choose!
This is Trasna, the crossing place.
Come!

CHAPTER 9

LITTLE GIRL, I SAY TO YOU 'ARISE'

THE FOLLOWING TRUE STORY WAS RECORDED in 2008 in the small sitting room of the Dublin community to which I belong. Iris told the story like this:

I was 25 at the time when 'she' came with the big news, 'a friend of mine has this company and they need help, it would be perfect for you, for your studies ... a part-time job in an accounting office'.

I was really excited, and the next day I was still excited. I remember I wanted to present myself very well and I wanted to get this job and to prove that I could do it. It was the normal excitement that you have when you go for a job interview, and you want to get it ...

It was a normal hallway and it was a normal room with computers, a completely normal office that you could imagine any where. They asked about my background, my experience, they didn't need to ask many questions because they knew it all. These two men burst in – I was thinking 'this is like some kind of hidden camera programme or something'.

But my second thought was 'this is too brutal, it is not funny'. I remember one was older, one was younger. I remember one had these big big eyes. The younger one was a bit more compassionate, he never sexually touched me or hit me. The older one was the aggressor, saying 'you are coming with us, you are coming with us'.

This was the first time I heard him mention my sister. Just obey us, just obey us. This was the first time I slowly saw that 'she' was involved, and they knew where they could find my little sister ... I think it was two days of violence, sexual, and mental abuse and then I was just there, and there was no such violence anymore.

I didn't cause any trouble because these people made it clear to me that if I don't obey whatever I am supposed to do for them they know where my little sister lives, they know where my mother lives. This is what was used. They realised they didn't have to hurt me physically anymore because they knew I am not going to disobey.

The first day was very brutal, it was rape. But every other experience was also a rape because I did not want it. But it was mental games more, degrading me in many ways, it didn't take so long, not days and days, but they would do something mentally or verbally and then they leave you alone and that is the worst I think, alone with your thoughts.

The second day they came with heroin. They knew that I had my own story with heroin five years before. I got out of that alone. I had like a one-year story of going back and forth but I was a winner and I was so proud of myself because I knew this was something big that I overcame and I won that game and I knew how quickly I would become addicted again.

This I was resisting. That is why I got many violent things, like rape and hitting, but very smart hitting because they don't want you to look hurt physically because clients are coming. I was really resisting, but then the first client came in. I realised why I was being held. And that I could not get away.

For the first few days it was so horrifying to accept this. This heroin that was present manipulating me was really helpful because it makes you numb, like a sedative. I will never forget the first moment of this first man coming into my room and I am even the one who has to make him feel relaxed, I am to seduce him.

I don't know how many I had, maybe five clients a day, but there are many girls who had ten, fifteen ... you being there trying to sell your body to someone who comes with the money, and then you had these thirty minutes of whatever it is called, I cannot call it any name, it is not sex, it is not making love, it is a body and it could well be a box where you put all this stress, anger and frustration and fear or whatever clients are putting ...

I adjusted quickly to what was happening, we have mechanisms of surviving, my mechanism was that I would play at being someone else – a student who was doing this for money...

I didn't have to take phone calls, that was done by the woman outside, but you would hear these conversations, it was like speaking about cabbage, is she fresh or is she not fresh?

It comes to the point when you really feel this is a trade, fresh meat at a market and the client wants to know what he can do with this fresh meat, how does it look like because there are so many others he can choose. He can come and decide you are too fat, or you are too ugly, or he can choose between eye colours.

Sometimes I would be moved elsewhere because prostitution is illegal. They would come and tell me to undress, and they would move me with a sheet, just a sheet over me, to degrade me. I would be blindfolded, yes. The whole thing was very unreal, still is, like a movie ...

The same lady that interviewed me the day I was abducted – later I heard her voice – she was the one making appointments on the telephone. And she was bringing me food, many times I would not see her. They tried to avoid any contact. Always there was something happening.

But then (after six months) for two days nothing happened. Silence. I don't hear the phone. I don't hear the footsteps. For weeks I wanted to get out, and I am observing. That woman on the phone put my passport under the door. I thought she is trying to make more trouble for me. If these guys find it that will cause me more violence.

Third floor, not so high and there were good balconies. I am a good climber. Some people would be scared. Somehow, I really felt I'm getting out. I had this feeling I will not be dead, I just wanted to make sure this is the moment, and it will be ok. I had a very bad outfit, a cardigan, supposed to be sexy clothes, but better than a blanket. I was climbing down, I felt I am not scared, I am climbing down. I went to a friend.

With all the people I met I really felt nobody will believe me, and it was true, many people took care of me but the first thing in their minds was 'it's ok, you probably chose this to finance your drugs, but we are taking care of you now'. This was really hard because I didn't choose it."

Iris later concluded that her passport had been returned because the brothel owners had a tip-off that there would be a police raid on the place. She had accepted our invitation to visit Ireland to speak to college students to raise awareness about human trafficking. A native of southeastern Europe, at the time of this interview she was living and working in Germany. As it happened, her only brother was studying in Dublin and he was sitting next to her as the documentary for our national radio station, RTE, was being recorded. I was sitting next to him on the sofa and could feel him trembling as he listened to his beloved sister's story.

Sacred Space

For me, that was a riveting experience. Now, years later, every time I enter that small room and recall the recording of that documentary, I feel I am in a very sacred space.

I had first met Iris in Geneva when she was among a group of five survivors of human trafficking who were recounting their experiences to an assembly of the UN. I had gone there with my colleague, Sister Maura O'Donohue,[1] who had returned to Ireland in 2003, saying she wanted to dedicate the rest of her life to raising awareness about the then little-known crime of human trafficking.

Maura had become aware of this during her work in the 1980s and 1990s, when she was heading the AIDS desk at CAFOD[2]. Under her direction, ninety-five HIV treatment centres had been established in several countries. In addition, she organized educational workshops in Africa and Asia. These had brought the problem of human trafficking to her attention. Many of these HIV workshops were held in seminaries and at assemblies of religious sisters.[3]

---

[1] See also Postscripts 5 and 6

[2] The London-based Catholic Agency for Overseas Development. Having specialised in Community Healthcare, Maura's medical work took her to eighty-three countries, as well as spending 14 years in Ethiopia.

[3] It was during these seminars that Maura received an appeal from religious leaders of diocesan congregations of sisters, begging her to help them

When Maura returned to Ireland, she joined the small community where I was living. That was great because we had been good friends back in my student days, but after that for thirty-five years we had hardly ever been on the same continent at the same time. In 2003 she had been granted funding from generous donors in the United States to cover travel and other expenses to get this anti-trafficking work going. She asked me to find the time to give her a hand.

One day in the springtime of 2004, she told me she had an appointment with an Austrian visitor in a Dublin hotel to discuss what could be done about trafficking. I dropped her off at the hotel and as I drove away, I asked myself 'where is she going to begin?' This was a topic very few people knew about. My mistake was that this was not a beginning. It was simply one more line of enquiry to add to the contacts Maura had been building up over recent years.

A short time later she met with colleagues from COATNET,[4] an international network of Christian organisations against trafficking. Representatives of the Churches' Commission for Migrants in Europe (CCME) brought a significant ecumenical dimension to those exchanges.

In October that year, Maura presented to the Irish Missionary Union a report on human trafficking, based on a recent study by the International Organisation for Migrants (IOM). It was a general overview of human trafficking, especially on trafficking in minors. Later that month I accompanied her to Sion in Switzerland for a 4-day seminar on Child Trafficking, attended

---

regarding the sexual exploitation of young sisters by some members of the clergy. See Postscript 6

[4] COATNET links 45 member organisations from Catholic, Anglican and Orthodox communities in 39 countries, and co-operates with other faith and civil society organisations worldwide.

by over 190 participants from a wide variety of disciplines – lawyers, magistrates, doctors, psychologists, government representatives, police, and NGOs.

The number of countries where human trafficking was known to take place came to 105, including Asia, Africa, Europe, the Americas, and Oceania. The issue of supply and demand was raised repeatedly. I learnt new words like 'paedo-criminality' and 'sextortion'.

The Swiss people took the issue of child sex tourism very seriously. They invited the tourism sector to commit to specific measures to protect children from sexual exploitation. They believed that at that time, more than two million children were being forced into the sex industry through this lucrative criminal business. With serious use of social media platforms, they made it possible for tourists, wherever they were going, to report any suspicion of a possible exploitation. "Don't look away" was their plea to tourists.

I came home from Sion with a heightened awareness of the patterns of child trafficking, the challenges presented, the lessons learned, the issues of unaccompanied minors, the disappearance of children, the difficulties in tracing traffickers, the practice of organ trafficking and – above all – the need for networking to address the challenges of prevention, protection, repatriation, and psychosocial support. It was a daunting prospect.

A month later, Maura was in London where she attended a two-hour meeting at the House of Lords. Her diary noted that "the Lords at the meeting were open about the UK being a destination and a transit country for trafficked persons. All agreed on the fact that the need for such trade must be removed, but they did not seem to have a solution."

Act to Prevent Trafficking

In Ireland, there was still little awareness of the issue, nor acceptance that Ireland could be a country that was a destination as well as a transit country for trafficked persons.

Maura gave a number of talks to different groups. People were interested, shocked at the information, but there was no tangible outcome. Then, in November 2005, the Conference of Religious of Ireland arranged an information session with a visiting Good Shepherd Sister from the United States, Sister Helène Hayes.

She spoke about the global problem of human trafficking to a gathering of some eighty religious women and men, and she showed a 20-minute video called *Fields of Mudan* relating the plight of a little girl of about six years of age who became trafficked and was locked in a trailer on the long journey to a brothel. The audience was dumbfounded.

When we shook off some of the effects of the stunning video, someone said "we have heard talks and seen presentations about this before and have walked away and done nothing. This time we must form a group to raise public awareness about this issue."

The first meeting of the group that was later named APT (Act to Prevent Trafficking) was fixed for December 19th, 2005. The first task of the Conference of Religious was to identify communities of Sisters who could provide safe housing for women who were rescued. At that time, the State and other charities had no such facilities.

Ireland was already a signatory to the Palermo Protocol to Prevent, Suppress and Punish Trafficking in Persons, Especially Women and Children, which opened for signature on 15

November 2000. This established UN criteria for addressing the problem of human trafficking. In 2005 the Council of Europe agreed a Convention on Action Against Trafficking in Human Beings.

But, as yet, Ireland had not passed the national legislation to enable the country to ratify the Protocol and – as far as we could discern – there was no sense of urgency about doing so. In May 2006, APT succeeded in getting a 15-minute slot to address the Joint Oireachtas Committee on Justice, Equality, Defence and Women's Rights. Three members of APT were chosen to present our concerns to this small body of Deputies and Senators and the rest of us were welcomed to the public gallery.

The first to speak used her precious five minutes to outline a job description.[5] Avoiding anything dramatic in her style of presentation, the appalling facts were revealed in a way nobody could forget: a career with flexible hours, no experience required, no high school diploma needed, no minimum age, special opportunities for poor women, single mothers, women of colour. The details of the services required and the workplaces left nothing to the imagination.

It was specified that benefits would be provided at the discretion of management who held no responsibility or legal redress for on-the-job hazards such as non-payment for services rendered, sexually transmitted diseases or pregnancy, or injuries sustained through performance of services. It was specified that accusations of rape would be treated as a breach of contract by the employee.

---

[5] This had been prepared by a US anti-trafficking group called *Whisper* based on the experiences of women survivors of trafficking.

The five minutes ended with the question 'how many of you would encourage a sister, daughter, wife, or partner to apply for such a job? Women don't apply for this work, they are tricked and captured into it. Such jobs exist. And Ireland has no legislation to deal with this crime.'

The second speaker used her five minutes to state that what we were looking for must be anchored in a human rights framework. The essentials must be outlined in terms of legislation, including dealing with the perpetrators, the issue of migration and support to the survivor.

She pointed out that this was a multi-faceted issue needing an inter-disciplinary approach. State and voluntary agencies would be needed in a coordinated and integrated effort to combat this evil. She went on to outline twenty points that would need to be included in the legislation and added a number of very practical recommendations including a public information campaign and ongoing international collaboration on this problem.

In the final five minutes, it was stressed that this cruelty is far bigger than a mere immigration issue. The diagram of a Problem Tree was used to show the root causes and their effects. Poverty is the driving force behind trafficking in persons. The question of profit, organised crime and seeing people as commodities were clearly labelled on the tree.

But central to it all was the demand for purchased sex. The enormous profits of gangs from the trafficking of persons are often compared to the earnings in the illegal drugs business and the arms trade.

But a key difference was pointed out – and how many times since has this been repeated – that a person captured by human traffickers can be used and sold not just once, but over and over again. And as the demand for commercial sex grows, so does the need to entrap more and more victims, the majority of whom are women and children.

Attention was drawn to the provision of sexual services at major sporting events, business conferences and political conventions. Our speaker cited Interpol regarding the huge profits gained in this low-risk business. The impact of this trade on the spread of HIV, still a big concern back in 2006, was also mentioned.

We left the Gallery in our Parliament Buildings wondering what impact this presentation might make on the politicians who were listening. Just as we were talking among ourselves, we were approached by Senator Mary White, who had been present and was deeply touched by what she had heard. 'You have to reach a bigger audience', she said. 'Why don't you prepare an audio-visual presentation of your message, and I will book the AV room here where you can invite all the elected members to hear what you have to say.'

Coming out of the Woodwork

The following days were busy, preparing the audio-visual and mailing personal invitations to every member of Parliament. Our friendly Senator advised us that their lunch break was from noon till 2 p.m. We should run our 30-minute presentation 4 times in that space. We did so, and up to one hundred members of Parliament heard the message. Some of our politicians invited our members to the bar after our presentation. It was remarked: "we thought you nuns had all gone away, and here you are coming out of the woodwork to hassle us".

We were not the only group advocating for this legislation, and in due course it was introduced and eventually passed. An

'Anti Human Trafficking Unit' was established within the Department of Justice. The woman leader of the Unit came to our next meeting of APT and asked us to tell her what we had been doing all our lives up to this. She and her staff became very supportive. Women detectives were given specialised training. We were hopeful.

In 2007 Maura asked me to book a flight for her to Northern Ingushetia where she had agreed to inspect projects for CAFOD. That clashed with a meeting of COATNET in the Middle East, so she asked me to represent her there. I got a flight via Dubai. When we landed, I stood in line next to a dark-skinned priest from Sri Lanka and we began chatting. I found he was going to the COATNET meeting too.

When we reached the immigration desk, I was signalled to go through, but he was taken aside, causing me some concern. Later we were reunited on the transport taking us to the hotel. 'Don't worry', he reassured me. 'I'm used to that. It happens all the time because of my skin.' During the Conference we were taken on several eye-opening field trips. I often sat with this priest and listened in awe to the huge extent of human trafficking from his perspective.

I remember alighting from our minibus one morning and being ushered into a modern complex, going immediately downstairs to an underground gallery. Our hosts, members of a local Christian charity, explained that we would meet with men and women who had been trafficked and were being retained – not detained – in this location, pending their repatriation. My understanding was that their repatriation would take place when some source of funding was made available from their country of origin.

Staff we met seemed to be very kind people, but I found the long wide underground corridor a bit daunting. There was no natural daylight. To the right a blank concrete wall. Maybe there were doors to some rooms off it. To the left a wall of wire from floor to ceiling ran the length of the corridor. We could see a corresponding wire wall at the back of the space and another wide corridor beyond that.

This large space was divided by inner brick walls into several 'rooms' each holding about thirty people, women in some and men in others. Each 'room' had a shower and two toilets in the far corner. The personal belongings of the occupants were hanging on the wire at the back in a variety of small plastic bags. I don't recall any furniture, but there may have been a table and a few chairs. My attention was entirely occupied by the young women who came up to the wire to greet us.

It didn't take long to figure out who among our group spoke which languages and I became engaged with a vivacious young woman from the Philippines. She told me that they take turns to cook meals and for that time they can leave this 'room' and work in the kitchen at the end of the corridor.

I must have asked her, somehow, no doubt awkwardly, if she found it hard returning into the locked-up area. I was bowled over by her reply. "Oh no, Sister, it is wonderful here. Everybody is so kind. We are safe here, no beatings, no rape, no insults. I sleep all night in the sleeping bag they have given me." She had no idea when she might get back to the Philippines, but for now she felt safe.

My priest friend was standing next to me, holding hands through the wire with two young women from Sri Lanka. Before we left, I noticed him emptying his pockets and giving them all the cash he had. As we got back into the minibus, he told me,

> *Those two girls were captured by the Tamil Tigers when they were eight years of age. Did you notice the markings on their skin? They escaped when they were fourteen, only to fall into the hands of the traffickers. We will have to work very hard to find a place of safety where they can be sent.*

On another field trip we were shown a photo of a beautiful young Indian teenager. She had been hired as a housemaid for a well-off local woman. Though the woman was kind, her husband was a vicious and violent predator.

One day while the woman was out of the house, he demanded sex from the teenage housemaid. When she resisted, he tied her to a kitchen chair and took a kitchen knife which he used to cut off her beautiful long black hair. The photo showed how she looked – I shall never forget it. Once freed, her hair would grow again, but how long would it take to recover from the trauma of her captivity?

Back at the Conference, listening to the stories and the efforts of delegates from different countries – especially those from Eastern Europe and the Middle East – gave me further exposure to the suffering this problem was inflicting on countless people.

The Swiss-born Bishop, Paul Hinder, Apostolic Vicar of Arabia, addressed us, encouraging us to never give up in our efforts to end this slavery. He outlined in detail the reality of migration in the world, and it was from him that I first heard the expression 'migrant partners'. Other sessions at this meeting showed the necessity of international collaboration in addressing the issue of human trafficking, the importance of credible and independent national rapporteurs, and the detailed and painstaking work of providing support to survivors. It was clear that networking of NGO actors and international state collaboration was paramount.

Bangkok

On the concluding night of that Conference when we were taken for a tour of the city and a local cultural meal, I got food poisoning. I felt quite ill while waiting for my connecting flight at Dubai. When I reached Dublin, I was admitted to the Intensive Care Unit at St. Michael's Hospital with a very arrhythmic heartbeat.

A few days later, when Maura arrived back from her travels in the Northern Caucuses, she called into the hospital and urged me to get better quickly as the following week we were booked to Bangkok. This was to attend an assembly organised by the Global Alliance Against Traffic in Women (GAATW).

This network of NGOs from all continents focusses on the exploitation of women migrant workers, whether trafficked or victims of economic migration. That event absolutely opened my eyes to the vast number of women who, through lack of educational opportunity, are forced to emigrate. While it affects women on all continents, I was particularly shocked by the extent of this problem in countries like India, Indonesia, Malaysia, Laos, and Vietnam.

As well as domestic servitude, I learned of boys and girls trafficked for performance in circuses, as camel jockeys, for begging, and as brides. GAATW conducted a survey in eight countries on all continents that revealed the 'collateral damage' suffered by people who were trafficked. Sometimes the very steps taken to counter human trafficking put added burdens on the victims of trafficking.

In many countries the laws focussed on migration rather than on the support and rehabilitation of survivors of trafficking. In some countries, excessive focus on victims of trafficking for prostitution tended to overlook the problems of those trafficked for construction work, agriculture, fishing, hospitality, and manufacturing industries, where highly exploitative conditions exist.

Sometime later, during another anti-trafficking meeting in Prague, we were taken to see the 'shop windows' of the red-light district. An Irish religious sister working there told us she gets phone calls from some of the women trapped there to come and pray with them while they are waiting between clients. 'They love me to pray a decade of the rosary with them' she said. 'I go down there every evening that I can.'

Back in Ireland, networking became a key priority for APT. We were already maintaining contacts with the Dublin-based frontline service called RUHAMA. Several members of APT volunteered with their services, including befriending survivors of trafficking, sometimes accompanying them to a Court hearing. Through the Irish Missionary Union, we kept up contacts with Irish missionaries who were meeting the problem in increasing numbers in dozens of countries. We also kept in touch with the US-based religious sisters, UNANIMA.

Establishing a European Network

As members of APT, we increased our contacts with a group acting on behalf of religious congregations in The Netherlands. They had already been working for ten years and had developed very useful services through collaboration with voluntary groups throughout the world. This network enabled a rapid response for victims of trafficking.

For two years we held monthly meetings by Skype, and gradually this group grew to include a small number of colleagues in Austria, France, Germany, Italy, Portugal, Spain, and UK. We set ourselves the task of establishing a European Network of religious women tackling the issue of human trafficking. We began meeting face-to-face in Den Bosch in the Netherlands and eventually on 25th March 2009 we went down to the Bank and registered our charity under Dutch law. We called it RENATE.[6]

The graphic artist I engaged in my other communications work in Dublin designed the logo. He also designed the small brochure we had written in English, French, Spanish, Dutch, Portuguese, Italian and German. This networking increased our capacity to share information, resource material and help survivors through our international contacts. It deepened our awareness of the size of the problem, and the global routes that were being used by traffickers.

However, that was not enough. We were aware that many of the countries of origin for trafficked women and children were in central and eastern Europe, while all our members lived in the western countries. We decided to translate our brochure into six languages of eastern Europe. Our colleagues in Den Bosch arranged the translations and the brochures were printed in Dublin. We travelled to Brussels to ask help from UCESM[7] to deliver our invitation to religious women in central and eastern Europe – asking them to contact us. They did. In

---

[6] Religious in Europe Networking Against Trafficking and Exploitation www.renate-europe.net.

[7] UCESM is the Union of the European Conferences of Major Superiors, which gathers 39 national Conferences in Europe.

2011 through RENATE, funding was sourced to bring a group of 77 religious sisters to the first truly European meeting in the Polish city of Trzebinia. Many of those attending were already deeply involved in the work of preventing the problem of trafficking through education or otherwise. Listening to the services they were providing to survivors of trafficking was deeply touching. At our Trzebinia conference, useful theological as well as practical papers were presented.

RENATE has been growing since then, providing support and sharing constructive ideas between its members. There is no central physical office or secretariat, but the Board meets in different countries a few times a year. The first thing we did was to arrange training for members in the use of social media. Some very practical training sessions on other topics and some international conferences have been arranged since then.

In Italy, with the amazing energy and dedication of Sister Eugenio Bonetti, who was among the founding members of RENATE, religious were active in many ports and places of detention of immigrants. There was a call to formally establish a global network of religious working to raise awareness of the problem, to support those with active rescue services and those raising awareness and engaged in political lobbying around the related legal issues.

The Justice Desk of the UISG[8] scheduled a meeting in Rome in 2009. National and Regional networks of women religious from all parts of the world were represented. However, our colleagues from Oceania decided they would support us from their home countries due to the high cost and the carbon footprint which their physical presence would have incurred.

---

[8] International Union of Superiors General.

That Rome meeting was a lively and very informative gathering. We discussed the best way the new global network would function. What would it be called? We divided into regional or common language groups and poured over possible acronyms. We tried out how they would sound in different languages.

When we gathered in the big assembly room for the report back none of the proposed names conveyed what we were about – until a gentle voice from the Asian delegation far across the room said, "We think it should be called *Talitha Kum.*" [9] The instant applause showed everyone's acceptance. Since then, *Talitha Kum* through its website and webinars has provided a great service.

Around the world, religious Sisters were fulfilling a special role in many countries in assisting survivors of trafficking to be reintegrated into society. At the same time, they were proclaiming that trafficking, including the rescue of those exploited through sex trafficking, is not only a women's issue. The whole of society needs to be challenged to work for the elimination of this heinous crime.

Three Priorities

When the time came to mark the tenth anniversary of the establishment of *Talitha Kum*, 86 delegates from 48 countries registered for the event. They represented 52 networks organised by religious sisters working to counter the crime of human trafficking. The Final Declaration of this event named three Priorities for Action.

---

[9] The little girl in the Gospel story of Mark 5:41 would represent for us all the women and children trapped by traffickers. Jesus said to her, *'Talitha Kum' – Little Girl, I say to you, arise.* www.talithakum.info.

- *The first concern* is the power differential between men and women in all sectors of society – economic, social, familial, political, cultural and religious.
- *The second priority* is the dominant model of neo-liberal development and unfettered capitalism which creates situations of vulnerability that are exploited by recruiters, traffickers, employers, and buyers.
- *The third issue* is unjust and inadequate immigration laws and policies coupled with forced migration and displacement which puts people at greater risk of being trafficked.

By this time, in most of our home countries various civil society groups had begun to address the issue of trafficking. Legislators and police forces who were acting locally were collaborating internationally. The Trade Union movement had become committed to the cause. In Ireland, members of APT joined an alliance of more than seventy agencies to form the 'Turn Off the Red Light' (TORL) campaign. This work was informed by research carried on throughout previous years by the Immigrant Council of Ireland, drawing on testimonies of survivors of trafficking.

The aim of the campaign was to raise public awareness about the dangers of prostitution and sex trafficking and to lobby the Government to introduce legislation to end the exploitation of women, men, and children in the sex industry.

It was felt that the best way to combat sex trafficking and prostitution was to tackle the demand for paid sex by the introduction of laws that proposed to target sex buyers. In recognition of the vulnerability of those involved and exploited in prostitution, it proposed the decriminalisation of those who sell sex and provide greater support to victims of trafficking and prostitution.

This approach had achieved some success first in Sweden and came to be known as the Nordic model. It was replicated in other countries of Europe and further afield. The legislation was enacted in Ireland in February 2017. The campaign was successful in raising awareness of the issue of human trafficking, using the whole range of communications media. However, convictions are very few.

It was now many years since the UN Palermo Protocol was initiated. Most national governments signed up to this, but it took several years before they ratified it. This was further strengthened in 2005 when the Council of Europe Convention on Action against Trafficking in Human Beings was adopted. This came into force in 2008 when 10 member countries ratified it. It has a reporting mechanism which is binding on States that have ratified it, and it conducts monitoring of the situation.

There is now a high level of cooperation between many countries and their law enforcement agencies, and yet, the outcome for victims of human trafficking is dismally poor. Current estimates show that 40 million people are exploited by traffickers, of whom 10 million are children. It is estimated that criminal gangs are earning up to 150 billion dollars a year through human trafficking. During the two centuries of transatlantic slave trade, around 15 million people were in slavery. The figures we are now learning about are truly shocking.

With so many agencies dedicated to the elimination of human trafficking all over the world, one wonders how the crime continues to be perpetrated on so many different fronts and goes unpunished. Very moving films have been screened in our cinemas. Shocking documentaries with witness reports have been shown on TV networks. Impressive dramatic productions have toured our parish and community centres, all raising awareness of this crime. But perpetrators of trafficking can change their tactics instantly, whereas passing legislation to keep up with it can take years.

Hidden in Plain Sight

Concerned citizens have been taught to observe rented properties in their neighbourhood and to contact the Crimestoppers number if they suspect possible victims:

- *Have I noticed faces at a window, looking stressed and never smiling?*
- *Are there children in a house near mine who rarely come out and speak little or no English?*
- *Have I noticed frequent visitors to a residential property – men arriving and leaving at unusual times?*
- *Are there cars or minibuses picking up foreign nationals at unusual times?*
- *Are children collected from school by different people each day, who are not related to them?*
- *Is there a child at a fast-food outlet in a shopping mall who looks nervous and is given no say in what is being purchased for him or her to eat.*
- *Have I been offered low price deals at my door, involving cheap labour, for cash?*
- *If I am offered a low cost car-wash that involves a couple of young immigrant workers with little or no protective clothing, do I not need to ask myself how much are they earning for their labour, and what are their living conditions?*

These crimes are well described as 'hidden in plain sight'. We won't see what is hidden if we do not know what to look for.

In a number of countries, courses have been provided for staff working in the hospitality sector. In Ireland in 2013, two Sisters of Mercy started such an initiative.[10] Since then their outreach has continued to grow and provides a very practical service.

They received great collaboration from hotel management groups and industry leaders which enables them to deliver workshops for management and staff. Once the hotels became aware of the indicators of risk, they were able to develop protocols in cooperation with the law enforcement agencies. As this work continues to bear fruit, they have begun working with hospitality training colleges and universities to ensure that future leaders in this sector will be aware of the risks.

The problem of human trafficking has led to a huge amount of research. The publication of victim impacts is heart-rending. Each survivor we may meet represents only the tip of the iceberg of those who remain trapped.

Santa Marta Group

When Pope Francis began his pontificate in 2013, he continued the denunciation of human trafficking, which had already been done by his predecessor, Pope Benedict XVI in many of his addresses and writings. On a very practical level, Pope Francis welcomed the expansion of an initiative of the Bishops' Conference of England and Wales.

Back in 2012, a unique partnership had been established by them with the Human Trafficking Unit of the Metropolitan Police in London. In April 2014, twenty-four police chiefs from several countries joined a group of Bishops in Rome. They stayed at Santa Marta, where Pope Francis has made his home,

---

[10] 'Mercy Efforts for Child Protection against Trafficking with the Hospitality and Services Sectors' (MECPATHS) https://mecpaths.com.

and the group they established became known as the 'Santa Marta Group.[11] Cardinal Vincent Nichols, Archbishop of Westminster, was appointed as the leader of the group.

At the end of that two-day conference in 2014 they signed a historic declaration. As senior law enforcement officials within the international community, they committed 'to eradicate the scourge of this serious criminal activity, which abuses vulnerable people'.

No time was lost in organising more conferences further afield. An event at the United Nations was jointly organised by the Santa Marta Group and the permanent observer mission of the Holy See to the UN. There were regional meetings in Latin America, Africa, and Asia, and one in Ireland which focussed on the maritime industry. At many of these events survivors of human trafficking were among the speakers.

At the 2016 Santa Marta Conference, a call was made for every Bishops' Conference to ensure there is a named bishop in their Conference to meet and engage with law enforcement officials. The need to accompany all victims of trafficking through the law enforcement process was highlighted. As the Santa Marta group has stated:

> *There is not a single solution to this complex and transnational issue. It requires the bringing together of the skills, wisdom and experience of committed people who work in very different national contexts.*

That – precisely – is the nub of it. The group met again in April 2023 in Vilnius, capital of Lithuania. The conference brought together law enforcement leaders, lawyers, judges, health

---

[11] The Santa Marta Group now has members in 35 countries — santamartagroup.com.

workers, lay and religious leaders. Keynote speakers highlighted the seriousness of this crime and the difficulties in combatting trafficking.

There was a clear appetite and desire among attendees to work together on awareness-raising, information exchange and other collaborative efforts. Organised crime groups that exploit the vulnerable and benefit from this evil crime can only be defeated by a coalition of good. They established a six-point strategy[12] that is designed to prevent and ultimately eradicate human trafficking. The plan will also focus on working with Governments and businesses to ensure that supply chains are slave-free.

The person who understands and best explains this to us is Kevin Hyland OBE. While working in the UK he became the first Anti-Slavery Commissioner and brings the experience of his high-level police work to the wider role he now fills on several international bodies. Now living in Ireland, Kevin criss-crosses the world in his efforts to link professionals and agencies in the fight against human trafficking. He makes it clear that two elements are essential in approaching a solution to the problem of trafficking:

> *One element requires the close collaboration of many sectors of society – governments, law enforcement agencies, health agencies, religious congregations and faith-based societies, trade unions, community groups, civil society, and students. If the situation is to be addressed effectively, citizens need to be active in keeping governments focussed on strategic planning and funding to tackle this crime.*

---

[12] https://santamartagroup.org/about/strategicgoals.

The second element requires action to address commerce in products that depend on slave labour. It is believed that 16 million enslaved people work in the private sector in businesses with which we interact daily – perhaps producing the T-shirts we wear, or the PPE in our health services, or the fish we import. It is known that children as young as four or five years of age are mining materials used in cosmetics, and – appallingly – mining the cobalt that is essential to the batteries for our mobile phones and for the electric cars and buses which are looked upon as a solution to our care of the planet.

Pull and Push Factors

Our demand for low-cost clothing and low-cost everything, constitutes one of two major 'pull' factors behind those forty million people enslaved by human trafficking. The other major 'pull' factor is the demand for sexual services.

The issue of ethical purchasing needs to become everyone's concern. The G20 nations have begun to take on board the issue of ethical procurement chains, but all businesses need to be brought on board if enslavement in low-cost production is to be ended.

There is also one major 'push' factor. The prevalence of poverty in many countries remains critical to the success of the traffickers. The World Bank estimates that the COVID-19 pandemic has pushed between 40 to 60 million people into extreme poverty. As a result, people already living in disadvantaged situations are becoming more vulnerable to being trafficked due to increased poverty, joblessness, and weakened social support structures.

The seventeen Sustainable Development Goals of the UN, together aim at addressing the above problems by 2030. Especially Goal 8.7:

> *Take immediate and effective measures to eradicate forced labour, end modern slavery and human trafficking and secure the prohibition and elimination of the worst forms of child labour, including recruitment and use of child soldiers, and by 2025 end child labour in all its forms.*

As a result of advocacy by concerned citizens of the United States, some courageous legislation has been introduced in the U.S. Congress to address this push factor in Guatemala, El Salvador, and Honduras. Called the 'Central American Women and Children Protection Act', it attacks the causes of human trafficking.

It authorises the State Department to provide assistance to these countries so that they increase protection to people in their homes and communities, linking the insecurity people feel with the migration issue, which in turn makes the people vulnerable to traffickers. The legislation specifically prohibits any funds going to governments. It must be channelled through civil society organisations. Experts acknowledge that there is no quick or easy solution to the problem of human trafficking. But this is one important step.

Can we hope for similar legislation on a wider global stage, protecting the vulnerable in countries of Europe, Africa, Asia, Oceania, and South America? What would it take to persuade consumers and businesses to use their purchasing power to eliminate slave labour at the sources of production? Many small steps could lead to one giant step to eliminate human slavery. Imagine setting 40 million people free! Is that too much to ask, or even hope for?

More recently we have become aware of something deeper. At an APT meeting where we were reflecting on the three priorities of *Talitha Kum,* one member said: "I am just thinking that there is a link between the rape of a woman through trafficking and the rape of the Earth through our neglect."

Pope Francis had already drawn a connection to this double challenge in *Laudato Si* where he outlined the task of addressing the needs of our planet.

> *It is clearly inconsistent to combat trafficking in the fur of endangered species while remaining completely indifferent to human trafficking, unconcerned about the poor … Concern for the environment thus needs to be joined to a sincere love for our fellow human beings and an unwavering commitment to resolving the problems of society.*[13].

Fatima Conference

In November 2022 our European Network, RENATE, held an important 5-day conference in Fatima. Back in 2009, when we registered this charity in the Netherlands, all the members were from religious congregations of women. By 2022 it embraced many lay men and women, all passionately involved in the work of raising awareness about the problem of human trafficking, lobbying politically, or providing assistance to survivors.

The 97 delegates came to Fatima from Albania, Austria, Bulgaria, Croatia, Czech Republic, France, Germany, Greece, Hungary, Ireland, Italy, Kosovo, Lithuania, Macedonia, Malta, Netherlands, Northern Ireland, Poland, Portugal, Romania, Slovakia, Spain, UK, Ukraine and the Vatican. We also had a

---

[13] *Laudato Si',* par 91 and par 123.

speaker from USA. The Portuguese team of RENATE had put enormous work into preparing this event.

Bishop José Ornelas, Bishop of Fatima and President of the Conference of Bishops of Portugal warmly welcomed the delegates and affirmed that human trafficking is one of the greatest challenges facing the Church today.

Morning prayer each day included a short video with a message from a survivor of trafficking. Reporting on the work of RENATE, the House of Prayer Task Group reminded us that every activity has to be accompanied by prayer. Contemplative religious communities and all our friends and co-workers are invited to become members of the House of Prayer which can be accessed through the website.

Two delegates came from the Vatican's Migration and Refugee Section, which is personally guided by Pope Francis. Flaminia Vola, the Regional Coordinator for Western Europe at this Vatican department, told us that the message of Pope Francis was that these people must not be shut out or left behind.

Her colleague who is Regional Coordinator for Eastern Europe and Central Asia, Yurly Tykhovlis, is a lawyer who has already spent six years with the Pontifical Council for Justice and Peace. It was heart-rending to listen to his account of the current work on both sides of the border in Ukraine, his native country. But it was inspiring to experience his passion for a new evangelisation. He stressed the need for a proactive position of our Church in all dimensions of public and social life, especially migration, human trafficking and peace-making.

Our theological reflection at the close of the first day[14] drew on the Gospel story of the Wedding at Cana. Mary noticed the young couple's plight. She saw their dignity was going to be destroyed. She needed to do something. It wasn't her role, but she stepped outside of that. There was a human need. You push out the boat, way beyond your comfort zone. That is what Mary did. It is about faith and expectancy. How do we reframe what impacts on us and how do we respond? Can we take what Mary did in the context of reading the signs of the times today?

Next day we heard graphic accounts of people-smuggling[15] that occurs between Algeria, Morocco, and Spain. We were moved by the desperation of people caught up in the most inhumane situations at sea in the Mediterranean. There was a plea that each European country would work to reform their immigration policies and be aware of our responsibilities towards people who have become undocumented. Our theological reflection at the end of the second day reminded us that we are called to be the innkeepers of the Good Samaritan story. Other choices would make us either robbers or indifferent bystanders.

Myria Vassilliadou, former EU anti-trafficking co-ordinator, spoke by video link, telling us of the challenges that face EU parliaments and institutions through the ever-growing methods which traffickers develop in their global efforts to secure enormous profits. Kevin Hyland, speaking of his years at

---

[14] Each evening, the theological reflection on the day's work was led by Irish group facilitator, Cora Lambert.

[15] People smuggling and human trafficking are different. Those smuggled pay for their transport to another country and are free if they arrive safely. Trafficked persons are unwilling captives, often controlled by mobile phone and surveillance. It is reported that some may even have had electronic chips implanted.

Scotland Yard, told the gathering, "I had helicopters, secret surveillance equipment, intelligence, and dogs, but the most important resource available to me were the elderly Sisters to whom I could bring a survivor whenever we found one."

US attorney, Rochelle Keyhan is a first generation Iranian American. She is CEO of *Collective Liberty* and recipient of several awards for her work against slavery, cyber-crime, and women's issues. She outlined important changes needed in the criminal justice approach to the crime of human trafficking.

Our problem today, she said, is that there are very few prosecutions for this crime. Only three prosecutions for every one hundred police departments in the United States – a country that has 17,895 police departments. She explained the need to change from the Vice Approach, which is prostitution-based, requires victim cooperation and routinely leads to victim arrest. This should be changed to an Organized Crime Approach, which is offender-focussed and based on data that is intelligence driven and minimizes the need for victim cooperation.

Which of Us Is without Sin?

Our final theological reflection was based on the story of the woman caught in adultery. We all know that one cannot commit adultery alone. She may not have been a victim of the man, that we do not know. But she was a victim of the system. The intention in the story is to judge her as a bait to trap Jesus – he could be accused of treating the Law of Moses nonchalantly or, on the other hand, breaking the Roman Law. The accusers cared nothing for justice.

Given how today's economy involves a whole cast of actors across continents involving supply chains and ordinary purchasers of goods, it is an economy in which we ask: "which of us is without sin?" Alongside this, we have human trafficking, a sophisticated network of a high profit, low risk industry. We were reminded:

> *In RENATE you have found your North Star, your purpose, your dream. Now your discernment asks: in the interplay between God's inspiration and human exploitation, discernment is a journey into the unknown among many uncertainties. But remember 'where two or three are gathered in my name, I am there among them'."*[16]

Very early on that Saturday morning as we waited for the coach that would take us from Fatima to Lisbon airport, I glanced at my fellow travellers and thought: tomorrow I will be at Mass in Dublin, she in Vilnius, he in Athens. Those over there in Rome, those others in Munich, these beside me in London, that big group in Tirana, others in Paris, Budapest, Prague, Bratislava, Valetta, Bucharest, Warsaw, Madrid ... and beyond. The harvest indeed is great, but given the size of the problem, the labourers are still too few.

---

[16] Matthew 18:20.

PART 2

CONCLUDING UNSCIENTIFIC POSTSCRIPT

I was not born for one country,
the whole world is my native land.

POSTSCRIPT 1

COMMITMENT

I CANNOT SAY WHAT KEEPS MY INTEREST in Søren Kierkegaard alive, but every few years I reach for my copy of his *Concluding Unscientific Postscript* and dust it down with a little nostalgia. As a 19th century thinker, he was unforgivably opposed to any change in the status of women, but I don't think he would mind my borrowing his title to introduce the remaining stories I would like to share with readers. Some of these stories describe adventures in faith in the lives of my missionary colleagues who recounted them personally to me. Others are stories I researched for our Yearbook *Healing & Development.* Like Kierkegaard, the structure of my *Postscript* is a bit unruly.

Kierkegaard's *Postscript* is a somewhat ironic attempt to flesh out ideas that he had begun to develop in an earlier, shorter work called *Philosophical Fragments.* In that book he provided the fundamental structure of his thoughts about Christianity. He hinted that he might have more to say later. The *Postscript* contains that 'more'. In this book he deliberately went against the grain, making Part 1 quite short, and Part 2 much longer. It is a difficult book to read.

When I was in Maynooth *Philosophical Fragments* was on our undergraduate course in philosophy. So were several other titles of his, including *Fear and Trembling, Either/Or,* and *Sickness unto Death.* These texts grapple with questions of faith and the Christian challenge as presented to Kierkegaard in the Lutheran Church of his native Denmark during the forty-two years of his life. His father was troubled with pathological feelings of guilt. Kirkegaard had to grapple with the effects of this early influence for most of his life.

He uses a pseudonym to author the *Postscript* and, only in a short three-page reflection at the end, does he add his own name and the date, February 1846. I probably never read the *Postscript* from cover to cover, but I carried this five-hundred-page hardback book in my luggage on my first journey to Tanzania and then back to Ireland, later to Brazil and back, and later still to USA and back.

I liked to read again a few passages that I marked when I came across them. These would be things that I want to think about for my own wellbeing. Kierkegaard would love that! A big goal of his was to get people to think – to think for themselves as individuals, to think about who they are and what makes them what they are. Who am I becoming and what is the process of that becoming? What is at the core my existence?

I find it amazing how many thinkers were influenced by his ideas even a century after his death in 1855. Most people regard him as the father of *Existentialism* – the philosophical reflection on 'existence' that dominated the century after his lifetime.

I like to think he might enjoy my simple stories too. They might relieve him of his melancholy. Much of his writing was an attempt to figure out the role of religious belief in a person's life. Brought up with his father's strict views, his early experience of religion was joyless, then a period of atheism, then a life of self-sacrifice, and ultimately frustration with a church that would not change in order to remain relevant through changing times. Kierkegaard concluded that we really cannot *be* Christian, we can only aim at being so.

He reminds me of a young man in the youth group I worked with in São Paulo years ago.[17] His name was Ziro. He would visit our little house fairly regularly, sit down at the kitchen table, prop his head on his hands and ask deep questions. He would not have had any tertiary education, so I doubt he came across Kierkegaard.

One day I decided to bring up the question of his excessive use of alcohol and hoped he might give this problem some thought. I said something like: "Ziro, wouldn't it make your mother very happy if you didn't get drunk so often? As a Christian do you think you might be able to find the strength to get on top of this problem?" He replied: "You cannot call me a Christian, for I am not a Christian. All I can do is try my best every day of my life to become a Christian." That was Kierkegaard in a nutshell.

An individual's development, as this famous philosopher saw it, may pass through three stages, though they may overlap. The first is what he calls the aesthetical stage. This is where, in our personal development, we experiment with ideas but do not commit to anything. Next comes the ethical stage. We realise this is the time for action; we make commitments. Finally, we embrace the religious stage; we recognise our failures and shortcomings, but we commit ourselves to God.

---

[17] In the Archdiocese of São Paulo at that time, candidates for the Sacrament of Confirmation had to be at least sixteen years of age, ready to make choices that would shape their adult lives. The age group in our youth ministry was about 16-24 years.

Without commitment, he suggests, we are like a stone that someone sets skipping across the surface of the water. As long as it has the momentum to keep skipping it does well. But, when it runs out of energy and stops skipping, it instantly sinks into the depths. Commitment keeps us skipping. It gives us direction as we enter an uncertain future.

Like Ziro, however, Kierkegaard could not 'be' a Christian. He could only strive towards that desirable goal. In the unique structure of the *Postscript,* three times he inserts an Appendix into a Chapter. The first Appendix in the middle of the book runs to forty-one pages! Then at the very end he writes the third Appendix. There he asks that nobody should take the pains to appeal to this book as an authority. He writes: "I have no opinion except the one that it must be the most difficult of all things to become a Christian."[18]

Like Ziro, he did not understand that Baptism initiates us into a two-sided commitment involving me and my Creator, whom we call God. This rite initiates much more than an effort to follow Christ. It confers membership of that community which theologians call the *Mystical Body of Christ.* The person who accepts their side of the baptismal promise is not 'trying to be Christian' but *is* a Christian. Mystery yes, but more than a mere challenge.

This rite that John the Baptist initiated at the Jordan River long ago introduced a new era of religious understanding. The old era that began with God's promise to Abraham is not abandoned. It is updated. The baptism of the new era is a promise that involves two 'signatories'. The Creator-God promises to journey with us, through thick and thin. The Son of God, Jesus Christ, born an infant at Bethlehem, would grow up and show

---

[18] Op Cit. p. 546.

us - in the three years of his active life - how to manage ours. Baptism is our "OK, count me in, I will listen to that teacher. I will adopt that way of life."

A person is, of course, free to face the ups and downs of life without engaging in this two-way promise. Some people don't know about it at all. There are millions of people who take another route through a different faith tradition that helps them to relate with their Creator and with everyone else. Others who were baptised think it is something that may have mattered as part of their early education but is not relevant to the busy life of a professional adult. At the same time, they *do* adopt the Christian way of life through their goodness, honesty, self-sacrifice, and generosity. Although they may not be actively seeking divine support as they do this, the God of Love who was a co-signatory to their baptismal promise has not opted out of their lives.

For Christians, baptism is an invitation to lean on that divine support all through life. It is a commitment to relate with those who share this Earth and care for it as a loving, forgiving human family. This is done in the knowledge that our relationship with the God of Love gives us the energy and shared skills[19] to do this as part of an extended community whose hallmark is love.

The emphasis should not be about do's and don'ts, which can create an unnecessary burden of guilt, but about the breadth and depth of our ability to heal everyday pain through everyday love.[20] This way of life is not for experts. It is for life-long learners. It is not for the perfect. It is for those who are willing

---

[19] Cf Paul's *Letter to the Romans*, Ch. 12: 6-8

[20] Cf Paul's *Letter to the Ephesians*, Ch. 3: 17-19

to say 'sorry' when they fail and pick themselves up and try again.

On this lifelong journey, one of my favourite quotations from the *Postscript* is:

> *Feeling is like the River Niger in Africa –*
> *its source is not known nor its outlet, but only its course.*[21]

Kierkegaard was never in Africa. He only left Denmark five times, four of them to go to Berlin where he studied for his doctorate. His mention of the River Niger is about the course of our feelings. It is part of his challenge to us to explore who we are as unique individuals. The way we manage the course of our feelings can tell us a lot about who we are. It is not the origin or the outcome of the feeling that he wants us to reflect upon. It is about its course. The 'why' behind the feeling invokes the 'how' of what I will decide to do in response to it.

I know that tracing the origins of any great river is a challenge. But we learn a lot as we study its course. Take the world's longest river, the Nile which has known five stages in its evolution so far. It rises somewhere south-west of Lake Victoria, meets six sets of cataracts, then flows for approximately 4,132 miles - touching the shores of Burundi, Congo, Rwanda, Tanzania, Kenya, Uganda, Sudan, Ethiopia, Eritrea, and Egypt. It divides into the White and Blue Nile rivers, which reunite at Khartoum before flowing north to Cairo after which it wriggles its way on till it reaches the Mediterranean.

Pointing to the exact beginning of the Niger is also a challenge but its course is amazing. A small river that begins in the highlands of Guinea flows northeast into Mali. Then it turns south again and flows through all of Niger before it crosses into

---

[21] *Concluding Unscientific Postscript, p.212*

Nigeria, irrigating as it goes, providing transport, working with power stations, while its banks offer a home to a great variety of wildlife. In places, it becomes a network of lakes, streams, marshes, and creeks. I crossed it on several visits to Onitsha, and further northwest near a small village called Barbo. I never crossed it without thinking about the course of my feelings.

The great Niger welcomes many tributaries along its way covering 2,600 miles. Then, as it nears its destination, it divides itself, as if to share its majesty and its magic. My colleagues in our community at Torugbene need a motorboat to bring health services to remote villages as the great River flows past their doorstep on its way through Delta State. On its inexorable journey to the Atlantic Ocean, it also traverses eight other states – Ondo, Abia, Imo, Akwa Ibom, Bayelsa, Cross River, Edo and Rivers State.

Kierkegaard had no idea how his comments on feeling would give rise to a lifelong river of thought for me. Another of his observations that I find nourishing to reflect upon is this:

> *"The evening's farewell to the day*
> *and to the one who has lived the day*
> *is a speech of mysterious meanings.*[22]

Our lives at their very beginning, and at their very end, indeed all along the way, are laced with mystery.

---

[22] Ibid, p.210

POSTSCRIPT 2

THE PHILOSOPHY OF PROSPECTIVE

I BECAME FAMILIAR WITH THE PHILOSOPHY of Gaston Berger in 1974 when an Italian Jesuit, Max Taggi, was travelling the world with a new methodology for facilitating renewal in Catholic parishes and religious communities. It became particularly popular with women religious, who quickly adapted to the imaginative planning it involved, eager to move away from the formal style of boardroom meetings they had inherited.

Max, who spoke fluent English, French and Spanish as well as his native Italian, was a fulltime facilitator with the *Movement for a Better World* (MBW).[1] This movement had been founded by the Italian Jesuit, Riccardo Lombardi in 1952 under the papacy of Pius XII. In 1965 it received Vatican approval for a permanent core group with a mission to promote processes of communitarian renewal in the wake of the Second Vatican Council.

MBW used the ideas of Gaston Berger (1896-1960) to develop methodologies for planning change in Catholic communities. These ideas were creatively adapted for parish planning and missionary commitments.

---

[1] Always referred to as MBW.

Max was invited to facilitate our General Chapter of 1974, which was held in Rome. The following year he asked if I could work with him at the Chapter of another Congregation in England. That began a series of commitments over the next five years. Working with Max was always great fun.

For several years after that I worked in team with experienced sisters and priests – sisters from Notre Dame and Franciscan communities, priests who were Jesuits, Franciscans, and Passionists and from the Society of Missionaries for Africa. In the 1970s we assisted several communities in developing their pastoral plans – in Ireland and the UK, then in the United States, and later in Nigeria – before the invitation came for me to go to India in 1993.

Gaston Berger was born in St. Louis, Senegal – where the University is named after him. He received most of his education in France. Working for some years in industry, his philosophy was grounded in practical matters. Having studied under Maurice Blondel and influenced by the phenomenology of Husserl, he became Professor of Philosophy at the University of Aix-en-Provence in 1944. This was after his engagement in the War effort in France in 1939-40. He combined his studies with his commitments as Regional Director for the Resistance.

After the War, his exceptional talents as a professor and his gift for establishing co-operative relationships internationally, led to his becoming Secretary General of the United States Educational Commission for France, which marked the start of the Fulbright Program in that country. In 1953 he was given responsibility for tertiary education by the French government and modernised the French university system. The establishment in Paris of the International Centre of Prospective Studies continued the development of philosophical studies of the nature of time as something that is not determined but is open.

This is the basic question explored in *Prospective.* Tragically, his life ended in a traffic accident in November 1960.

Berger's philosophy, and the methodologies of future planning which derived from it, had proved successful in the business world. MBW saw that we could add a faith parameter to Berger's wisdom. With theology and Scriptural reflection, *Prospective* had the potential among committed religious groups to be personally renewing for those involved, while also creating imaginative ways to tackle social justice issues.

Two key theological points were identified behind Berger's thinking. One is Creation and the other is Hope.

In past times we tended to look upon Creation as an historical event. Before Vatican II, it was thought that God did this once, for all time, and everything subsequent to that act grew from it. More recently, theologians had seen new and deeper insights into Creation. It was accepted that Creation is an act that is continuously happening. God is continually creating, continually willing the Universe to 'be'. We are not just the objects of Creation, but co-creators. Creation implies a very special partnership between God and us humans.

Hope is important too. The future lies before us. Our attitude towards it depends on our degree of Hope. Making a 'pilgrimage in time', i.e. exploring the future, gives us the possibility of greater freedom than we know now. As we stand here and now, we are bound by the 'immediate'. While we are over-immersed in solving immediate problems, we can be blind to the possibilities of the future.

Berger's concept of the future was important. It is not merely that which follows the present. The future is that which is different from the present, and even more, the future is what is open. Because it is still open, we can determine the future, partly at least. We can build up our own future. Of course, if we do not plan, it will come anyway. We can wait for it to arrive and do nothing. In that case, others will determine how it will be for us. On the other hand, we can be responsible and prepare for the future. We can direct, at least partially, how it will be. That is planning. It is our outlook that will help us shape our future.

There were important principles to be followed in drawing up a methodology:

It must be simple enough for all to learn quickly. It must save time by arranging for different groups to work simultaneously on different subjects. It must ensure that all participants are fully engaged in all stages of decision-making on every subject, whether they are good public speakers or not.

As we evaluated the past and discussed the present, we would begin to look to the future. Every step included an invitation to reflect upon the Scriptural mandate in relation to our situation. Then we would ask "Must the future be the same as the past?" We would leap forward to an imaginary time when our ideal situation was in place. Dreaming? Yes, but not to be dismissed as such. We would challenge the present with that imagined future. We would try to identify the possible and plan towards that goal.

The English edition of *Shaping the Future: Gaston Berger and the Concept of Prospective* introduced me to subjects like 'social science and forecasting', 'the nature of time', and 'education for a world in acceleration'. Now well thumbed, it is the most cherished volume on my bookshelf. This collection of ideas was edited jointly by the Nobel prize-winning cardiologist André

Cournand[2] and the philosopher Maurice Lévy, both of whom had worked with Gaston Berger as his ideas developed.

In 1979 on a visit to New York, I had the opportunity of meeting André Cournand. We had been in correspondence, and he was very interested to know that church groups were using *prospective*. By that time, he had retired from his professorship at Colombia University. However, it was there at the Medical Faculty that he invited me to meet him. Our first encounter was in the library which bore his name. A small-sized gentleman, he still used the white coat worn by any hospital consultant in those days. Though he had become an American citizen, he never renounced his European background nor mastered the pronunciation of English that we are used to. His culture was very French, but his patients and students understood him well.

Soon after that, he and his wife, Beatrice,[3] entertained me at their brown-stone home in New York city. A few years later they invited me to stay with them at their farm at Great Barrington, Massachusetts, where Beatrice taught me that the water should be boiling on the stove before you go outside and pluck the corn from its stem. Another time I had a memorable summer's evening with them at an outdoor performance of *The Tempest* at Tanglewood – the summer residence of the Boston Symphony Orchestra.

---

[2] André Cournand was born in Paris in 1895 and died in USA in 1988. Like Edith Stein and Marie Martin, Ludwig Wittgenstein and Teilhard de Chardin, he had interrupted his studies in 1914 and served for three and a half years at the front as an assistant battalion surgeon. Later in life he revolutionised cardiac surgery, for which he was awarded a Nobel Prize

[3] Cournand's first wife, Sibylle Blumer died in 1959, aged 58. In 1963 he married a research colleague, Ruth Fabian. She died unexpectedly in 1973. Then in 1975 he married Beatrice, a physician herself, who was the widow of his great friend and colleague at Columbia, Alfred A. Berle.

After the performance, this ninety-year-old professor with a long list of distinguished awards drove me carefully along the Turnpike back to Boston. He seemed to be happy in the company of someone who was interested in *prospective* about which we talked a lot. He asked questions too about my faith, the issues of good and evil, my concept of God, and my understanding of an eternal future. This great man died in 1988, so he has all the answers now.

POSTSCRIPT 3

THE DIVIDED HEART

REV. JAIME WRIGHT WAS A VERY WELL-KNOWN Presbyterian minister whose American-born parents had been missionaries in Brazil. He worked tirelessly and secretly with Cardinal Evaristo Arns and Rabbi Henry Sobel, copying one million pages of documentary evidence about 'the disappeared' during the repression of the 1970s. This work led to the publication in 1985 of the book *Brasil Nunca Mais,*[1] a human rights history of the period. Jaime's own brother, Paulo, who had been a State Deputy in Santa Catarina, was one of the 'disappeared', lost without trace.

Jaime and his wife, Alma, became good friends of mine. He was Secretary to the Board of the Ecumenical News Agency, *AGEN,* and we had a lot of contact during my work there. Though Alma and I only met a few times, we spoke quite regularly when I would phone their home to ask Jaime something. In fact, I related with her in much the same way that Edith Stein related with Malvine Husserl. It was a womanish thing. I always felt I had Alma's support.

In 1987, when I was asked to return from Brazil to Ireland, I was given only 48 hours to give my answer. Late that evening the phone rang in our house in Jardim Princesa on the periphery of São Paulo. It was the Regional Leader of our work

[1] Brazil Never Again

in the Americas calling from New York. After the usual pleasantries, I remember her words: "I've just had a call from ..." and the phone line went dead. A few minutes later it rang again. "Sorry about that, the line went down. How are you all? I was telling you I just had..." and down went the line again.

It was bedtime, I remember, and I was tired. It was half an hour before the phone rang for the third time. "The Irish Missionary Union are asking if you would return to Ireland and work there, and they need an answer in two days. Please phone me then." I never knew whether the line dropped or whether she just hung up. This was devastating news.

The days of 'blind obedience' had gone out with Vatican II. The new system was nearly worse! It was called 'discernment'. It was an assignment you chose freely. Leaders would gently ask if you thought it was right for you at that particular time. The burden of decision was on your own shoulders.

I consulted my community in the four small groups we were - dotted around the periphery of São Paulo. That Archdiocese was no longer considered an area of primary mission, and we were researching new areas far to the north and towards the interior of the country, looking at places where we felt we could make a new commitment. When our Regional Leader had come on Visitation from New York some time earlier, she challenged each of us personally: ask yourself 'is all of you being used'? We were all looking at our future, but nobody was considering it might not be in Brazil.

My colleagues were of no help to me at all. They kept throwing the ball back into my own court. Write down ten reasons why you should go, and then ten reasons why you should not, it was suggested. I did so, but that didn't clarify anything for me. My Dad would soon be eighty, and maybe it would be good to be near him as he grew older. But a desk job ... who would want that again! I'd already spent half my life behind a desk.

I phoned Alma Wright and explained to her my sense of confusion. She listened very patiently for a long time as I ran my pros and cons past her. When I stopped talking, she immediately replied: 'You must go. Times are changing and this is the time for you to change too.' She did not hesitate and from that moment neither did I. Then she broke the news to me that she and Rev. Jaime were in the same situation. They had just decided to accept a request from their Leadership to move from São Paulo to Vitória.

The next day I sent my decision to New York, and they sent it on to Dublin. Now the goodbyes. Hardest was my parting with my little dog *Principe.* Would he grasp the significance of this? He was always with me on my rounds and at every meeting. He had his own wire basket secured to the carrier of my Yamaha. Surely, he would miss all that. I resolved that I would never have a dog of my own again.

I was in tears as I said goodbye to my community and parish friends at Guarulhos International Airport. On the flight to Rio, as the hostess was handing me the complimentary orange juice, there was turbulence. Wet and sticky, the juice spilled all down my white jacket. I didn't care. What I looked like wouldn't bother me when I arrived in New York. I would have deeper feelings to deal with. Neither did I care when I discovered that my luggage had not been put on board that commuter flight.

The jet that would take me from Rio's Galeão airport to New York seemed huge. My eyes were stinging. Once boarded, I took out my diary and wrote the lines I headed *Galeão.*

My luggage is not on board
that is to say
letters and gifts, clothes
and other trappings –
perhaps they will come tomorrow
like the airline said …

This seatbelt fastens me in –
that is to say
holds my body here lest I should fly
back where I've been:

São Paulo, people town,
pulse of our poor world's ailing economy
one-time hope of the migrant
now smog-bound stage of the urban myth
my much-loved school
where I've learnt to read
reality – inside and out.

Parting is hard to spell
in Latin America.

We're moving now
this window seat lets me look out
for the eastern ink-blue line
that will herald tomorrow's dawn
but I still look down on
Rio's rain-washed runway.

Its neat-rowed navigation lights
beneath this great jet's roar
burn silently
the color of forget-me-nots.

It was not a long journey from Kennedy airport to our house at City Island from where our work in the Americas was co-ordinated. The community was warm and ensured I lacked nothing, as I awaited the arrival of my luggage in a day or two. But that word 'welcome' – so sincerely uttered – pierced deeply each time I heard it, reopening the wound I was trying to allow to heal. How could I feel welcome when I wasn't myself at all? After a breakfast I barely touched, I escaped upstairs to my room and wrote the lines I headed *En route to reassignment.*

Great silver bird you carry me too far
you soar beyond my limits
too soon you set me down
where I am not –
at least not yet.

You carry passengers like me
people who move slowly
who change at a price
from south to north
from west to east
and otherwise.

You place no worth on
what you'll never hold
that part of us that does not dance
to the sound that calls the flight
that is not bound by place
separated by distance
but rather measures –
in each one differently –
the rhythm of our journey:

That which we hold
and that which we let go

that which we fear
in what we do not know
that which empowers us
to travel yet afar
that which we build together
no matter where we are.

In our long association with Benedictine spirituality, the strength of stability is an important concept. Stability reduces stress and contributes to good mental health. Benedictine monks take a vow of Stability which binds them to live in one Monastery for life. Globe-trotting missionaries couldn't do that! Our Stability is our commitment to our assignment wherever that might be.

During those in-between assignment days, I couldn't wait for the hour when stability would return to my life. The process was slow enough. When I reached Dublin, where I spent most of my growing-up years, the focus was on preparations to celebrate 1988, the millennium of the city's foundation. New coins were being minted but I felt totally disenfranchised despite the joy of seeing my father and family again.

In my parish church in Booterstown, the plush red carpet around the altar gave rise to feelings of total alienation. It felt like a far cry from the carpenter's workshop of Nazareth. At the same time, I couldn't say there was anything wrong with this beautiful church that had stood there for the people through thick and thin for almost two hundred years.

For months I was looking at everything in the northern hemisphere upside down. This was not helped by the fact that at my work in the Irish Missionary Union every day I was hearing of the challenges faced by Irish missionaries in the southern hemisphere. This yo-yo existence continued for months. It felt like my body and my soul were in separate hemispheres.

In that crazy state of mind, I was invited to Nigeria as a facilitator at the MMM Area Assembly. The reflections were to be based on the movie *The Color Purple,* which would be shown at the opening session. I booked an outbound flight to Lagos from Schiphol airport in early February and a return flight at the end of March. At the gate next to mine, a plane for Rio de Janeiro was called and the people sitting beside me got up. Absent-mindedly, I got up and followed them into the queue for the boarding gate. The hostess looked at my boarding card sympathetically. "This flight is for Rio. Your ticket is booked to Lagos", she said. The pain I thought had gone was suddenly back again.

Thankfully, things looked up quickly after that. Days of happy reunion with old friends in Nigeria had great healing properties. When I returned to Booterstown it was Holy Week. Landing in Europe from Africa I was a changed person.

Easter Sunday fell on 3rd April that year. A sheet of paper dated 8th April 1988 bears the heading *In Search of Home:*

January

Millennium lights bedecked the sky
Though winter tides were wild and high
And Dublin's coastline all forlorn
Festivities notwithstanding.

February-March

'Springtime' they called St. Brigid's Day
A cock-step stretched each welcome morn
But most of me was far from home
As Carnaval was pending.

At Amsterdam they called a flight
For Rio – was I hearing right?
They boarded it a gate away
But I was bound for Lagos.

Through Amekoko's mega-slum
And Mafoluku's laden heat
Ibadan's million hot tin roofs
Okitipupa's winding creek.

Late night discussions in Benin
Of suffering caused by structured sin
And how transform each woman's pain
To freedom soon gestating.

April

The palms are blessed and Holy Week
With rites of reconciling peace
And broken bread and word revealed
Prepare the way for freedom's seed.

The women find the stone unrolled
On resurrection's magic morn
As death lets go of every hold
With freedom's brand-new dawn.

In sunshine Dublin's coast is warm
A new world's ancient town
And all of me has found a home
In freedom's victory born.

POSTSCRIPT 4

TWO FRIENDS CALLED MAURA

As a teenager in the Boarding School run by the Presentation Sisters in Mountmellick, Maura O'Donohue was present when the film *Visitation* was shown. A classmate of hers was a day pupil who lived in Mountmellick, Maura Ramsbottom. As the film ended and the credits rolled up the screen, Maura O'Donohue decided she would become a Medical Missionary of Mary as soon as she finished her secondary education. The film had what the famous French catechist, Pierre Babin, would call 'modulation' – a certain quality of physical vibration, using vision and sound, producing psychological effects.

Maura Ramsbottom went off to train as a primary school teacher and enjoyed a carefree life for several years before she, too, decided her calling was elsewhere. Although a few years older than me, these two Mauras became my closest life-long friends. Another teenager who was present at the film that day was Nano Rhatigan. She also was touched by the 'modulation', joined MMM, and studied dietetics. We later worked together in Tanzania.

Maura R, as she was known everywhere, shared a flat in Dublin with a few other young teachers. She taught in an inner-city school. One day the Diocesan Examiner called to see how much the children whom Maura was preparing for First Holy Communion actually understood. Maura stood back and let him take the centre floor as he put his questions to the children. 'Who would like to tell me the story of Adam and Eve?' he asked. A little boy shot up his hand straight away.

> *There was this beautiful garden and God made Adam and Eve and put them in it, and they were havin' a great time. It was a smashin place. They could eat all the oranges and pears and bananas they wanted. But God said they were not to eat the apples, not even at Halloween. Then a great big ugly snake came along. He told Eve to try the apples and she did. And she gave a bite to Adam. God was mad angry with them for not doin' like he told them and ... and ... and ..."*

Everyone waited, holding their breath to hear what happened next. "That's very good", said the young priest, trying not to put pressure on the little fellow. "Can you remember what happened next?" The little Dubliner racked his brains and then he rushed it out:

> *"God was mad angry with them, so he was, and he sent the pair of them down the country, and they had to live there for the rest of their lives."*

Maura and her teacher friends planned carefully their first holiday together in Italy. They spent a while in Naples and Maura fell in love with Capri. The others all got married and never saw Capri again. But Maura got back there many times during her studies in Rome. She absolutely loved Italy. In those days, we were staffing the *Clinica Mediterranea* in Naples, and Maura went down there from Rome between terms. From there it was only a short hop over to Capri.

Once, when we were working together in our Central Administration team, she asked me to help her to book a tour of Africa for a series of scripture studies she had been asked to conduct for all our communities. It took many weeks of correspondence before we could plan that journey. It could not be done 'as the crow flies' because the communities had other priorities and could not be free for Maura's course at the time that suited us best. It had to be fitted in with their other commitments, student nurses' examinations, and so on. This meant Maura had to zig-zag a bit. When we went to the Travel Agent in Dublin to make the bookings, the young woman who sat down with us just could not understand. "But if you are going to Angola, you should go there after Nigeria, not fly over to Malawi and then back west again." Yes, we knew the geography of Africa, and we knew that would be more economical, but there was no use going to Angola when the communities were not available.

I had planned the final flight of this trip back to Ireland from Angola through Rome. 'Wouldn't it be more direct and cheaper through Lisbon?' Maura had asked me. I replied: 'Why would you come any other way than you have always chosen?' When I went to pay the deposit, I told the travel agent to allow three days before her last flight from Rome to Dublin, knowing Maura would relish a few days to herself in the eternal city.

Maura was a great teacher, a biblical genius who was much in demand. However, she had her limitations. Once, while on home leave in Ireland, she spent a few days with her aunt, whose family had a pub in Athy, Co. Kildare. I also stayed with her over that pub on another occasion when we were passing by on holidays.

One morning after Mass in the local parish, her aunt stopped to talk to a neighbour. They both had small grandsons with them. The boys got a bit bored as Maura's aunt was telling her friend all the wonderful things Maura could do and all the faraway places where she had been working. Maura felt embarrassed. She didn't recognize herself in the description, and felt it was a bit 'over the top'. Then she overheard her nephew tell the other little boy the discovery he had made the night before: "She can't do the Rubik Cube ... hasn't even read the book!"

During my final year in Maynooth, I stayed there all summer completing my Master's thesis on *Responsibility and Revolution*. The other students had all gone home, so it was a lonely place. The early Fathers of the Church up in the College Library had a lot to say on the subject, but I found their writings, all in Latin, a poor substitute for human company.

Maura came over to stay with me for a week. She knew well I was flagging in my attempt. Each day she would read what I had written and give me her comments, usually very challenging but assuring me it would be worth the effort. Sunday came and it was time for her to return to Drogheda. I remember it was a very hot summer's day. After lunch we walked to the bus stop in the main street. When she boarded the bus and I waved her goodbye, I turned to walk back to my studies alone. It struck me then, like a thunderbolt: Heaven is presence - the eternal presence of Love. Hell, if such exists, must be eternal absence.

Maura had what you could only call an addiction to Nigeria and its people. One day in Lagos, I asked her "Are you the only expatriate on the DELES team?" To her it was quite an irrelevant question, and she was slow grasping what I wanted to know. I watched as she closed her eyes and nodded her head ten times in a circular motion – as if going around a circle of people at a meeting. Then she opened her eyes and replied: "Oh yes, I must be - why did you ask?"

Reflecting on the encounter in John's Gospel between Jesus and the Woman at the Well,[1] Maura would ask her students: What kind of world does this conversation between Jesus and the Samaritan woman open up for us?

It is a world of dialogue, she would say, where questions are encouraged, and even unasked questions do not pass unnoticed. An understanding of dialogue and the readiness to engage in it is the key to truly receiving the message of Vatican II. The church is in the contemporary world, the Council states, and must be involved in the two-way process which dialogue implies.

True dialogue calls for respect for each one involved in the process. It calls for a commitment to try to understand the perspective from which the 'other' speaks or acts and, above all, it involves a genuine openness to understanding their age, education, beliefs, and lifestyle. It is a world where we recognize what needs to be left behind and are prepared to leave it. It is a world of adventure, a world of risk, a world that changes constantly.

She would also draw on the spiritual school of St. Benedict in which the work of the Medical Missionaries of Mary is grounded. Benedict specifies the importance of listening with 'the ear of the heart'. Edith Stein and her contemporary philosophers would later name this the gift of empathy. Maura would give an example of that:

> *It is the art of deep listening. Imagine a large group in a room. Among them is the mother of a baby, and the baby is in another room. If the baby makes even the smallest sound the*

---

[1] Jn 4:7-26.

mother is likely to be the person who hears it before anyone else because she is listening with 'the ear of her heart'.

Years later I was making my fifth visit to Malta, researching the places where Marie Martin worked during WW1. I was helped by Emmanuel and Josephine Balzan, the parents of Irene, one of our two Maltese sisters. They kindly offered me their holiday apartment in Bugibba each time I went. That year, Maura was in Ireland on leave from Nigeria when I was making my booking. 'Would your piggy bank allow a budget-flight to Malta?' I asked her. She said it would and off we went. Irene's Dad met us at the airport, where he was an engineer, and drove us to Bugibba.

In vain could I keep Maura's attention on the reason for my visit there. She was too deeply attached to Saint Paul to have a heart for much else. Time was scarce to cover all I needed to do, but to satisfy her, I agreed to investigate the possibility of a visit to the small island where Paul had been shipwrecked. It is described very graphically in Acts of the Apostles by Luke,[2] who must have been with him on that voyage. Tourists could visit the island if they had purchased an expensive all-day trip on a cruiser that would take them to many islands including Gozo. That was not in our budget, and we didn't have the time even if we had the money.

We left our research around St. George's Bay and took the bus further along the coast to St. Paul's Bay where we found a fisherman mending his nets on the slipway. I told him my plight. No problem. Come back in an hour and we'll take you over. It was just a short distance across the bay – should take less than half an hour to get there. Maura was 'over the moon'.

---

[2] Cf Acts Ch 27 and 28.

We went off and had coffee – another of her Italian cultural delights. When we returned to the slipway, the fisherman had the row-boat ready for us. He introduced us to his 13-year-old son who would take us out to the island. Maura was not a swimmer. She looked at me a little nervously as we got into the boat. "Don't worry", I assured her, "I've done a course in life saving." When we stepped on to the island, she forgot I was even there. She was in another universe - completely absorbed by the spot where Paul had been shipwrecked.

I was very concerned about a bad cough she had and begged her to get it investigated before returning to Nigeria. But all I would be told is 'it's much better today'. With all our medical skill, how nobody could stop her leaving our Motherhouse for Africa a few weeks later, I will never understand.

The two Mauras didn't see a lot of one another after they both finished their theology studies in Rome shortly after Vatican II until about 2006 when we were all back in Ireland. Sadly, Maura R had returned from Lagos to have the health check she should have had much sooner. It might have been too late even then. This was the first time the two Mauras and I were together in Ireland after nearly forty years of work abroad.

When she came to visit our house in Dublin, to celebrate, as a surprise we had booked a table in an Italian pizzeria in Wicklow Street. We knew she would love that, and she did. We went to evening Mass in Clarendon Street first. I didn't cop on when she was unable to read the menu, telling me she needed to get her reading glasses changed. Maura O'D understood more than I did. After the meal we drove her back to Drogheda. Getting into the car for our return journey to Dublin, Maura O'D breathed a sigh of relief. 'She is much too ill for us to be able to manage', she said. Very soon after that Maura R was admitted to Beaumont Hospital in Dublin.

In south County Dublin there is a shopping mall in Cabinteely where its founder, Ben Dunne and his wife, had built a small Oratory. There was Mass there each weekday at 4.30 pm. Maura O'D and I were just leaving the Oratory when my phone rang. Maura R told us the news she had just been given. Primary cancer in her lungs had spread to her brain. That is why she was falling so frequently. That is why she had not been able to read the pizza menu.

Now that the news was confirmed, we were heartbroken. We should not have been shocked, but we were shaken. Before going to the carpark, we called to the nearby pharmacy and bought a little canister of Arnica tablets to help steady us as we faced the evening traffic - known in Ireland as the 'rush hour' or more accurately in Nigeria as the 'go slow'. An accident somewhere caused a long tailback, and it took us two hours to drive across the city to Beaumont.

After greeting Maura R in her bed, I went down to the Chapel for an hour, while Maura O'D drew on her medical knowledge as they went through the options together following the booklet provided by the Oncology department. The two Mauras agreed it should be palliative care rather than surgery. "Sure look", said Maura R when I returned and heard her decision: "I've had seventy-five great years. I'll be ready to move on to what is waiting next when the time comes. Just pray the drugs keep my brain working as normally as possible for as long as I am here. That is all I ask."

For all of us, the remaining months of her life were very difficult. Maura had no siblings, but her cousins would come and go, and we would talk about the loss that we were facing. No more hilarious dinners in the Clontarf Golf Club where they were members and had occasionally invited us to mark special occasions. Her cousin gave me a packet of papers. He said they were precious. It contained Maura's early correspondence with Mother Mary Martin and some drafts of her theological writings which had been stored in their attic.

Before she transferred from our Motherhouse Infirmary to our nearby nursing facility, Áras Mhuire,[3] several friends were helping her pack her things for the move. The last day I visited her in the Infirmary, she handed me a sheaf of papers saying with serious, pleading eyes: "Will you finish this job for me? I've taken it as far as I can". It was her research on the early correspondence of our foundress. As I left the room she called after me: "Be careful with all that stuff". I didn't turn as I didn't want to upset her with my tears.

Maura had spent those otherwise difficult months confined to bed in the Infirmary pondering over all the collected correspondence of Mother Mary Martin. She selected brief quotations that would be a source of energy for busy missionaries, whose days rarely allow much time for reading.

Back at my office, I phoned my graphic artist and asked him to come over. I showed him the work Maura had completed and told him what we needed. I explained that the final product would have to be compact enough to be delivered to each member of our communities around the world. Brendan knew exactly what had to be done.

Back in his studio he designed small cards, three inches square, on which the quotations could be printed back and front, each one bearing a unique number and the year in which that letter had been written. He told me I'd find a man in a small workshop at the back of a house at the back of the Cherry Tree pub in Walkinstown. He would design little folding plastic boxes that would hold the cards. I drove over there next day

---

[3] The Irish words for 'The Residence of Mary'.

and met this other artist with a different set of skills who designed exactly what was needed. Maura was very happy to see the finished job.

Christmas and New Year came and went. We were now into 2007. When I called to see Maura in late January, she was feeble, but able to walk as far as the door with me as I was leaving. She said, "I'd say it will be about three days from now before I move on". "You'll be fine then", I replied. "Meet you later", and we hugged our final *au revoir*.

Three days later, in the afternoon, the call she was eagerly expecting came. It was the 25th of January, the Feast of St. Paul – the same one who was shipwrecked on that small island off the coast of Malta, and who gave his name to that great city in Brazil, the same place where I learned to read reality.

POSTSCRIPT 5

CLARE WOMAN OF THE YEAR

When Maura O'Donohue was nominated Clare Woman of the Year I was invited to the presentation ceremony as a guest. She had been my close friend for almost fifty years but for thirty-five of them we were rarely on the same continent at the same time.

Once, we had a coffee together between flights at Heathrow, she flying East and I going West. Her work over many years took her to 83 countries. I can list them all. She was so often abroad she held three current Passports because two of them would likely be in some Embassy waiting for a Visa. And some Embassies might not like to know she had been in certain countries they didn't think were so nice. Maura thought they were all wonderful places. Grozny in Chechnya was the place where she felt most overwhelmed by a sense of helplessness though the local people there inspired her no end.

After the Award Ceremony dinner Maura was asked to share some of her reminiscences. She told them about the time she was researching the needs of rural communities for the Ministry of Health in Ethiopia. Her specialisation was in International Community Medicine. She carefully drew up her research questions, and mapped the territory they would cover, bought the tents they would need for their months visiting the remote villages, and so on. Given the terrain, she was surprised when the questionnaires the staff were compiling showed the unanimous responses to the question: "Are your roads (a) mud roads, (b) graded roads or (c) all-weather roads?" She asked the staff to return to the village and check about that. "The respondents confirmed they are all-weather roads", she was told. "The people told us these are the only roads they have, and they use them in all weathers."

"Tell us another story", our hosts asked when the applause died down. She took the microphone again and told them about the time she was joined by a visiting researcher on her travels in Ethiopia. The area was home to people who survived in the most sparse conditions. As they left one small dwelling and walked on along the narrow path, the visitor asked: "Do you often leave a family without being given a gift?" Maura replied: "Did you notice anything in that home that they might have used as a gift for me? It is unusual to call to a home where they don't have coffee to offer while I complete my survey. That family where we had visited were among the poorest of the poor."

They walked on for half a mile or so, when they heard a man's voice calling them from behind. It was the father of the previous homestead they had visited. They turned and walked back to meet him. He smiled and handed Maura an egg. "We felt so badly that we had to let you go on your way without any gift for your journey. But after you left our hen laid an egg – here you are, please accept it."

A first cousin of Maura's was a priest in the Archdiocese of Dublin. One day I called to visit Fr. Michael O'Donoghue when he was Parish Priest of Kill o' the Grange. I asked him was the story I had heard true. He confirmed that one day when he happened to be passing Drogheda he decided to drop in to our

Motherhouse and see if Maura might be there. He explained to the young lady receptionist that he was her cousin. Then he waited quite a while as she went off to enquire. He said it was true that, when she returned, she told him Maura was not there and nobody knew where she was. She added: "The community leader rang London, but they don't know either. Maybe on your way back to Dublin you should drop in to the Airport and get her paged. She just might be there or at least they might be able to give you some information. They would know more than we know here, and they are always very helpful whenever we are looking for a Sister."

From 2003 for twelve years, Maura and I had the happiness of living and working and travelling together until her final diagnosis with leukaemia in September 2014. Maura had entered medical school at University College Dublin in 1950 and lived in the MMM student house at Rosemount before her novitiate. A few months after she began her 'pre-med', a young friend from Kilfenora took the train to Dublin and made his way to Rosemount. He asked her for the umpteenth time was she sure she was doing the right thing? But she had found her North Star and reminded him that there are lots of good fish in the sea. She graduated from University College Dublin in 1957.

There were three MMMs in that group of students. Anne Ward and Deirdre Twomey both went on to obtain Fellowships in Obstetrics & Gynaecology and devoted their entire lives to the people of Nigeria. Their classmates also included Dom Colbert, whose later work in Africa became legendary, and Sister-doctor Carmel Garvey of the St. Louis Congregation.

Maura's first assignment as a junior doctor was to Anua in Nigeria. There she was able to avail of the ongoing tuition provided by Sister-doctor Margaret Mary Nolan, a snatch of whose story is included in Chapter 2. Maura made her final profession of vows there in 1959. When our foundress arrived in October that year, she asked Maura to be her companion on the rest of her tour of all existing missions and all those to which she had been invited to establish new services. The rest of that story is also told in Chapter 2.

During the Christmas holidays of 1969 Maura told me she felt called to contemplative life. She wanted MMM to start a contemplative branch which she would be willing to get going. Many years earlier, our foundress had spoken to her about this, saying it was a dream she hoped one day would become a reality. A small number would live there with a life-long commitment. Others could go there for a shorter period to recover and refresh after strenuous and sometimes dangerous work overseas.

Maura thought the time had come to act on this dream of our foundress. Her request was declined, but she was advised to go and investigate a number of Benedictine communities in Europe to which she could transfer. I was devastated! Her spiritual director was a monk at Glenstal, Dom Columba Breen, whom I greatly respected. He had written about the early days which forged close ties between our foundation and his monastery, which he summed up with the words: "These are the deep designs of God that we dare not call coincidence".[1]

Maura wrote to me often from various Benedictine monasteries over those months - more than one hundred pages of handwritten letters. I was still studying at Maynooth and was hugely concerned. "I wonder if Dom Columba is looking at the whole picture?", I asked myself. A vocation is not entirely a personal matter. In any walk of life, it is a gift to more than

[1] Cf *The First Decade*, p13.

the individual who feels attracted to deploy their talents in one way or another for the service of others.

During holidays in Drogheda that Easter my parents came to visit me. "Would you like to go for a drive?" my Dad asked. Would I what ...? Never one to miss a God-given opportunity, I replied "Sure, let's go to Glenstal. There's someone down there I'd love to see." My parents were both turning 60, which I thought was much too old to drive a journey of 155 miles each way. My Dad agreed to let me take the wheel.

When we reached the monastery, I rang the bell and asked to see Dom Columba. My parents held hands and went for a walk in the magnificent grounds. I told Dom Columba what I thought, what Maura had written to me about her discernment, and I begged him to consider the bigger picture, which he did. Maura returned to Ireland soon after that, ready for the work she now knew was hers to do for the rest of her life.

Decades later I asked her how she felt now about the contemplative life, and she replied: "I think I understand it a bit better now. Monastic life is important for the Church and for the world. But everyone doesn't have to be in a monastery to be contemplative." In the months before she died, I confessed to her about that visit to Dom Columba, and that I still had all the letters she wrote to me at that time. She wanted to read the letters, but I told her the handwriting was illegible. I saw no need to go back there now. She agreed that I had probably done the right thing in going to Glenstal that Sunday. I knew for certain that I had.

As a young doctor, Maura had suffered cerebral malaria in Nigeria which nearly took her life. She was rushed back to Drogheda where the Consultant in the Tropical Unit advised that the only country in Africa that would be suitable for her was Ethiopia. After fourteen years there[2] she was recalled to Europe and took up work with CAFOD as the problem of AIDS was hitting the world. She travelled extensively giving workshops to religious communities, seminarians, priests, and healthcare workers. It was on one of these trips that the problem of the abuse of religious sisters by priests was brought to her attention. She told me: "The superior of one diocesan congregation stood up and shook her fists at me and begged me to bring this issue to Rome and get a solution."

On her return to London, Maura brought this to the attention of Cardinal Basil Hume who asked her to write a report to be submitted to the Vatican. When she did so and was summoned to Rome, Cardinal Hume asked one of his Auxiliary Bishops to accompany her, along with the Director of CAFOD. Maura would never speak about her report except to colleagues in professional dialogue, but it was shared with women religious leaders who were members of the International Union of Superiors General (UISG) in Rome.

They were gravely concerned. When no immediate action was taken by the Vatican, after a while they became impatient. Some of those leaders decided to release Maura's report to the *National Catholic Reporter* in Washington, DC. Publicly, Maura continued to maintain her silence. As a medical doctor, she felt bound by the Hippocratic Oath not to speak about information that came to her attention in the course of her professional work. She received an amount of hate mail from people who could not face the truth and felt it should not be revealed, much less explored for the protection of victims. For the next twenty years, Maura bravely bore this suffering. Many years later I

---

[2] See also below on Stories of War: Ethiopia.

read in the Dictionary of Irish Biography: "In February 2019 Pope Francis's announcements on the sexual abuse of women religious by catholic clergy brought her to international attention as major international publications – including the *New York Times* and *Die Zeit* – referenced her ground-breaking 1994 report."[3]

At the beginning of Maura's final illness, we were still living in Booterstown. In St. Vincent's Hospital, I sat at her bedside the evening she was given the diagnosis that her condition was incurable. She thought the Consultant said 'five weeks' but I think she may have got that wrong. That night we spent a long time selecting the readings for her funeral Mass. A few days later, on September 8th, she would move to Áras Mhuire, the nursing facility beside our Motherhouse in Drogheda. Trying to be cheerful as we walked to the car, I said: "Remember you and I left our homes another year on September 8th to go to Drogheda."[4] She replied: "This is part of the same blank cheque we signed the day we did that."

We had been working on a joint assignment, researching the development of the charism of MMM. Our team included our colleague, Sister-doctor Geneviève van Waesberghe, who was still working among communities in the Great Lakes Region of Africa. We were in regular contact by email. Working from a tiny folding table in the corner of Maura's room we got our book to the printer by Christmas.

When Maura woke each morning, she would text me to say it was time to come. When Easter was near and as leukaemia increasingly took over, she would sometimes ask me to pray quietly with her, apart from sharing the Divine Office as we

---

[3] See Dictionary of Irish Biography at www.dib.ie.

[4] She made the journey in 1950 and I did so in 1961.

did three times every day. She asked if we could afford to buy a little bottle of cologne for each of the staff who were caring for her. I bought these and little greeting cards on which she signed a personal message for each of them.

Often, she would say to me as I was helping her from her wheelchair into the car to go out for a coffee some morning or for a sunset drive along the banks of the River Boyne: "This dying business is very difficult."

From the day she was first given her diagnosis the previous September, she asked me to ensure that no extraordinary measures would be taken to keep her alive. "I want to die naturally in this bed", she said very emphatically. The day we arrived at *Áras Mhuire* she had made this very clear on her admission form and signed a 'do not resuscitate' mandate.

By the time Easter came around the Palliative Care team had taken over. We knew it wouldn't be long now. Maura's niece who was a Nurse Manager in Navan Hospital, came over to Drogheda on many evenings. I was so glad to see her coming. After she left, I would wheel Maura up to the dining room and make a cup of tea. We called this our nightly visit to the Royal Hotel. After that we would spend a short time in the Oratory. Back in her room at 9.45, we would play a CD from a Benedictine community of sisters in Belgium and listen together to their singing of Night Prayer before I left.

Maura's relatives in Dublin, would come quite often too, as did her two brothers who travelled from County Clare now and then to spend a few hours with her. Several times a week we would have video calls to her sister in Cleveland, Ohio. Those eight months passed as happily as any road towards the call of death can be.

In the last days of April, the Nurse Manager asked if I would like an armchair in Maura's room where I could nod off during the night hours. No dying resident of Áras Mhuire was ever left alone. Members of our Motherhouse community would come and stay a while and then quietly leave, whispering to me to call them if I wanted company during the night. Before dawn on May 3rd, having spent three or four quiet nights by her bedside, I was aware that in Nairobi - two hours ahead of us - the delegates to our General Chapter which would close that morning would be gathering for breakfast. As I opened my laptop to write them an email, I noticed Maura had just drawn her last breath.

She had promised that she would always be at my shoulder to call upon whenever I needed help. 'Which shoulder?' I asked. 'That one', she replied pointing to the left. I booked the top space in the same grave, where our mutual friend, Maura R, had already been buried.

'You will not be laid to rest', I had often warned each of them during their final days. 'You must spend your heaven doing good on Earth.' Two weeks after the funeral of Maura O'D, while I was dealing with my sense of loss in the *Tearmann* healing centre in Glendalough, a little-known ailment I had since childhood disappeared forever. I figured Maura was telling me that heaven is indeed all we hoped it would be.

POSTSCRIPT 6

WAR STORIES

FROM THE FIRST WORLD WAR TO THE PRESENT TIME, war has been a sad and tragic theme in the exciting adventure of the Medical Missionaries of Mary. In the course of my eighteen years in our Communications Department, I asked a number of my colleagues to tell me about their personal experiences of war to share with our readers and donors. Previous editors of our publications had done likewise.

Nigeria 1968

The civil war began on 6 July 1967 and ended on 10 January 1970. Looking back some years later, Frederick Forsyth, former RAF pilot and investigative journalist, author of best-selling thriller novels, wrote:

> *At the very heart of the vortex was a group of Catholic and Protestant missionaries, with their local colleagues, women and men who, but for the war, would probably have continued in humble and anonymous pastoral work among their people until called away by age, infirmity or God. But strange events often produce the needed people. Some remained inside the fighting enclave, shepherding their flocks away from the firing lines, running the feeding centres, refugee homes and orphanages, tending the sick ... appealing*

for help, distributing relief food and giving many the Last Rites.

He wrote disparagingly of those authorities who had never heard

the rattle of machine guns between the palms,
the crack of mortar in a crowded village square,
the singing hiss of an incoming bomb
nor the whimper of a dying child.

In October 1968 our annals recorded: "Coming ... coming ... coming ... everyone could see war coming ... The stillness of the quiet, dark sky was disturbed by a crackling ball of fire that left a trail behind it ..." This was the climax to a long series of signs of approaching war. It was no longer coming – it was here.

At the beginning of hostilities, we operated general and maternity hospitals, training schools, all with numerous out-stations attached, four hospitals in Calabar Diocese, one in Ikot Ekpene Diocese, seven hospitals as well as many Leprosy Settlements in Ogoja Diocese. The warfront has passed through all of these with varying degrees of hardship and war damage. No Sister suffered personal physical injury. The present position is that all our missions are still to the good, though all impaired, naturally, some of them more so than others.

Our nursing Training Schools, except at Ogoja and Ikom, are out of operation at the moment. Staffed by 38 MMMs and those they have trained, all our places except three are still 'in production'. The great heartbreak of the Sisters staffing them is the frustration of so much food and drugs 'so near and yet so far' – only a trickle is getting through.

Sister Mechtilde Robinson was assigned to Ikom Joint Hospital in 1967. She recalled:

A few months later bombs fell, and we knew there was war. The army came to Ikom from Obudu. One morning we found that all the staff and patients had left the hospital. We stayed on to mind the hospital with the help of some staff living nearby and the Holy Child sisters joined us. Bishop McGettrick visited us to make sure we were alright. Because the army was coming to take over, the Blessed Sacrament was removed to a safe place and the light was switched off. This was very sad.

Sister Áine Lucey gave the following account of her 1968 experiences in Ikom to our Editor in 1972. At that time, for her security, it was published without specifying who told the story:

For some time, political unrest was mounting. Minorities began to move back to their region of origin, and we began to experience an influx of refugees. Many of these refugees were not natives of the area but had come in search of employment. Soon everyone was suspect. There was tension and more tension and at times frayed nerves. Our compound was constantly searched for infiltrators, houses were searched, people were detained for questioning. Even missionaries were detained on one or two occasions. There were many checkpoints on the roads. We only travelled when it was absolutely essential and always heaved a sigh of relief when we came within a radius of about fifteen miles or so of our own station and were greeted with a friendly smile and 'Welcome Sister'.

Many people carried guns, real or mock, and mass demonstrations were the order of the day. Some parts of the country were still practically completely unaffected by these events. The military leader very aptly described the situation when he said, 'We continue to live under explosive tension guised in treacherous calm.' The business world continued to function as though all was normal. Our thoughts were distracted for a time by the announcement that an epidemic of smallpox and meningitis was feared. Mass vaccination campaigns were arranged. Soon our first case was admitted. When it became evident that we were within the epidemic zone, we erected a canvas tent at the far end of the compound in a successful effort to contain the dreadful disease and prevent it from spreading to other patients. Most of these smallpox patients were refugees or people who had close contact with them.

One calm evening when we came out from supper, the stillness of the quiet dark sky was disturbed by a small crackling ball of fire that left a trail behind it. A rocket? A fall-out from a satellite? It did not resemble a falling star. Each one had her guess. The next day we learned that it was soldiers at the border informing the capital city of the Region that war had started. We wondered what next. Strangely enough, tension snapped. Soon we were informed by the army that our hospital would be used as a casualty clearance station. Two army doctors were sent to take up duty but there were no casualties. When we questioned them, they told us, like good soldiers, that they were following instructions and knew nothing. We began to grow accustomed to explosions in the distance – to the extent of even persuading ourselves that they might be caused by hunters in the bush or blasting in the quarry. Then, suddenly, all the children and practically all the women were evacuated from the area. The missionaries were the only expatriates left and the people did not conceal their deep admiration and gratitude. The hospital staff seemed to be completely unaffected by the mass exodus. Not even one member resigned and the vast majority of them were from distant places. They remained, cheerfully and willingly carrying out their duties.

When war came, we knew its horrors! One Sunday morning when we returned from Mass we noticed a bus outside the hospital. We had never seen a bus in the area before. We took a hurried breakfast and went on duty. For the first time we witnessed the gruesome effects of war. From now on, subjects which to us had been the topic of a novel or film were to become stark cruel reality – no glamour but plenty of challenge. It was an experience which I now greatly appreciate, and which proved most educative. We were to witness the horrors and widespread effects of treachery and betrayal side by side with stalwart patriotism, warm generosity and courage. Noble heroic deeds gave us courage and a new will to continue in the face of difficulties. Most of the soldiers who were admitted to the hospital were Catholics, the vast majority of them excellent ones, who took advantage of their visit to hospital to receive the Sacraments. Missionary priests who still lived in the area were able to hear their confessions and attend to the dying at the battle front. Later, displaced indigenous priests and clergy of other Christian faiths were appointed army chaplains and this relieved considerably the burden of the overworked missionaries.

Our hospital was now indeed a military hospital. Only one ward was left for civilians. Extra beds were put up in every available space and we also had the use of five houses outside the hospital for battle casualties. New procedures had to be adopted. Instructions to our patients included: 'Please unload your gun and check the barrel'. The most able-bodied of the patients were requested to deposit guns, rounds of ammunition, and hand grenades at the office before going to the wards. An officer collected the remainder. As well as dispensing medicine and looking after the patients' physical and spiritual needs we had to boost morale. Morale was of paramount importance.

Although we experienced extreme suffering, life was not without its bright side. We received courage from each other and supported one another. Once 'the boys' got over their initial pain and fatigue, they were usually ready for a chat and a joke. We endeavoured to have a film twice a week for them, but they only appreciated war films from which they could learn tactics. Sometimes we played records and the more able-bodied danced. But the 80 soldiers were never off duty. They were always alert for a strange sound, a plane, or distant shooting.

The shelling started unusually early one morning. They seemed to be prepared to keep at it non-stop. For days now it had been coming gradually nearer, but today it instilled fear into every heart. When we went on duty at 7.30 am, we were not greeted with the usual cheery welcome. Those who were well enough were fully dressed, awaiting orders to go to the Front. Every man was on edge and alert. We took consolation from the fact that a large bridge, which we knew to be mined, lay between us and the advancing army. Retreating soldiers arrived in large numbers soon after we went on duty. They were exhausted, dejected, down-hearted men. They had spent weeks in the trenches without a break, the sound of shelling blasting their eardrums, often without food or water or a night's sleep.

Soon there was a tremendous explosion. A helicopter on a bombing mission had exploded and disintegrated almost immediately after take-off. This dampened morale considerably. The casualties soon poured in, most of them suffering excruciating pain as well as extreme mental anguish. Many of them were deaf or dumb or both, from shell shock. Some were at death's door. Others went to their Creator just on arrival or shortly before it. That day morale was extremely low, the will to fight was gone. The men were completely played out and exhausted. Soon there was another large explosion. We knew it was the bridge. This meant our people had lost a village.

We continued to receive heavy casualties throughout the afternoon. Just before nightfall we received our orders. Everyone was to leave the area before morning as it was within shelling range. We joined the band of wandering refugees and had that most frustrating experience of being displaced persons. It was an education in itself and taught us how little we really understood the drives and instincts, the anxiety and anguish which lay behind these people's surface behaviour and emotional reactions. But our suffering was not as intense as that of the native people. There were many convents on the periphery of the battle zone where a warm welcome, a good meal, and shelter always awaited us. At night we could rest peacefully in clean bed linen.

Our indigent refugees had to trek their weary way for many miles until well outside the war zone where they would meet a refugee camp where conditions according to any standard, were often appalling – overcrowding, bad sanitation, scanty food, disease already prevalent. Or they would return to their village of origin, if, fortunately, it was in a peaceful area, where their kith and kin gladly shared their frugal meals and earthly possessions with them, pleased to know that at least a few more women and children were safe. Some of these people had had to flee at least twice previously.

We all shared the relief of being away, at least for the time being, from the noise of the battle front. There were no clouds of smoke in the distance, but we no longer had firsthand information of how the fighting was going. We lived in fear and wonder. All, irrespective of creed or nationality, entertained a common desire that God would hasten the day when 'mercy and faithfulness shall meet each other, justice and peace shall embrace'.

Sister Christine Gill recalls that it was April 1968 when Afikpo was bombed and one of our nurses was among the first fatalities. This was heartbreaking for all the Sisters and staff at the hospital. Years later Sister Christine told me:

We were very busy as we had many casualties and no time to grieve for our lovely Rose. I remember fighter jets were spraying bullets. We were in the middle of an operation in the theatre when the windows were blown in, so we had to leave and take cover. Another very loyal staff nurse we had was Felicia, who insisted on travelling with the Sisters whenever we had to go out. She felt it was better for us to have a local person with us who could speak on our behalf. She was with us when we were all captured and marched to the river. I remember we had a white pillowslip that we waved as a sign of surrender. As we walked along silently, a young soldier took a rosary beads from his pocket and asked Sr. Sarto to bless it for him. She made the Sign of the Cross over it, and he said, 'Thank you Mam'.

On arrival at the beach, we wondered 'What next?' A small group of high-ranking soldiers were waiting for us. Mosquitoes and sandflies were not an issue at this stage. One said, 'How will we get the Godly people across the river?' Another said, 'Make them swim it'. Another said, 'I want no trouble with their Jesus and their Peter'. Eventually, Felicia cried out 'we no fit use gun'. It resonated with one officer. His grandmother lived in the same village she came from. They got canoes to take us across the river. As darkness fell, it felt like a

Gospel scene. Felicia remained with us when a Land Rover was brought to move us to Ugep. She remained for a while before moving back to her home village.

For two months we lived like the wonderful local people, going to the river as they did for all our needs. Several years later when we were back in Afikpo and had got the hospital back to normal, visitors came to see us one day and introduced us to their baby son. It was our former staff nurse Felicia, and her husband – the army officer who had ordered the canoes to take us over the river.

Dr. Godfrey Hinds had filled the post of General Surgeon at Afikpo since 1949. Sister Deirdre Twomey was Obstetrician & Gynaecologist. They were among the motley crowd taken prisoner that day at the hospital. Years later Deirdre let me photograph pages and diagrams from her Diary, some of which was written in the Irish language lest it be seized at a checkpoint. She told me:

On looking back now, I can say that being able to stay on with the people through the war was a tremendous privilege. It was frightening when we experienced the bombs, the bullets, the shells, and we had the sadness of famine as well. But we also experienced the wonderful power of the prayer of the people. Everyone walked around with the Book of Psalms in those days. At the hospital we were inundated with casualties. Air raids usually took place over the marketplaces. We might have between fifty and one hundred civilians brought in after an air raid. We were totally exhausted from the days and nights of work. I remember one night Sister Brigid said, 'we'd all die bravely if only we could get one good night's sleep'.

We also treated the soldiers. We accepted whichever band of soldiers had gained control of the mission area to which we were assigned, and we treated them if they were wounded just as we treated everyone else who needed our care. We didn't take sides, except to be always on the side of the suffering people.

When I said, 'eventually you were all captured?' Deirdre replied: 'Well, 'liberated' is the word the federal army used.'

For three days we had stayed under the dining room table, knowing from the heavy bombing and shelling that the nearby town was being taken. Patients who hadn't run away home were taking shelter under their beds in the wards. Student nurses hid under the beds in the dormitories. On the third day, a band of soldiers came up to the dining room window and shouted to us to come out, or they would shoot into the house.

Dr. Godfrey Hinds went out first, holding up a white handkerchief in one hand and his stethoscope in the other. The rest of us followed. We were marched down the road towards the river, holding our hands in the air at first. The distance is about three miles. After a while they said we could put our hands down and walk quietly. The worst thing was seeing the bodies of all the young men killed along the roadside. We were sixty people in all, sisters, priests, patients, students, staff. The soldiers helped us to carry some of the patients. That night we were ferried across the river in canoes and motorboats, the bullets still flying over our heads. Once we reached the far side, the soldiers – seeing how hungry and weak we were – opened their army rations and shared them with us.

Then Dr. Hinds told the soldiers there was a Catholic mission a little further up the river, and asked if we could be held there. They agreed, so we all moved into that mission, just as we were. The clothes we were wearing were all we had with us. Luckily the expatriate lay staff who had been forced to leave that mission in a hurry had left their clothes behind. We opened their tin trunks and togged out for the work ahead.

Before long, we were allowed to begin clinics for the people in that area – and they were so many! Here, you can see the record for October 31, 1968. We saw 1,173 patients that day.

As I took a photo of her diary, I asked how on earth they could have counted them when they were so overwhelmed with work! Deirdre replied:

We used to start the clinics at 7 o'clock in the morning and work right through until after five o'clock in the evening. Fr. Cathal McBride got everyone into one place, while the staff and I set up our clinic on the veranda of an abandoned school. He let patients through 50 at a time, and the nurses triaged them. Either the nurses treated them themselves or directed them to Dr. Hinds or to me depending on their symptoms. So that day Fr. McBride counted 23 groups of 50 and then 23 people in the last group.

Sister Joan Cosgrove recalls that when they were allowed back to Afikpo after the fighting had moved further east, they were very busy caring for the sick among refugees who had been in the bush for months, living on whatever they could find. She was Pharmacist at the hospital. The International Red Cross and other international teams set up a programme providing food for two large camps in the area, with about 5,000 refugees in each. This rehabilitation programme was gradually phased out after the war ended.

Things had returned to the normal busy life of a hospital and nurse training school when I visited there in 1979. But the first photo I took was of the bullet holes in the Oratory furniture. Twenty-five years later, some of the MMM Sisters who were part of that 'liberation' had been assigned to different missions in different countries. But they managed to arrange their leave so as to return to Afikpo together to recall those experiences and to give thanks for their safety, and for all the development that had been achieved since peace was declared in 1970.

Uganda 1978

By February 1978, the people had had enough under the regime of terror of Idi Amin who had seized power from Milton Obote six years earlier. More than 200,000 had been killed. Rumours abounded that the Tanzanian army joined by Ugandan rebel fighters were about to invade from the south and reinstate Milton Obote. These were confirmed when a number of Sisters from indigenous Congregations arrived on foot from the border area with Tanzania, one hundred miles to the south of Masaka. Celebrations marking the centenary of the arrival of the first Catholic missionaries in Uganda were taking place in Kampala. The invading army waited until they were over.

> *When we heard bombs exploding in the distance, everybody who could walk left the hospital compound at Kitovu. Before long the first bombs were dropped around the strategic town of Masaka just 2 km away from our hospital. Patients who could walk, nurses and other staff, ran away to whatever safety they could hope to find at home. Nine nurses and two young men working in the Laboratory couldn't get home as they lived in the area from where the army was advancing. We stayed in the compound with them, until the bishop came up and said we should all go out to Kategondo, the senior*

seminary 14 miles away. Eventually, when the six of us did go, we brought the nine nurses, and the remaining patients with us, but the two young men stayed at Kitovu. It really wasn't any safer at the seminary, but we were all together there – the tutors and some students who couldn't get home.

For nine days, bombs were dropping all around us. It was very frightening, even during the day, from early morning. Some of the planes flew low. After nine days, word came from Masaka that if we didn't go back the whole hospital would be looted. Two Sisters went to talk to the Officer in Charge of the invading Tanzanian Army to negotiate our safe passage. We were stopped every few hundred yards. Having spent years in Tanzania ourselves, we spoke fluent Swahili, and they were friendly. One of them even knew the MMM Hospital at Dareda. We called in to tell the bishop we were back, then drove up the hill to Kitovu. It was so weird, no people, no staff, very scary – especially if you saw soldiers approaching. People started to come back when they saw we had returned. We began outpatient clinics. We had no electricity, just enough gas to boil a kettle in the morning. We rigged up an old stove on the veranda and lit a fire to do the cooking. Planes still kept flying over. Three bombs dropped on our compound, one just 100 yards from the back door.

Once Masaka was captured, the Army moved on to take Kampala. At one stage, they were defeated by Libyan reinforcements fighting for Idi Amin. The survivors came back one evening and camped on our compound. But there was no sign of them by morning. Eventually they got to Kampala and took it. On Good Friday, we were in the Oratory in Kitovu, ready to begin the ceremonies, when we heard a car coming into the compound. The Commander, who had earlier been billeted in St. Henry's School nearby, came in. 'We have routed Amin', he said. Life started to come back to normal – but it took a long, long time before anything like a lasting peace was established.'

Ethiopia 1978

Mengistu Haile Mariam, who fled Addis Ababa in 1991 for asylum in Zimbabwe, faced charges of crimes against humanity in Ethiopia. Tens of thousands of opponents of Mengistu's military Marxist regime were murdered during the 'Red Terror' campaign in 1977 and 1978. During that time, senior pupils from the country's secondary schools were trained as 'agitators' to rout the 'evils of imperialism'. Some 20 boys and girls arrived at the hospital run by MMM at Gambo, and forced the closure of an entire block so they could be installed there. For well over a year, they engaged in agitation among the staff and local farmers' organizations. Nobody could prevent this happening, not even the local Health Authorities. These young agitators had authority to hire and fire staff, commandeer hospital vehicles, and interfere with hospital management according to whim.

The doctor, Sister Maura O'Donohue, could not see a patient without one of these young people present. If she discharged someone, they could – and often did – issue a counter command. Every Friday, they would call a meeting of the staff, at which Maura would have to sit through an interrogation session lasting up to five hours. It didn't matter how you answered, you would be accused of exploitation and imperialism.

After a year, hostility grew, and tension was building up. The Sisters knew the time was coming when they would have to flee. Over a period, seriously ill patients were referred to a larger hospital. All the others were gradually discharged, but some had not left due to the counter-orders of the student agitators. This is how the final moves were recorded and given to me by Maura:

> *Another Friday meeting. This time I insisted a second Sister would accompany me. I told her to bring the keys of the hospital with her. They were very hostile all through the meeting that went on from 5 pm until 9 pm. On leaving, we slipped the keys to a trusted member of staff and had a quick word with a driver whose family did not live locally. 'Come at 3 am', we whispered. Back in the convent we made tea, and I went through the files, packing essential records, while the other three Sisters packed my bag as well as their own. At 3 am, our driver crept in. We were ready. Silently we pushed the two landrovers out onto the road, our driver in one, with one of the Sisters[1] at the wheel of the other. 'Let it roll down the hill before you start the engine, and don't put on the lights'. It was 15 km to the main road. Once there we would be relatively safe. But first there was the narrow makeshift bridge just beyond the hospital compound. Reaching it, we saw it was blocked on the far side by a huge tree trunk. With a steady nerve, the Sister in the first landrover drove up the embankment. We all clung on as she negotiated the almost perpendicular ditch. We got by. The second landrover was on our tail. They too made it. Relief. We stopped at the Military Barracks and handed an envelope to the Guard. In it was a letter saying we had to leave because of disturbance. By 8 am we were at the bishop's residence, explaining our situation. A kindly Frenchman, he thought a good rest at the nearby convent would be all we'd need before returning to Gambo. But we knew it was more serious than that. We ignored his well-meaning advice and headed for Addis Ababa, reaching*

[1] Sister JoAnn Mullen

the offices of the Ministry of Health before they closed. There, the Secretary of the Ministry understood the misguided zeal of the youth corps. He took immediate action and instructed the Provincial Medical Officer to have them removed and to negotiate our safety with the local leaders. Six weeks later, they accompanied us back and provided a guard to ensure that we could re-open the hospital and do our work without further interference.'

Sudan 1986

Sister Nina Underwood told me the following story which took place long before the country we know as South Sudan was created in 2011:

In July 1986 Sister Nancy Lyons, a Maryknoll Sister, and I were working in Southern Sudan. We lived in the Government controlled city of Juba, but our work was mainly serving people who were sympathetic to the SPLA and had been displaced by the war between the Khartoum government and the SPLA rebel forces.

One Saturday around 11 a.m. as we returned to our mission, we saw a group of about 20 men running away with medical equipment from our dispensary. Thinking it was a bunch of ruffians, I leaned on the horn and thought we had chased them off. But they returned armed with AK47 automatic weapons, and we had to dive under the car to avoid the bullets that were zinging around us. Luckily a grenade they threw in our direction didn't explode. We managed to crawl to our house, a pre-fab and no way bullet proof. We crawled into the chapel, but eventually heard them approaching. We shouted to them that we were missionary Sisters. They told us to come out with our hands up. We did.

Some of them were as young as 15 or 16 years. They grabbed our watches, crucifixes, glasses, sandals – anything they might be able to sell, and then dragged us across the compound. They tried to march us barefoot through the bush, but the thorns tore my feet, so I dropped to my knees and said 'shoot me now or give me back my Birkenstocks, I cannot go another step'.

By evening we reached a huge prison camp, and joined about 1,000 people being held there, almost all men and boys. Those guarding the camp were disciplined soldiers. We felt safer there than with the group who had captured us. They had radio contact and were pretty well organized. The Commander interrogated us – didn't we know they had told all expatriates to leave the area so that they could finish off the war? They were not impressed by the fact that we were providing medical care for their own displaced people.

However, as translators they found us useful since they had looted much equipment and needed our help to translate the instructions on how to use it. They treated us well, gave us a mosquito net, food, and a Bible, but sent a political emissary to indoctrinate us. We were held there for about a week. It was a miracle that neither of us became ill with the water we had to drink.

Meanwhile, unknown to us, international efforts were being made to secure our release into the hands of the Government army. The most horrendous part was the first time they attempted to release us. A 12-hour cease-fire had been arranged during which we were to be handed over. But one side broke that and we had to return to the prison camp. A new plan was devised. I was to carry a white surrender flag while walking with them to the banks of the Nile where a man named Marino would meet us with a boat to take us to the 'safety' of the other side – controlled by Government troops. Three other prisoners were sent with us, all older Kenyans, one woman and two men, no longer of use to their captors.

When we reached the Nile, we called in vain for Marino, but there was no boat and no Marino. Night was coming on. The soldiers accompanying us didn't know what to do. Their orders were to deliver us safely across the Nile. Instead, they lit a huge fire to drive away the mosquitoes and told us to lie down. They argued for a long time, but eventually it became quiet. As dawn appeared we realised we were alone.

One of the Kenyan men said he could lead us towards the Government camp, but it would have to be through the marshes as the pathway would be strewn with landmines. All day long we walked, without food or water. After many hours we came close to where the Government army were dug out. Evidently, they knew we were to be released by the SPLA. When they saw us coming, they shouted to us to run to the trenches. They began shooting over our heads, believing SPLA soldiers were behind us.

We had to wait while paratroopers were flown in from Khartoum to 'rescue' the two American women. These were polite and well dressed, and they asked us how we wished to be carried across the swamps to meet up with the army trucks that would take us to Juba. It upset us greatly that our three fellow prisoners, local people captured at the same time as us, were not coming with us.

In Juba we were interrogated on what we had seen at the prison camp. We were carrying letters to them from the SPLA, which seemed to anger them very much. So, they decided to expel us. We got a chance to talk to the archbishop, who told us not to worry, he would try to arrange for us to come back quietly when we felt ready. On August 15th we were deported, flown by military plane to Nairobi. I made my retreat there, and a month later got a pass to cross back into Sudan from Uganda, through SPLA controlled territory. The local church people put on a tumultuous welcome and said how upset they had been when they heard about the way we had been treated by their own people.

Rwanda 1994

The appalling situation in Rwanda unfolded during the early months of 1994. When it seemed the genocide might be easing, the Irish bishops asked Trócaire to urgently organize a humanitarian response. Trócaire asked us if we could provide essential personnel to set up emergency health services. Going in ahead of us, the experienced Trócaire team would arrange the logistics and the funding.

Sister Geneviève van Waesberghe, my friend since our novitiate and student days, was a member of our Central Leadership Team at the time. A graduate of the Medical School at University College Dublin and a native French speaker, her decades of experience of medical work in East Africa had also made her fluent in Ki-Swahili. She volunteered to lead a team of MMMs into Rwanda.

Geneviève had a *profound* sense of the special relationship between war and the healing professions. During World War I, her Dutch grandmother was a refugee in London when her mother was born. During World War II, her mother was a refugee in Belgium when she herself was born. For many years working in the Great Lakes Region of East Africa, she presented her Dutch passport as she criss-crossed borders in her ministry of healing. Dutch passport notwithstanding, she had never lived in the Netherlands nor spoke the language of her ancestors. Her origins classified her as displaced, migrant, refugee. Luckily, she received her education in the impressive school system in France during the era when the philosopher, Gaston Berger, was influencing educational circles there.

Despite the ever-supportive love of her brothers and sisters who all became naturalised French citizens, I sensed that her deepest roots were those she had put down in East Africa – first in Tanzania running a remote hospital in the Diocese of Sumbawanga; surviving a plane crash while living for a decade among the Maasai at Loolera; healing the mental anguish of child soldiers in northern Uganda; or among women held in a remand prison in the Democratic Republic of Congo.

She was steeped in the spirituality of St. Benedict - who in turn pointed his followers to the roots of the Benedictine way of life in the practise of St. Basil, the fourth century priest who is credited with founding the first ever hospital in Europe. These deep roots stabilised and nourished Geneviève's entire adult life. I was acutely aware of this as I listened to the story she told me of her 1945 train journey after the armistice. Though not yet three years of age, she never forgot the day when, together with her older brother, she travelled from Belgium to France where her parents had settled when they got married:

> *I still remember the day my mother – who was pregnant – my eldest brother, and I travelled back from Brussels to Paris in a train filled with liberated soldiers. On arrival in Paris, accommodation was found for us in a Printing Press. A few days later we returned to the Ardennes covered with scabies. Papa was waiting for us, but our house was uninhabitable, and the farm totally destroyed. For a while, a war widow gave us hospitality until our house was somewhat rehabilitated. A few weeks later my mother gave birth to Xavier who died shortly after birth. Restarting life in the Ardennes was rough*

and remained a struggle for years. Even our well had been affected by the bombings and was no longer springing up with water. As kids, we had to go down to the village each day to collect water for the house. Then in 1947, Elizabeth was born and died some months later. Her death affected me deeply. In the area, medical care was almost non-existent. However, in the midst of great difficulties my parents' faith in God seemed unshakable. God became central in my life, and I began also to dream about a better future for women and children. I wanted to care for the sick.

On the flight from Dublin to Bujumbura, capital of Burundi, Geneviève was joined by Sister Siobhán Corkery, a nurse-midwife who had many years of experience in Nigeria and had been waiting for a visa to take up a new assignment in Brazil. They were promised that others would follow very soon - and they did once arrangements could be made to cover the work in which they were currently involved.

On landing at Bujumburu, the first task was to buy a Land Rover with funds from Trócaire. Next, they located the Apostolic Nunciature to inform the Nuncio of their plans and ask any advice he might have. He seemed quite surprised and said: "Nobody is coming for my help to get into Rwanda. Everyone else is coming to ask my help to get someone out." Below is the first of several letters to our MMM Associates and supporters that Geneviève sent me in the months that followed:

We went in on 13th June. There were 20,000 displaced persons in Cyanika by then, mainly squatting in the Church, in the priests' house and the dispensary. I cried when I saw the people so miserable, sick and hungry. No sanitation. The priests' house and the dispensary were badly looted. We were shown the room where Fr. Joseph had been hiding for three days before being killed. He had chosen to stay with the people.

Recently, we discovered that about 7,000 people had been killed in Cyanika. A few are buried on the dispensary ground, some 250 in the priests' courtyard and there is a huge mass grave near the sisters' convent.

To get to Cyanika we had to negotiate 17 checkpoints between the Burundi border and Butare, a distance of about 30 kms, and 15 more checkpoints after we got a pass to travel on to Cyanika.

A house was rented for us in the village. The first night in our new house we prayed in thanksgiving to have reached Cyanika safely. Siobhán and I shared a room to feel safer. We did not like having a checkpoint just outside our house! But we were tired and slept well.

Soon Cyanika had 45,000 displaced people. The eucalyptus forests on the hillsides were being cut and small huts called blindés were being built. Thousands of displaced people were occupying the health centre, so we agreed to start our work in a classroom of the secondary school. Trócaire had arranged that a Medical Assistant would be recruited for us – his name was Jean Marie Vianney – and an auxiliary nurse called Philomena. We asked for some interpreters. Ernest, Damascene, and Marie Thérèse came along. With them, Siobhán and I began to organize our base. Early in that afternoon, we saw some 400 very ill patients, with cerebral malaria, severe malnutrition, people with pellagra and beri-beri.

Our second day was a Saturday. At 8 am we were at work. Hundreds of people were already queueing – motionless and in total silence. We saw 700 patients that day. We were struck by their silence. Also, when someone died, there was not a tear. It seemed the people were numbed by too much suffering.

That evening, thanks to the logistical skills and the backing of the Trócaire team, Sister Leonora arrived from Dublin.

We rejoiced when Leonora arrived. She did not waste any time. She was on duty Sunday morning. We thought of doing only emergency work on Sunday, but the people were so sick we could not leave them ...

When Fr. Tom McDonnell SPS joined our community, it was a real blessing. He spends his time with the sick, visiting the families of those who died in our camp. He got the parish council together again and at the Sunday Masses began a process of reconciliation. In our community, our times of liturgical celebration have become very important. We bring to it the events of the day. Each day is different, so all liturgies are also very different. We have shared our tears and we have been silent. We have found healing, encouragement, strength and hope in our celebrations ...

In mid-August began our three epidemics of dysentery, meningitis and measles. I, too, got typhus and had to go to Nairobi. A young English doctor came to relieve me and took care of mainly meningitis patients. Some of our staff became ill and the number of patients kept going up. One day we had 1,400 patients, mostly very sick

On TV you have seen a lot of atrocities, but little is being said of the love of the people of Rwanda. Many have given their lives to save others, regardless of the ethnic group. The Christians left are a real sign of hope, but they need support and encouragement at this time, to know they are not left alone. Last week I visited Kabaho, a Marian Shrine which has been a centre of prayer and of formation for Christian life for many years. In April it was also the scene of terrible massacres. 10,000 people died there. We stood in the church where nothing is left but the crucifix on the wall behind the altar and the blood of the Rwandese people splashed on the walls. But the Marian shrine is intact and each day at 4.30 pm a group of 30 people pray. One of the local Sisters said to me: "Geneviève, in Rwanda now is the favourable time to live the Gospel."

Liberia 1994

When Sister Bridget Murphy received an invitation to visit her old mission at Ganta in Liberia, the people said they wanted her to come so they could show her how the work had been built up once again. And they wanted to say 'sorry' for the way she and Sister Giovanni McCormack had been treated during the terrible fighting that had driven them out as refugees. It was a joyous reunion, even if the peace was still uneasy. A few years later, in our house on Highland Ave in Boston where Sister Brigid was then in charge, she told me how she had escaped with her life back in September 1994:

The situation had become more volatile. The 'Presidential Guard' sent to protect the TB and Leprosy Settlement at Ganta were little more than child soldiers. They were armed but untrained. Looting and robbery were frequent. They were more violent than the regular army that had been there before. When everything was taken and we had nothing left to give them, we felt our lives were at stake. There were still TB patients in the wards, and leprosy patients in the small houses they occupied. Most of the local staff had gone, except for three or four. One evening these young soldiers came and took the last things we had, all our money and Father Larry's motorbike. They locked the two of us in a bedroom, waved a knife at us, and said they would be back later. We were very scared and just put our lives in God's hands.

After about an hour, we figured they had gone. It was getting darkish, about 6 pm. Time to make a decision. The room where they had locked us had a window without burglar bars on it. We could make our escape if we acted quickly. We climbed through the window and jumped the 4-ft. drop into the back garden and crept around to the back of one of the leprosy patient's houses – an old man who had been with us a long time. He went out and made contact with one of the staff, Henry, a young man who had stayed because he was in charge of TB patients. It was near 10 pm when Henry came. 'Remain here', he said while I go and see how safe it is.'

By now the soldiers had returned. They were shooting throughout the whole compound, so we had to keep out of the way. Then Henry came back and said, 'let us go, I know the way'. He led us on foot through the rice swamp. It was very wet. Where the drains were deep, he lifted me across. Eventually, after three hours of this terrain, we got to a safer place near to the border with Guinea. Henry brought us to a house that belonged to relatives of his who had fled that morning. There was no food, but we were safe there for the night. In the morning, Henry went to a corner where he had some coins buried and dug them up and gave them to us. It wasn't worth five dollars in all, but his kindness touched us. We were refugees now. Henry was afraid to be seen with us in daylight, so we said goodbye and he returned to the hospital. We made our way to the border and tried to cross. It was quite difficult. They wanted money. Eventually we got across into Guinea, probably the only two Irish among 40,000 refugees who crossed that day. The Guinea soldiers also wanted money. All I had was a medal with Pope John Paul II on one side and

Our Lady of Perpetual Succour on the other. Shiny gold in colour, they thought it was worth the $50 they were demanding. Taking it, they said 'you can go'. In Guinea we met up with the UNHCR and they took us as far as the Catholic Mission. We spent the next two weeks there, trying to get help for the patients we had left behind. We were able to make arrangements with the Ministry of Health in Guinea who undertook to ensure shelter for any leprosy patients ready to move. But many said they would rather stay and die where they were.

Some of our staff came over and we were all together in a hostel belonging to Catholic Mission in Guinea, who were very good to us. All the time we were trying to get visas to get back into Liberia through the capital, Monrovia. We succeeded, and the staff were reunited with their families there. When we had done what we could to ensure the Leprosy Programme could keep going from Monrovia, we left for Germany to report to the German Leprosy Relief Association, and from there we made our way back to Ireland.

Angola 1975-2003

For most of the time from 1975 until 2003, civil war wracked Angola. MMMs have been there through it all. The Portuguese had begun the colonisation of Angola in 1483 and there was a long independence struggle. This intensified during the1960s as one African country after another broke free from their colonial rulers. The group to whom the Portuguese eventually handed over power had links with the Soviet Union. When Civil War broke out, they supplied a proxy Cuban Army to do their work. Western powers backed another faction. Later, South Africa, then in the grip of Apartheid, invaded from across the Namibian border in a violent attempt to keep

Communism out of its area of influence. As the war ebbed and flowed, our hospitals at Chiulo and Cuamato in the south of the country were under the control of each of these forces at different times. Always admitting wounded soldiers like any other sick people in the district, it was made clear to everyone that we did not take sides. We treated people because they were sick or wounded.

When I was Congregational Secretary in the mid-1970s, news of the violence in Angola was in the global media every few days. The Irish government advised all Irish citizens in Angola to leave the country. Families of our sisters there were constantly asking us for an update on the situation and hoping the sisters would do as the Irish government advised. Much easier said than done! Missionaries become immersed among the people they have come to serve. Withdrawing from two hospitals was not a decision to be made at a distance of thousands of miles. The leader of our Motherhouse community in Drogheda had many years of experience in Angola and spoke Portuguese fluently[2]. She was willing, even anxious to go. But flying into the capital city, Luanda, and going from there by road was not an option.

She flew to Namibia and made her way to an unmanned border crossing that she knew well. There she would be able to find a young person she could hire to cycle the 75km journey to Chiulo and deliver a letter asking one of the community to come down and meet her three days later. She lodged with a local religious community on the Namibian side of the border. On the third day she returned to the crossing point to wait for whoever who would come down. She explained the anxieties in Ireland about their safety and said she would come back

[2] Sister Veronica Tarpey

again in three more days to hear how the community felt about the situation.

As soon as the sister who had come to the border had crossed back over the Cunene River on her return journey to Chiulo, that strategic bridge was destroyed by bombing. That was the only possible route out. The bombed bridge and increased warfare in the area put an end to any further discussion about the subject. The travelling sister flew back to Ireland with the answer. The sisters' families accepted the reality and increased their prayers for the safety of their loved ones.

The 30-bed hospital at Cuamato, south of the Cunene River, could not remain open as a hospital due to the fighting. Local trained staff could continue to manage it as a Health Centre, and two sisters, one a surgeon and the other a nurse, would drive by jeep the 80km from Chiulo every two weeks. They would stay overnight. When the fighting in the area was particularly bad, they would cycle, diving into the undergrowth every time they heard a plane overhead.

On reaching the Cunene River, they would face the trickiest part of the journey. The sisters and staff who accompanied them from Chiulo would climb across the half-submerged railing of the bombed bridge, carrying their kit on their backs. The Bishop of Ondgiva Diocese, along with his Vicar and his Secretary and some helpers, would be waiting with towels on top of the tall structure that remained on their side of the river. They would rig up ladders and ropes and some would go down to the water's edge to help the team from Chiulo to climb up. When they had dried off, the Diocesan team would drive them to the hospital where people would have been patiently queueing.

Life at the hospital in Chiulo was fairly safe, but every journey beyond that was a risk. The sisters recall one occasion when soldiers shot at the tyres of their Land Rover which served as an ambulance, causing it to overturn into the bush. Luckily nobody was seriously hurt, though the vehicle was a write-off. The commander was very annoyed with those soldiers who had ignored the red cross painted on the roof and sides of the vehicle and the white flags held out through the windows. He radioed for a helicopter, which took them first to the army camp where they were given tea, and where they accepted the apology. Then they were airlifted back to the hospital.

Further north, our Lubango community Diary shows the following records for May and June 2001:

> *May 8: Sixty children taken from an orphanage were marched for a terribly long distance, released because of international pressure; many had to be transported on the backs of others because of the condition of their feet when they returned.*
>
> *First week of June: Moxico – a plane of food belonging to the World Food Programme was bombed and completely destroyed. Flights, and hence food supply to the area, are suspended.*
>
> *Melange: – A vehicle went over a mine killing 19 passengers with many more very seriously injured.*
>
> *June 4: – A car passed over a mine but in a forbidden area. One person killed and a priest very badly injured.*
>
> *June 6: Namakunde, Kunene Area where there is a big market – many houses burned down, and a blind 70-year-old woman stabbed to death. 20 people kidnapped. Ordinary people are searching for peace and harmony, wondering how long they must be the pawns of militarization.*

Eventually, on 4th April 2002, a Peace Treaty was signed. For MMM that was a most significant date. Our foundation was on 4th April 1937. On the 25th anniversary of our foundation, 4th April 1962, as communities around the world were celebrating the Jubilee, two brave women left Chiulo and made their way eastwards to establish the small mission hospital at Cuamato[3].

With peace restored we could celebrate the 50th anniversary of our arrival in Angola and of the religious profession of Sister Brigid Archbold. I was invited, along with all the sisters who had previously worked there. On the morning that we left Lubango at 4 am for the fifteen-hour drive to Chiulo, above us the Milky Way - with its estimated 100 billion stars - streamed across the entire sky. That was an absolutely spectacular, unforgettable experience.

On reaching Chiulo, it was touching to see how many graduate nurses from several cities made the long and difficult journey back to the hospital where they trained. They now held senior positions in healthcare in different parts of the country. Days ahead of the Jubilee Mass, people came from afar and built an amazing camp in an area close to the hospital. Everyone was so happy as we mingled and chatted! They brought gifts of chickens and goats and rice and maize and eggs, while the local community presented us with nine head of cattle to feed the crowd which was expected to be very large.

For several memorable days, enthusiastic school children and musicians rehearsed the liturgy. Bishop Fernando Guimarães Kevanu would be coming from Ondgiva. I filmed it all. One of the local leaders who spoke at the dinner after that memorable Mass said:

---

[3] Sisters Brigid Archbold and Benedicta Friel

The sisters were always with us, whether in times of joy or in times of sorrow during the war situation in our country. Without let up, we saw them crossing the Rio Cunene by canoe, or on foot with water to their shoulders, going to help our people of Xangongo and Cuamato-Ombadja. Our words cannot describe this satisfactorily, but the birds and the trees could tell you.

POSTSCRIPT 7

WHAT HAPPENED TO CHARLIE?

TWO OF THE GREATEST DISASTERS OF WORLD WAR I were the 1915 campaign to capture the Turkish peninsula of Gallipoli and in 1916 in France, the battle for the towns and villages north of the River Somme. During both these campaigns, Marie Martin, who later founded the Medical Missionaries of Mary, nursed wounded soldiers in Military Hospitals. The devastating news she received in Malta just after Christmas of 1915 that her younger brother Charlie was missing in Serbia, moves me to this day. I believe it is to Charlie, killed in action a few months before his 21st birthday and just four months after he sailed to the war, that we owe the foundation of the Medical Missionaries of Mary. His death led Marie to discover what really mattered.

When Charlie joined the 6th Infantry of the Royal Dublin Fusiliers and set off for training in the Army Camp at the Curragh in Co. Kildare, he believed he was only interrupting his studies at Trinity College Dublin. A body of correspondence to his family gives us a good insight into what followed after that.

About 2012, I came to know Professor Susan Schreibman.[1] At that time, she was responsible for research in Digital

[1] Dr. Schreibman is currently Professor of Digital Arts and Culture at Maastricht University.

Humanities at Trinity College Dublin. She invited me and Maura O'Donohue to meet the team of post-graduate students who had opted to digitally transcribe the Diary that Mrs. Mary Martin had written for her son, Charlie, when he was reported missing. The young men and women we met at TCD were full of enthusiasm and questions as Maura and I gave them the historical background to the work they were about to begin. Soon after that, Dr. Schreibman transferred to Maynooth University. From there, I invited her to come with me to our Archives in Drogheda.

Before Mrs. Martin died in 1955, the family had moved from Greenbank in Monkstown to St. Margaret's on Cross Avenue in Booterstown[2]. Maura O'Donohue was then a medical student at University College Dublin. Every Tuesday, it was her job to visit St. Margaret's, and after dinner with the family, give the elderly Mrs. Martin her medication and help her to get to bed. This was so that Ethel Martin could have the evening free to attend her weekly meeting of the Legion of Mary. Maura got to know Ethel very well and asked her to make sure that when the time was appropriate, any correspondence her mother had from Marie or from Charlie would be placed in the MMM Archives. Marie was never aware of this and might not have agreed, but after her mother's death Ethel did as Maura had asked.

Ethel, too, had gone to her eternal reward by the time Susan Schreibman and I embarked upon digitizing the correspondence. Wearing white cotton gloves Susan would steady each

---

[2] St. Margaret's was the new name given to the house called *Dunamase.* This is where Kevin O'Higgins, Minister for Justice in Ireland's first government, was living at the time he was fatally shot on his way to Mass in Booterstown on 10th July 1927. The house has since been renamed *Dunamase.*

document as I carefully photographed it. She then took the collection back to the Digital Hub at Maynooth and prepared them for eventual publication on the Internet. Our friend, Andrea Martin, whose father, Larry, was a first cousin of Marie and Charlie and Ethel, became our ally. A Media Lawyer, I often consulted her opinion as we began to explore this treasure-trove. Andrea and I were invited to take part in a dialogue broadcast by RTE television on the upcoming historic centenary of the Easter Sunday of 2016. Hosted by Ryan Tubridy, it invited families to recall the sufferings and the legacy of Irish men and women who served either in Ireland's national War of Independence or during World War 1.

Here's what we found as we trawled the Archives:

On 29th April 1915, writing from Gaugh Barracks at the Curragh Camp, Charlie told his mother he was happy to have met his sister, Ethel, and other family members at the Curragh Races earlier that week, but he had lost his bets on every single horse. They would be leaving from the Curragh Siding next day at 4 pm for the North Wall on the Liffey. (That is where his grandfather and granduncles docked their tall ships in the previous century.) From there they would sail for more training at Basingstoke.

On 24th June a letter from Basingstoke said he had been very busy and would be leaving next day for Greenham with twenty men to pitch tents for the remainder of the Battalion who would be joining them for training. It was now believed they would not be going to France but to the Dardanelles. They had all ordered shorts and helmets. His next letter on 3rd July reported that all the equipment had been issued. They hoped to be moving soon and were all in great form.

There was talk that they would be travelling on Mauritania, which had been requisitioned as a troopship. That meant they ought to have a good voyage. He had hoped for another spree to London. Last time there it looked eerily empty. But another visit wouldn't happen now. They had a very strenuous time out at Newbury Common where they spent two nights practising digging trenches. They had to work eight hours non-stop through each night. He sends his mother some khaki drill, asking her to get the family tailor, Phillips, to make up a jacket for him, with the stars on the shoulders. Remind Phillips to allow for shrinkage in the wash! He sends her a blank cheque to pay Phillips when it is done and asks her to send it on after him. He had tried to get it made up locally, but all the tailors were choked with work. He also says "I am sending you my commission. Please give my love to everyone at home. Thank Ethel for her photo and tell her I have not had time to get taken in my proper kit."

Two days later, July 5th, he is reporting to his mother that the weather has been intensely hot. They will be moving soon. "We are all in great form about the move and, if only we have a good boat, we ought to have good sport on board. No one seems certain whether we are going to Alexandria first or going straight to Gallipoli." There are no facilities in Basingstoke for storing spare kit, so he will send it all home and hopes it won't be in the way. I feel sure Mrs. Martin would have had no difficulty finding a nook for it somewhere on their lavish five-acre property in Monkstown.

On 2nd August a postcard to his mother from Cairo tells her they are all 'still alive and kicking', the weather is A1 and they are all very fit. But he has not heard anything of his older brother, Thomas, who was also believed to be in Cairo. He was serving with the Connaught Rangers. He was wounded early in their operations and shipped back to the hospital on Bere Island in Co. Cork.

Another postcard bears a date stamp showing 3 pm on 21st August at Gizira, Cairo. The rubber stamp on the reverse shows its arrival at Blackrock Post Office in Dublin at 5.45 pm on 30th August. Charlie writes "This is a spot we spent a fortnight in on the way out. The picture hardly does credit to the beauty of the place." The caption at the top of the black and white photo is written in red: *Vue géneral de port de Métélin"*. In that photo I can count at least a dozen troop ships in the bay.

It turned out to be a very good boat, the one they got in the end. Not the *Mauritania* but the *SS Megantic* of the White Star Line, built at the Harland & Wolff shipyard in Belfast and launched on 17 June 1909. Before the war it had been carrying passengers mainly between Liverpool and Montreal.

Charlie's letter to Marie, dated 4th September 1915, is on headed notepaper "On Board the SS Megantic". Although he has appeared light-hearted in his correspondence with the rest of the family, he has a serious message for her:

> *Dear Marie,*
>
> *I had the good fortune to receive two of your letters here and I cannot express my gratitude. A letter is easily worth a £5 note and the effects last longer than the cash does. Perhaps you would like to hear what these sisters do out here. On the hospital ships, they are kept going 18 hours a day and they practically do all the dressings themselves. Thomas will tell you about them. It was very funny meeting Sister Brasil; she had been asking Douglas about me the day before. As soon as I arrived on board, she recognised me at once. She was on night duty and kept fearfully busy, but we managed to have several chats ... She said she would write to you. At hospital*

in Cairo, I was very lucky. We had an Irish matron who was very nice to you and allowed us plenty of liberty ... I used to sleep out in the open surrounded by a mosquito net. I never found the mosquito net the slightest good as I always woke up with a few new bites ... It was nearly the hottest time of the year for Cairo – sightseeing was quite an effort. The Bazaars are very interesting but quite beyond the purse of the average Briton. The hotels and gardens are fine, but the theatres were slightly off the mark, finishing at 2 am. As we had to be in by 9.30. it was a matter of difficulty climbing the railing with one hand. I did not go very often.

I am sorry they sent Gerald Gartlan back so soon but all the same I think he is lucky to go to France. Everybody that has been in both places said France is quite a picnic compared to this show. I am sorry to hear you are still suffering from the mania for nursing; I was hoping that you would have shaken it off by now. It quite pains me to hear that Violet is also a victim. Has Ethel disappeared off the map; no one seems to have mentioned her. You gave me a fearful scolding in one of your letters. I'm sure I must have deserved it, but I cannot think how. Please don't do anything foolish in the way of trying to get out to France. You would do much better work in Ireland.

Best love to all,

Charlie

On 21st September, Charlie sends a charming postcard to his sister, Violet, for her birthday. From the *People of Egypt Series No. 13*, it shows a colourful Nile Sailor standing on board a vessel, his back to blue water and a blue sky with white clouds and palm trees on a distant shore. On the back he writes: "We are getting on splendidly. We are resting here for a couple of days. Best wishes for a Happy Birthday and many returns thereof. Charlie"

After that, Mrs. Martin received two Field Service standard printed Post Cards bearing Charlie's signature and the dates 4th and 24th October, with the pre-printed message "I am quite well."

Then, amazingly, a handwritten sheet of notepaper got through. It bears the letters "M.S.7" where the address would normally be, and is dated 16th October 1915, but on our copy, somebody has written 'Nov on envelope'. Could he have been confused about the month, or did the letter take a month to reach Dublin? It is addressed to his sister Ethel:

> *Thanks ever so much for your many letters which I'm afraid have gone unanswered. I got a box of food from you also the other day, which I greatly appreciated. When we are on out-post duty and have to stand for (up) to an hour before dawn a cup of hot soup is really a godsend. The other parcel has not arrived yet, but the postal service seems to be much better here, so I hope to get it in a day or two. Since my last letter home, we have pushed on about five miles and are in Bulgaria at last. The French have been doing great work, especially the Artillery. I am so glad Thomas has got extra leave. I hope he will bring some stuff out for me ... I am in the best of form and my appetite would alarm the housekeeper. Best love to all. I hope Marie will enjoy Malta. Personally, I thought the glare from the white houses and street appalling. Don't forget the Plum pudding.*
>
> *Your affec. Brother,*
>
> *Charlie*

The rest was silence. Charlie never knew about the letter dated 29th December 1915, from the Brigadier General in Salonika, which would have advised him:

> *I have much pleasure in informing you that you have been brought to my notice by your superior officer for your gallant conduct during the recent operation in Serbia. I have forwarded the recommendation to higher authorities for consideration.*

Like Marie in Malta, Mrs. Martin sought information about his whereabouts everywhere she could. A letter from London dated 6th January 1916 informed her that Charlie was reported missing between 6th and 11th December 1915. It gave her the names of two other Lieutenants of his Battalion who were hospitalised in London and who might have some more information and promised that if any other officers of the Battalion arrived home, they would advise her of their arrival and their addresses.

There was a small glimmer of hope when Marie received a letter from the British Red Cross in Malta, dated January 21, 1916, regretting that they could offer her no news 'but meanwhile it is just possible that the reason why there is no trace of this officer in the Mediterranean Hospitals is because he is upon a Hospital ship which has sailed for England.'

A letter to Mrs. Martin from the Hellenic Red Cross Section of Prisoners of War in Athens, dated 23rd March 1916, bearing the reference number 5293-419, said:

> *In reply to your letter of 6th January 1916, we have the honour to inform you that the Red Cross at Sofia has notified us that Lieutenant Charles Andrew Martin, 6th Royal Dublin Fusiliers, does not stand actually on the Prisoners of War list*

which we have in hand. As soon as we get any news of him, we will inform you.

Another letter Mrs. Martin received around the same time from the Red Cross in Geneva, bearing the motto *Inter Arma Caritas,* conveyed a similar message. On May 25th she was writing to the American Legation in Sophia. But the search for Charlie among prisoners of war was futile.

After the War Office had confirmed Charlie's death to Mrs Martin in June 1916; after his posthumous award for bravery had been granted; after the Royal sympathies were received; the Martin family did not give up on their efforts to find out what exactly happened to Charlie. In Malta, Marie had managed to locate and speak to some of the men who had been under his command at that last fateful battle. They told her how brave he had been, how he had commanded them all to retreat but held the position himself to ensure cover while they did so, even after he had suffered two bullet wounds.

In 1917, two sisters whose brother was also in Serbia, and still a prisoner of war, were contacted. At last, details of what happened after Charlie's men had retreated down that hillside were revealed. The letter from this prisoner-of-war to his sisters was picked up by the Army censors. Mrs. Martin received a letter dated 27 September 1917 from the War Office, Alexandra House, Kingsway, W2. It bore the reference C.2. Casualties. S/4895/8.

Madam,

I am directed to inform you that a letter from Lieutenant W.E. Gilliland, Norfolk Regiment, a prisoner of war in Bulgaria addressed to his relatives in which he refers to the death of Lieutenant (Acting Captain) C.A. Martin, 6th Battalion, Royal Dublin Fusiliers, has been brought to the notice of the

Secretary of the War Office by the Postal Censor. A copy of the extract from this letter relating to Lieutenant Martin is enclosed. The information, it will be seen, strengthens the decision already made by the Army Council and I am again to express their sympathy with you.

I am to add that should such be your desire publication would now be made in the official casualty lists.

I am, Madam,
Your obedient servant,
(Signature) R.C. Fowler

COPY:

Depot des Prisonniers de Guerre
Philippopolis, Bulgaria.
14th August 1917

My very dear Sisters,

You also ask about a Charles Martin, Royal Dublin Fusiliers. If you mean Lieut. C.A. Martin, I have learned the following facts. He was hit in the arm and leg, but carried on, subsequently he was hit again as far as I can gather, in the stomach, the bullet lodging somewhere in his spine. He was picked up on the morning of 9th December 1915 by the Bulgarians and taken to a dressing station where it was found that he was paralysed from the hips downwards. Everything was done for him, but he died probably on 10th December. The above facts were given to me by a Bulgarian Medical Student, a candidate officer who attended to Lieut. Martin doing all that was possible in the circumstances. I met this medical student the night I was captured, and he and the Doctor in charge dressed my wound and provided me with a meal of hot tea toast and cheese at a small field dressing station. They also found me a shake down for the night – straw and blankets which were indeed welcome, for not only was it cold but I was dog tired having had some forty hours with precious little sleep.

Not long ago I met this gentleman in Philippopolis; he recalled our meeting and told me about Lieut. Martin. He did not know Martin's name, but from a description he gave of the officer, he answered my recollection of Lieut. C. A. Martin, Royal Dublin Fusiliers ...

Sg. W. E. Gilliland. Lieut.

That is not quite the end of the story, however. Decades later, a member of the Irish police force, the Gardaí, was on duty in Dublin when his patrol car was involved in the search for a stolen motorcycle. That took him to a field along a side road in Rathcoole off the N7 highway. The patrol did not find what they were looking for. However, that night after he had come off duty, Garda Tim Fitzgibbon decided to return to that field and have another look for some clues. In the ditch between the field and the road he found a packet of sodden papers. He brought them home and put them at the back of the hot press to dry them out.

The packet contained letters addressed to Mrs. Martin, Greenbank, Monkstown, Co. Dublin. They contained several documents and letters revealing the search for information about what happened to Charlie. There was also a hand-written letter from Charlie to his Uncle Charlie written when they were on the Bulgarian frontier. And, critically, a letter dated 4th January 1916 from the senior officer who had sent Charlie's company forward on 6th December to hold an advanced position at what is known as the Rivit Ridge in order to delay the Bulgarian advance.[3]

The Martins had long since left Greenbank when these letters were found in the ditch. Despite much effort, Garda Fitzgibbon failed to find a relative to whom these precious documents could be returned. He put them in his attic. Many years later when he retired, he took down the package again. What happened next was recalled by Andrea Martin in a radio production by the Irish national broadcaster in *Sunday Miscellany* on RTE Radio 1. The piece was titled *Lest we Forget* from which the following is an extract:

> *In mid-November 1915, a sudden change in the weather devastated the 6th Battalion of the Royal Dublin Fusiliers in Northern Greece. Those who had survived the slaughterhouse of Suvla Bay the previous August, now found themselves ill-equipped and hungry, with only lightweight uniforms to protect them against the wind, rain, and ice. They had been sent to support French troops resisting a Bulgarian attack on Serbian Macedonia.*
>
> *On 8th December, a young Lieutenant with that battalion, twenty-year-old Charlie Martin from Dublin, became lost on a hillside in the mist. Seriously wounded, he was captured and died shortly afterwards in a Bulgarian medical field tent.*
>
> *Charlie, had he lived, would have been my father's first cousin. He came from a wealthy Catholic family; loyal first to the Catholic Church and then to the British Crown, and with a distinct sense of Irish identity. The family was sympathetic to John Redmond's Home Rule movement. We know*

---

[3] My copies of all this correspondence are water damaged. Hopefully the National Library of Ireland has been able to improve the legibility of some of them.

this from the diary kept by Charlie's mother, Mary Martin, in the period January to May 1916.

Charlie and his brother Tommy had both volunteered to fight. Their sister, Marie, had volunteered as a nursing assistant with the VAD – Voluntary Aid Detachment – first in Malta and then in France.

The diary was written by their mother after Charlie had been reported missing in action in December 1915, to keep a record for him of what was happening at home in Dublin. It opens on 1st January 1916: "Dear Charlie, Since I heard you were missing as well as wounded, it has occurred to me to write this diary in the form of a letter. We hope to hear from you soon…and later on, when you read this you will know what has been happening."

The diary spans the period of the 1916 Rising … It ends quite abruptly on 25th May with an entry about the cancellation of a tennis party because of rain.

A century later, one voice was still missing from this family patchwork of wartime voices – that of Charlie himself. But, through outrageous serendipity, that missing voice was finally heard in 2017.

Mary Martin's 1916 diary, which had been lost for years, had surfaced in the National Library. It had been chosen in 2012 by Professor Susan Schreibman, now Professor of Digital Humanities at NUI Maynooth, as the ideal subject for a digital research project by a group of her post-grad students. The result of the students' work is fascinating. The digitised diary can be found online by simply googling 'Mary Martin'; which is exactly what retired Garda Tim Fitzgibbon did 5 years later in 2017.

While searching on farmland in Rathcoole in the early '90s, for a stolen motorcycle, Garda Fitzgibbon had found a rolled-up ball of papers in a ditch, sodden and rotting. He brought the bundle home and put it at the back of his hot-press to dry out. The outer papers disintegrated when he retrieved the bundle from the hot-press, but the papers at the centre, while damaged, were still legible.

These papers contained references to Mary Martin and included two letters home from Charlie, both written in early November 1915, probably his last letters home.

Asked what prompted him, over twenty-five years after finding the papers in a ditch, to google "Mary Martin" and to then locate Professor Schreibman and deliver the papers to her, Tim Fitzgibbon said, "It was as if I was being pointed in the right direction by the persons referred to in the papers".

Writing to his mother, Charlie's tone is comforting and upbeat: "We sleep out in the open with a waterproof sheet and a blanket over us, but we are all so fit we rather enjoy it... the 6th Company officers mess together. I have three songsters among them, so we have very cheery evenings."

He also writes to his uncle, still cheery in tone, but slightly less gung-ho. "I shall have to bring you out here after the War", he writes "the country round here is most interesting". He speaks of his battalion's progress though Serbian territory; "..we advanced about 20 miles, in several places building the roads as we went...we have been subject to a fair amount of shelling....I am at present on an outpost on a hill 3000 feet up from Battalion Headquarters and all water has to be carried up by hand so washing is a thing unheard of.

We are getting very fit and after Suvla this is quite a picnic...the sun is shining all day – the nights are a bit cold".

Charlie's handwriting is readily legible and elegantly-formed, using pen and ink in the letter to his uncle but pencil in the letter to his mother. The reason for this becomes clear in the closing paragraphs of that letter: "My beautiful writing case was missing from my kit when I got back. So if it could be replaced on the quiet as a Christmas present, I should be delighted."

Charlie Martin never saw Christmas 1915. And his cheerful letters belie the horrors experienced by his regiment that brutal winter in Macedeonia. From the tone of the letters, we hear the energetic voice of a brave young man who clearly loved life, loved his family, was hopeful for the future despite the circumstances, and didn't expect to die. But young lives are lost in wars. Is that why his voice echoes back across the intervening century, via the Internet and a ditch in Rathcoole; to remind us...lest we forget?

By yet another extraordinary coincidence, a staff member at RTE remembered that decades earlier there had been a robbery at the home of two elderly sisters who were relatives of the Martins. They lived in Sandymount. As a student at Trinity College, he had availed of hospitality with these two ladies who wanted to feel they had the security of a trusted young man in the house at night. He was not there when the robbery happened, but he knew that a precious packet of letters had been stolen.

Andrea and I shared a love for this young soldier whom we had never met. She presented me with a copy of the letters Tim Fitzgibbon had found. We both felt the originals should be housed at the National Library of Ireland. The Director kindly arranged a reception to which Garda Fitzgibbon and his wife, also surviving elders of the Martin Family, Dr. Susan Schreibman and representatives of MMM were invited. The letters were formally handed over to the National Library. Andrea presented a framed picture of Charlie to Garda Fitzgibbon who has given it pride of place over the mantel piece in his home.

Now, as I put down my pen, my thoughts turn to the future of our 'extraordinary adventure' that was so bravely, if unwittingly, initiated by Charlie. Once again, the reality and the threat of war features in every news bulletin we see or read or hear. If only a way could be found to resolve differences without resorting to armed conflict! The future is still open. The attitude of *Prospective* is summed up by the Boston-born thinker Adolf A. Berle:

> *So, there will always be adventurous groups of people who seek not only to relieve present evils but also to foresee future perils, searching out ways to prevent their arising, or in any case conquer them when they appear. In longer vision, people will carry on the work of discovering intellectual tools and philosophic principles, in the hope of enlarging the capacity of generations yet unborn to confront conditions and dangers no dawn has yet revealed.*

Leaning Against the Dawn

ACKNOWLEDGEMENTS

THESE STORIES WOULD NOT HAVE BEEN MINE to tell had I not had the privilege of encountering great thinkers like Julius Nyerere, Paulo Freire, Pierre Babin, André Cournand, Gordon Foster, Godfrey Nzamujo, Thomas Berry and Kevin Hyland – all of whom I met in person –- and amazing people among whom I have lived in grassroots communities, like Manuela, Zélia, Bruno, the twins Pedro and Paulo, their sister Cristina, and Iris who broke free from captivity in Central Europe.

Marie Martin, who founded the Medical Missionaries of Mary, pioneered the way that led me to experience life in the bustling cities and remote villages that inspired these stories. All those who followed her, especially those who shared my tent along life's way, have also contributed by ideas or encouragement as I wrote down what you read here. I recall a night long ago in São Paulo when a few of us were sharing the situations in which we had found ourselves since getting out of bed that morning. I realised 'in this extraordinary adventure of ours there is a story per person per day'. Whether mentioned in the book or not, to each of my missionary colleagues, both women and men, I feel a great debt of gratitude.

I am grateful too for the encouragement and the critical review of my text from those who generously gave their time to teasing out the ideas. Their scholarship and understanding of mission were generously shared. Like true friends, some of them told me things I didn't want to hear - to bin large sections of what I had written and start again several times when I thought I was finished. I am particularly grateful to Gina Menzies, Fr. Donal Dorr, Deirdre Rudden, Fr. Gerry Kane, Andrea Martin, Sister Eilis Coe, Fr. Thomas Tusuubira and Mairead McGrath.

My brother, Leo, has been an inspiration, supporter, and honest critic through all the years. To each idea in this book, he has devoted serious thought. I give thanks for this, his insights and his patient listening to the ups and downs of a writer's challenge in our weekly phone calls.

I am privileged to live in the dynamic parish community of Booterstown on the southern shore of Dublin Bay. The encouragement of our parish priest, Monsignor Ciarán O'Carroll, and many friends who have taken the time to read early drafts of these stories has kept me going. Their interest and support, their friendship and love are deeply treasured.

To my publisher, Joe Holland of Pacem in Terris Press, I owe a debt of thanks for his assistance and encouragement and for his patience as I dealt with life's interruptions.

To you, the reader, let me say thanks for your interest. I write these stories for one reason only — that the ideas of the great people who have influenced me may be further explored by people like you.

ABOUT THE AUTHOR

Born in Waterford, Ireland, Isabelle Smyth joined the Medical Missionaries of Mary in 1961.

She was among the first group of women to graduate from Maynooth University where she obtained an M.A. in Political Philosophy and an L.Ph. from the Pontifical University.

She subsequently obtained a Diploma in Sociology & Social Research at University College Dublin, later studied Clinical Pastoral Care at Methuen, Massachusetts, USA and qualified in Digital Communications with the City & Guilds of London Institute.

She has filled hugely rewarding assignments, first in hospital administration in Tanzania and then as Congregational Secretary from 1973 to 1979, followed by pastoral ministry in the Archdiocese of São Paulo, Brazil, 1980-1987.

While in Brazil she became English editor of the ecumenical news agency *AGEN*. She was recalled to Ireland to work at the Communications Desk of the Irish Missionary Union (1987-1991) and later as Director of MMM Communications (1993-2012).

During this time, she reported on frontline missionary work while visiting communities and filming in Angola, Benin, Ethiopia, Kenya, Malawi, Nigeria, Rwanda, Tanzania and Uganda, and during events in India, Hong Kong and the Philippines.

In 1998 she received a Fellowship to attend a course at the National Archives in Washington DC. She then began the digital documentation of over 100,000 images taken between 1910 and 2012

At the turn of the 21st century, she served as Secretary to the Irish Missionary Millennium Project that digitised more than one hundred historical films of several Irish missionary societies.

During these years she also chaired meetings of the Overseas Advisory Committee of Trócaire and served as a member of Trócaire's Executive Committee.

She did extensive research on World War I in Malta and at the battle scenes of the Western Front.

Since 2004, working with religious women and men against human trafficking she attended events in Switzerland, Poland, Romania, the Czech Republic, Netherlands, France, Belgium, Italy, Portugal, Thailand, and the Middle East.

She is now engaged with pastoral teams in Dublin in the parishes of Booterstown and Donnybrook.

BIBLIOGRAPHY

Chapter 1: Empathy: A Meditative Task

Batzdorff, Susanne M, (1998), *Aunt Edith: The Jewish Heritage of a Catholic Saint*, Springfield, Illinois, Templegate Publishers

Borden Sharkey, Sarah (2023), *Edith Stein's Finite and Eternal Being, A Companion*, New York: Lexington Books, Kindle Edition

Costello, G. J. (2024), *Edith Stein's Realms amid Posthumanism's Evolving Landscape: Conversations on the subject of "Subjectivity"* In François-Xavier de Vaujany, S. Gherardi, & P. Silva (Eds.), Organization Studies and Posthumanism: Towards a More-than-Human World. Routledge.

_______ (2023), *Lifepower as a Metaphor in Edith Stein's Philosophy of Psychology: Salient Questions for Psychoanalysis and Transhumanism*, In D. Goodman & M. Clemente (Eds.), The Routledge International Handbook of Psychoanalysis, Subjectivity, and Technology (1st ed.). Routledge.

_______ (2023), *Edith Stein and the Teaching of Design and Innovation: Empathy, Community and Human Creative Achievement*, 7th Biennial International Conference of the International Association for the Study of the Philosophy of Edith Stein (IASPES)

_______ (2020), *Responsibility and the Wizard-of-Oz: Looking behind the Digital Screen with Edith Stein and Emmanuel Levinas*. 10th Organizations, Artifacts and Practices (OAP) Workshop on "Collective Responsibility and Accountability in an AI era " on-line event at University of California, Berkeley, June 24th-26th 2020

Gelber, Lucy & Leuven, Romaeus, translated by Oben, Freda Mary (2017), *Essays on Woman from The Collected Works of Edith Stein*, Washington DC: ICS Publications, Kindle Edition

Gelber, Lucy & Linssen, Michael, (2000), *Knowledge and Faith,* Washington DC: ICS Publications, Kindle Edition

Koeppel, Sister Josephine, ODC, translator (1993), *Edith Stein: Self-Portrait in Letters,* Washington, DC, ICS Publications

_______ *(1986) Life in a Jewish Family, Edith Stein: An Autobiography 1891-1916,* Washington, DC, ICS Publications

Lebech, Mette, (2015), *The Philosophy of Edith Stein: from phenomenology to Metaphysics,* Bern, Switzerland, Peter Lang Ltd.

Peoples, Katarzyna, (2021), *How to Write a Phenomenological Dissertation,* Sage, Publications Kindle Edition

Ruiz Scaperlanda, Maria, (2017), *Edith Stein, The Life and Legacy of St. Teresa Benedicta of the Cross,* Manchester NH: Maria Sophia Institute Press, Kindle Edition

Sister Teresia de Spritu Sancto ODC, (1952), *Edith Stein,* London: Sheed & Ward

Stein, Edith, (1916) *On the Problem of Empathy,* Translated by Waltraut Stein, Washington, ICS Publications

Terego, Alex, (2013), *Edith Stein, Philosopher, Mystic, Martyr, Feminist,* Kindle Edition

Chapter 2: A life Lived in Empathy

Breen, Dom Columba OSB, (1948), *'Pre-natal Days',* in *The First Decade,* Drogheda, MMM Publication

Barnes, Joseph, (1948), *'The Outlook for the Leper of the Future'* in *The First Decade,* Drogheda, MMM Publication

Brittain, Vera, (1978), *Testament of Youth,* London, Virago Press

Buchanan, Andrew, (1948), *Visitation, The Film Story of the Medical Missionaries of Mary,* Dublin, The Richview Press

Carey, Ruth, (1975), *The Seed of an Idea,* Drogheda, MMM Publication

_______ (1957), *The Diary of a Medical Missionary of Mary,* Dublin, Browne & Nolan

Duff, Mary, et al (2005). Nursing Education in Drogheda 1946-2004, Drogheda, Nursing Education Commemorative Committee

Ekop, Ekaete, (2020), *Hidden Harmony,* FeedaRead.com

Ezeani, Chinyeaka C., (2019), *Interculturality in Religious Life,* Abuja, Nigeria, Paulines Publications Africa

Forristal, Desmond, (1990), *The Second Burial of Bishop Shanahan,* Dublin, Veritas

Hogan, Edmund, (1990), *The Irish Missionary Movement,* Dublin, Gill & Macmillan

Kiggins, Thomas SPS, (1991) *Maynooth Mission to Africa,* Dublin, Gill & Macmillan

Mellett, James CSSp, (1963), *If Any Man Dare,* Dublin, Fallons

McGettrick, Thomas (1988), *Memoirs,* Nigeria, Diocese of Abikaliki

Morris, Frank SPS, ed. (1979), *Reminiscences of Bishop James Moynagh,* unpublished

O'Rourke Magdalen, (1999), *Early Memoirs of MMM,* Drogheda, MMM Publication

_______ (2000), *A Profile of Mother Mary in the Foundation Days of MMM,* Drogheda, MMM Publication

Purcell, Mary, (1987), *To Africa with Love, The Biography of Mother Mary Martin,* Dublin: Gill & MacMillan

Strub, Elizabeth Mary, (1993), *Mother Mary Amadeus Atchison SHCJ and Crisis at Anua, Justice in Rome,* Rome, Society of the Holy Child Jesus

Ramsbottom, Maura, (1971), *He went about doing good,* Study of Jesus' Healing Ministry presented at the Pontificum Institutum Regina Mundi, unpublished.

Sartre, Jean-Paul, translated by Barnes, Hazel (1969) *Being and Nothingness,* London: Methuen & Co.

Smyth, Isabelle et al, (2015), *If you only Knew the Gift,* Drogheda: MMM Publication

Spain, Alex W., (1948), *Beginnings* in *The First Decade,* Drogheda, MMM Publication

Suenens, Leon Joseph, (1962), *The Nun in the World,* London, Burns Oates

Chapter 3: The Crisis of Capitalism

Atkinson, Anthony B., (2015), *Inequality, What Can be Done?* Harvard University Press

Ayiro, A. A., et al, (1971), *Taamuli: A Political Science Forum,* University of Dar es Salaam

Benedict, Pope, (2009), *Caritas in Veritate,* Vatican Publications

_______ (2000) *Introduction to Christianity,* San Francisco, Ignatius Press Communio Books

Berle, Adolf A. (1954) *The 20th Century Capitalist Revolution,* Harvest Publishers

______ Gardiner C. Means (1932) *The Modern Corporation and Private Property,* NY, The Legal Classics Library

Boushey, Heather et al, (2017), *After Piketty: The Agenda for Economics and Inequality,* Harvard University Press, Kindle Edition

Broodryk, Johann, (2002) *Ubuntu: Life Lessons from Africa,* Pretoria: Ubuntu School of Philosophy, Kindle Edition

Bruni, Luigino (Ed), Translated by Gold, Lorna, (2002) *The Economy of Communion,* NY: New City Press, Kindle Edition

Delson, Jeanne Philippe, (et al Eds.), (2017), *Anti Piketty, Capital for the 21st Century,* Washington DC: Cato Institute, Kindle Edition

Esteva, Gustavo et al, (2013), *The Future of Development,* University of Bristol, Policy Press

Francis, Pope, (2023) *Laudate Deum,* Vatican Press Office

_______ (2022) *Desiderio Desideravi,* Vatican Press Office

_______ (2020) *Fratelli Tutti,* Vatican Press Office

_______ (2015) *Laudato Si,* Vatican Press Office

_______ (2013) *Evangelii Gaudium,* Vatican Press Office

Friedman, Benjamin M., (2021), *Religion and the Rise of Capitalism,* NY: Alfred A. Knopf, Penguin Random House, Kindle Edition

Johnston, Douglas and Sampson Cynthia (Eds), (1994), *Religion, the Missing Dimension of Statecraft,* NY: Oxford University Press

Mazzucato, Mariana, (2021), *Mission Economy: A Moonshot Guide to Changing Capitalism,* London: Penguin Books, Kindle Edition

Mutaha, A. Z. (et al), (1976), *Cooperatives in Tanzania: Problems of Organisation,* Dar es Salaam: Tanzania Publishing House

Mwakikagile, Godfrey, (2006), *Tanzania under Mwalimu Nyerere,* Dar es Salaam: New Africa Press

McKenna, Joseph C., (1997), *Finding a Social Voice, The Church and Marxism in Africa,* NY: Fordham University Press

Pabst, Adrian (Ed), (2011), *The Crisis of Global Capitalism,* Eugene, Oregon: Wipf and Stock, Kindle

Piketty, Thomas, (2017), *Capital in the Twenty-First Century,* Cambridge MA: The Belknap Press of Harvard University Press, Kindle Edition

Proctor, J.H. (Ed), (1975), *Building Ujamaa Villages in Tanzania,* Dar es Salaam: Tanzania Publishing House

Tumbo, N.S.K. et al ((1977), *Labour in Tanzania,* Dar es Salaam: Tanzania Publishing House

Chapter 4: The Teaching Method of Paulo Freire

Doggett, Aileen and McVicar, Janet, (1990), *Handbook for Health Workers: An Introductory Training Course in Primary Health Care,* Nigeria, Ibadan, Ambassador Publications

Freire, Paulo, (2021), *Pedagogy of the Heart,* Bloomsbury Academic.

_______ *(2018), Pedagogy of the Oppressed, 50th Anniversary Edition,* Bloomsbury Academic

_______ (1996), *Letters to Cristina, Reflections on my Life and Work,* Routledge

Gordon, Richard, (2006), *Quantum Touch: The Power to Heal,* Berkeley CA: North Atlantic Books

Kilroe, Stephanie, (2019), *Anne Hope, the Struggle for Freedom,* London, Darton, Longman, Todd

Mukwege, Denis (2021), *The Power of Women: a Doctor's Journey of Hope and Healing,* NY: Flatiron Books, Kindle Edition

Timmell, Sally J. (2021), *You Can Never Go Back,* London, Darton, Longman & Todd

Chapter 5: Theologies of Liberation

Allen, Lisa, (2021), A *Womanist Theology of Worship: Liturgy, Justice, and Communal Righteousness,* Maryknoll NY: Orbis Books

Balasuriya, Tissa, (1990), *Mary and Human Liberation,* Colombo, Sri Lanka: Centre for Society & Religion

_______ (1977), *The Eucharist and Human Liberation,* Colombo, Sri Lanka: Centre for Society & Religion

Beaudoin, Tom (1998), *Virtual Faith: The Irreverent Spiritual Quest of Generation X,* San Francisco: Jose-Bass Publishers

Boff, Leonardo, (2022), *Thoughts & Dreams of an Old Theologian,* Translated by Francis McDonagh, Maryknoll, Orbis Books, Kindle Editon

Bosch, David J., (1991), *Transforming Mission: Paradigm Shifts in Theology of Mission,* Maryknoll NY: Orbis Books

Chittister, Joan, (2002), *New Designs: An Anthology of Spiritual Vision,* Erie, PA: Benetvision

_______ (2000), *Life Ablaze: A Woman's Novena*, Franklin, WI: Sheed & Ward

Cone, James Hal, (1969), *Black Theology & Black Power,* Maryknoll NY: Orbis Books

Ellis, Marc H., (2004), *Towards a Jewish Theology of Liberation,* Waco, TX: Baylor University Press

Eugenia, Sister M, (Ed), (1991), *New Horizon for Dialogue,* Dhaka, Bangladesh: Xaverian Centre for Inter-religious Dialogue

Gutiérrez, Gustavo, (1975), *A Theology of Liberation: History, Politics and Salvation,* Maryknoll NY: Orbis Books

Koyama, Kosuke, (1974), *Waterbuffalo Theology,* Maryknoll NY: Orbis Books

Mallon, James, (2014), *Divine Renovation: From a Maintenance to a Missional Church,* Toronto: Novalis Publishing Inc., Kindle Edition

Mascall, E.L., (1968), *Theology and the Future,* London: Darton, Longman & Todd

O Murchú, Diarmuid, (2013), *God in the Midst of Change,* Maryknoll NY: Orbis Books

_______ (1997), *Reclaiming Spirituality,* Dublin: Gill & McMillan

O'Gorman, Frances, (1983), *Base Communities in Brazil,* Rio de Janeiro: Francisco Alves *Publications*

O'Sullivan, Owen, (1997), *The Silent Schism: Renewal of Catholic Spirit and Structures,* Dublin: Gill & Macmillan Ltd.

Radford Ruether, Rosemary, (2013), *My Quest for Hope and Meaning,* Eugene, OR: Cascade Books

_______ (1996), *Women Healing Earth: Third World Women on Ecology, Feminism and Religion,* NY: Maryknoll: Orbis Books

Song, Choan-Seng, (2002), *Third-Eye Theology,* Eugene, OR: Wipf and Stock Publishers

Zagano, Phyllis, (2022) *Women Religious, Women Deacons,* New York: Paulist Press, Kindle Edition

Chapter 6: The god 'E'

Babin, Pierre (1991), *The New Era in Religious Communication,* Minneapolis, MN, Fortress Press

Chiona, James, Archbishop of Blantyre, et al (1993), *Choosing our Future,* Episcopal Conference of Malawi

Lanier, Jaron (2018), *Ten Arguments for Deleting Your Social Medica Accounts Right Now,* Vintage Digital

_______ (2014), *Who Owns the Future?* London: Penguin Books, Kindle Edition

Zuboff, Shoshana, (2019) *The Age of Surveillance Capitalism,* London: Profile Books, Kindle Edition

Chapter 7: The Challenge of Interfaith Collaboration

Brown, Malcolm (Ed), (2914) *Anglican Social Thought,* London, Church House Publishing, Kindle Edition

Cohn-Sherbok, Dan, (1992), *World Religions and Human Liberation,* Maryknoll NY: Orbis Books

Coward, Harold, (1988), *Sacred Word and Sacred Text, Scripture in World Religions,* Maryknoll NY: Orbis Books

Cozzens, Donald, (2004), *Faith that Dares to Speak,* Collegeville, MN: Liturgical Press

Fernando, Antony with Swindler, Leonard. (1985), *Buddhism Made Plain, An Introduction for Christians and Jews,* Maryknoll NY: Orbis Books

Lane, Dermot A., (2011), *Stepping Stones to Other Religions,* Dublin: Veritas Publications, Kindle Edition

_______ Ed. (1999) *New Century, New Society, Christian Perspectives,* Dublin: Columba Press

McLeod, Melvin, (2015) *Twenty-first Century Buddhists in Conversation,*

_______ (2006), *Mindful Politics: A Buddhist Guide to Making the World a Better Place,* Boston, Wisdom Publications

Musk, Bill, (1989), *The Unseen Face of Islam,* Eastbourne, UK: Monarch Publications Ltd.

Nolan, Albert, (2009), *Hope in an Age of Despair,* Maryknoll NY: Orbis Books

_______ (2006), *Jesus Today: A Spirituality of Radical Freedom,* Maryknoll NY: Orbis Books

O'Collins, Gerald, (2013), *The Second Vatican Council on Other Religions,* Oxford University Press

O'Hanlon, Gerry, (Ed), (2017), *A Dialogue of Hope: Critical Thinking for Critical Times,* Dublin: Messenger Publications

O'Mahony, Kieran J., (1999), *What the Bible Says About the Stranger,* Dublin and Belfast: Irish Commission for Justice & Peace and Irish Council of Churches

Panikar, Raimundo, (1981), *The Unknown Christ of Hinduism,* Maryknoll NY: Orbis Books

Race, Alan and Rao, Seshagiri, (Eds), (1993), *World Faiths Encounter,* Oxford: World Congress of Faiths

_______ (1982). *Christians and Religious Pluralism,* Maryknoll NY: Orbis Books

Rowlands, Anna, (2021) *Towards a Politics of Communion,* London: T&T Clark, Kindle Edition

Sri Ramakrishna Math, (1911), *The Condensed Gospel of Sri Ramakrishna,* Madras: Sri Math

Storey, Celia and David, (Eds) (1994), *Visions of an Interfaith Future,* Oxford: International Interfaith Centre

Swami Saradananda, (Ed), *Notes of Some Wanderings with Swami Vivekananda by Sister Nivedita,* Kolkata: The Bramachari Gonendra Nath Udbodhan Office, Kindle Edition

Thich Nhat Hanh, (1999), *Going Home: Jesus and Buddha as Brothers,* USA, Riverhead Books

_______ (1997), *Transformation and Healing: Sutra on the Four Establishments of Mindfulness,* UK, Full Circle Publications

Chapter 8: The Cosmic Christ

Berry, Thomas, (2009), *The Christian Future and the Fate of the Earth,* NY, Orbis Books

_______ (1992), *The Universe Story,* San Francisco, Harper

Berry, Thomas with Clarke, Thomas, (1991), *Befriending the Earth,* Mystic CT: Twenty-third Publications

Boff, Leonardo, (1995), *Ecology & Liberation, A New Paradigm,* Maryknoll, Orbis Books, Kindle Edition

Corbis Bookshley, Thomas, (1971), *The Spirituality of Teilhard de Chardin,* London: Collins Fontana Library

Dixson-Declève, Sandrine (et al), (2022), *Earth for All: A Survival Guide for Humanity,* Canada: New Society Publishers, Kindle Edition

Deane-Drummond, Celia (2017), *A Primer in Ecotheology,* Eugene, OR, Cascade Books

Delio, Ilia, (2013) *The Unbearable Wholeness of Being: God, Evolution and the Power of Love*, Maryknoll NY: Orbis Books

Dorr, Donal, (2020), *A Creed for Today, Faith & Commitment for Our New Earth Awareness,* Maryknoll NY: Orbis Books

_______ (2018), *The Pope Francis Agenda,* Dublin: Veritas Publications

_______ (2008), *Spirituality, Our Deepest Heart's Desire,* Dublin: Columba Press

_______ (2000), *Mission in today's world,* Dublin: Columba Press

Everest Media, (2022), *Summary of Thomas Berry's The Great Work,* Everest Media LLC, Kindle Edition

Feehan, John, (2016), *The Dipper's Acclaim & Other Essays,* Dalgan Park, Ireland: Columban Ecological Institute

______ (2015), *Reflections on the presence of God in creation,* privately published

Flinders, Tom, (2011), *Thomas Berry's Sacred Sound*. Petaluma, CA, Two Rock Publications, Kindle Edition

Freeman, Laurence OSB, (2014), *Beauty's Field: Finding God in Unexpected Places,* UK, Canterbury Press

Forster, Dion A., (2007), *Christ at the Centre: Discovering the Cosmic Christ of Bede Griffiths*. Amazon, Kindle Edition

Greene, Herman F., (2000), *Understanding Thomas Berry's Great Work,* Teilhard Association for the Future of Man

Haught, John F, (2021), *The Cosmic Vision of Teilhard de Chardin,* Maryknoll NY: Orbis Books, Kindle Edition

King, Ursula, (2015) *Spirit of Fire: The Life And Vision Of Teilhard de Chardin,* Maryknoll, NY: Orbis Books

Lyons, J.A., (1982), *The Cosmic Christ in Origen and Teilhard de Chardin,* Oxford University Press

Molyneaux, David et al (1990), *Between the Flood and the Rainbow: JPIC World Convocation, Seoul,* Rome: IDOC Internazionale 90/2

_______ (1990), *The Emerging Cosmic Spirituality,* Rome: IODC Internazionale 90/4

McDonagh, Sean, (2018), *Laudato Si': An Irish Response,* Dublin, Veritas Publications

_______ (2006), *Climate Change: The Challenge to All of Us*, Dublin, Columba Books

_______ (2005), *The Death of Life,* Dublin, Columba Books

______ (1990) *The Greening of the Church,* London: Geoffrey Chapman

_______ (1987), *To Care for the Earth: A Call to a New Theology,* London: Geoffrey Chapman

O'Leary, Daniel, (2017), *An Astonishing Secret: The Love Story of Creation and the Wonder of You,* Dublin: Columba Press

Raymaker, John (et al), (2013), *Spiritual Paths to An Ethical & Ecological Global Civilization,* Washington DC: Pacem in Terris Press, Kindle Edition

Rezende, Ricardo, (1994), *Rio Maria, Song of the Earth,* Maryknoll NY: Orbis Books

Rohr, Richard (2021). *The Universal Christ*, Random House, SPCK

Terego, Alex, (2013), *Pierre Teilhard de Chardin and the Cosmic Christ.* Kindle Edition

Chapter 9: Little Girl I say to you Arise

Cork, Matthew and Kemp, Kenneth, (2013), *Why Not Today? Trafficking, Slavery, the Global Church and You,* Chicago: Moody Publishers

Lohan, David, (2022), *At Freedom's Crossroads: Making Sense of Modern Slavery,* Cork, Ireland, Frederick Douglas Anti-Slavery Press

Postscript 1: Commitment

Kierkegaard, Søren, (1941), *Concluding Unscientific Postscript,* NJ: Princeton University Press

Postscript 2: The Philosophy of Gaston Berger

Cournand André and Lévy, Maurice, (1973), *Shaping the Future: Gaston Berger and the Concept of Prospective,* NY: Gordon and Breach Science Publishers Inc.

Heidegger, Martin, translated by Macquarrie, John and Robinson, Edward (1962), *Being and Time,* London, Blackwell

Postscript 6: War Stories

Byrne, Tony CSSp, (1997), *Airlift to Biafra,* Dublin, Columba Press

Colbert, Dom, (2018), *No Tears Left: Further Memories of an Irish Doctor Abroad*, Dublin, SPRINTprint

Fernando, Jude Lal, (Ed), (2021). *Faith in the Face of Militarization,* Eugene OR: Wipf and Stock Publishers, Kindle Edition

Postscript 7: What Happened to Charlie?

Lecane, Philip, (2015) *Beneath a Turkish Sky: The Royal Dublin Fusiliers and the Assault on Gallipoli,* The History Press, Ireland, Kindle Edition

Titles in Portuguese

Azevedo, Marcello, (1986), *Comunidades Eclesiais de Base e Inculturação da Fé,* São Paulo: Edições Loyola

Brunelli, Delia, (1988), *Libertação da Mulher,* Rio de Janeiro: Publicações da Conferência dos Religiosos do Brasil

Falcetto, Claudino, (1988), *Nova Evangelização e Vida Religiosa,* Rio de Janeiro: Publicações da Conferência dos Religiosos do Brasil

Freire, Paulo, (1983), *Educação Popular,* Bahia: Diocese de Juazeiro

Freitas, Maria Carmelita de, et al, (1989), *Inserção: Novo Modo de ser da Vida Religiosa,* Rio de Janeiro: Publicações da Conferência dos Religiosos do Brasil

Galilea, Segundo, (1978), *Teologia da Libertação,* São Paulo: Edições Paulinas

Gonzáles, Carlos Ignácio, (1986), *Teologia da Libertação,* São Paulo: Edições Loyola

Guareschi, Pedrinho A., (1981), *Comunicação e Poder,* Petropolis: Vozes Ltda.

Gutiérrez, Gustavo, (1975), *Teologia da Libertação,* Petropolis: Vozes Ltda.

Hortal, Jesús, et al, (1991), *A Igreja católica diante do pluralismo religioso no brasil,* São Paulo: Edições Paulinas

Ianni, Ocravio, (1982), *Dialética & Capitalismo,* Petropolis: Vozes Ltda.

Iriarte, Gregório, (1986), *Leitura Crítica para a Interpretação da Realidade,* São Paulo: Edições Paulinas

João Paulo II, Papa, (1989), *Carta aos Religiosos,* São Paulo: Edições Loyola

J. Simões Jorge, (1981), *Puebla, Libertação do Homen Pobre,* São Paulo: Edições Loyola

Libánio, João Batisa, Ed, (1992) *Santo Domingo, Conclusões,* São Paulo: Edições Loyola

_______(1985), *Fé e Política,* São Paulo: Edições Loyola

Mafei, Maristela, (1985), *Sangue na Terra: A Luta das Mulheres,* São Paulo: Ícone Editora Ltda.

Matos, Henrique Cristiano, et al (1986), *Falam as Contemplativas,* Rio de Janeiro: Publicações da Conferência dos Religiosos do Brasil

Mesters, Carlos, (1985), *Os Profetas e a Saúde do Povo,* Belo Horizonte, MG: Editora Littera Maciel

Przyklenk, Bishop João Batista, (1979), *Guia Ecuménico Popular,* São Paulo: Edições Paulinas

Rebré, A., (1982), *A Libertação do Oprimido no Antigo Testamento,* São Paulo: Edições Paulinas

Santos, Theotonio dos, (1983), *Conceito de Classes Sociais,* Petrópolis, RJ: Vozes

Saroni, Fernando, Ed. (1987), *A Solidariedade nas práticas de libertação na América Latina,* São Paulo, Editora FTD SA

Singer, Paul, (1983), *O Que É Socialismo Hoje?,* Petrópolis: Edição Vozes

Soncini, Nélia A., (1992), *Culturas Oprimidas e a Evangelização na América Latina,* Santa Maria, RS: Gráfica Pallotti

Sobral, José Joaquim, (1989), *Comunicação e Missâo da Igreja,* São Paulo: Edições Paulinas

_______(1987), *Uma Caminhada Ecumênica,* São Paulo: Edições Paulinas

______ (1986), *Guia para o diálogo católica-judaico no brasil,* São Paulo: Edições Paulinas

Souza Lima, Luiz Gonzaga de, (1979), *Evolução Política dos Católicos e da Igreja no Brasil,* Petropolis: Vozes

Vier, Frederico, (1986), *Sobre os meios de Comunicação Social,* Petropolis: Vozes

OTHER BOOKS FROM
PACEM IN TERRIS PRESS

AFRICANA STUDIES

THE METHODIST CHURCH IN AFRICA
SINCE 1820
Pianapue T.K. Early, 2020
Forward by Bishop David Greaves

DJUANKAYU
THE BASSA-AFRICAN CREATION STORY
A Postcolonial Practical Theology
Pianapue T. K. Early, 2020

AFRICAN ENCOUNTER OF FAITH & CULTURE
Ritual & Symbol for Young People
in Tiv Society of Central Nigeria
Clement Terseer Iorliam, 2020

BOTTOM ELEPHANTS
Catholic Sexual Ethics & Pastoral Practice in Africa:
The Challenge of Women Living within Patriarchy
& Threatened by HIV-Positive Husbands
Daniel Ude Asue, 2014

HUMANITY'S AFRICAN ROOTS
Remembering the Ancestors' Wisdom
Joe Holland, 2012

CATHOLIC SOCIAL TEACHING

SUMMARY & COMMENTARY FOR PACEM IN TERRIS
The Famous Encyclical Letter
of Pope John XXIII on World Peace
Joe Holland, 2020

CATHOLIC LABOR PRIESTS
Five Giants in the United States Catholic Bishops Social Action Department
Volume I of US Labor Priests During the 20th Century
Patrick Sullivan, 2014

CATHOLIC SOCIAL TEACHING & UNIONS
IN CATHOLIC PRIMARY & SECONDARY SCHOOLS
The Clash between Theory & Practice within the United States
Walter "Bob" Baker, 2014

PACEM IN TERRIS
Its Continuing Relevance for the Twenty-First Century
(Papers from the 50th Anniversary Conference at the United Nations)
Josef Klee & Francis Dubois, Editors, 2013

100 YEARS OF CATHOLIC SOCIAL TEACHING
DEFENDING WORKERS & THEIR UNIONS
Summaries & Commentaries for Five Landmark Papal Encyclicals
Joe Holland, 2012

THE "POISONED SPRING" OF ECONOMIC LIBERTARIANISM
Menger, Mises, Hayek, Rothbard: A Critique from
Catholic Social Teaching of the Austrian School of Economics
Pax Romana / Cmica-usa
Angus Sibley, 2011

BEYOND THE DEATH PENALTY
The Development in Catholic Social Teaching
Florida Council of Catholic Scholarship
D. Michael McCarron & Joe Holland, Editors, 2007

CHRISTIAN HISTORY, THEOLOGY, & SPIRITUALITY

THE NEXT STAGE OF CATHOLIC RELIGIOUS LIFE
Postmodern Lay Mystical-Prophetic Communities
Based on Ecological Spirituality
Joe Holland, 2020

ROMAN CATHOLIC CLERICALISM
Three Historical Stages in the Legislation of a Non-Evangelical,
Now Dysfunctional, and Sometimes Pathological Institution
Joe Holland, 2018

CATHOLIC PRACTICAL THEOLOGY
A Genealogy of the Methodological Turn to Praxis,
Historical Reality, & the Preferential Option for the Poor
Bob Pennington, 2018

SAINT JOHN OF THE CROSS
His Prophetic Mysticism in the Historical Context of Sixteenth-Century Spain
Cristóbal Serrán-Pagán y Fuentes, 2018

POSTMODERN ECOLOGICAL SPIRITUALITY
Catholic-Christian Hope for the Dawn of a Postmodern Ecological Civilization Rising from within the Spiritual Dark Night of Modern Industrial Civilization
Joe Holland, 2017

JOURNEYS TO RENEWED CONSECRATION
Religious Life after Fifty Years of Vatican II
Emeka Obiezu, OSA & John Szura, OSA, Editors, 2017

THE CRUEL ELEVENTH-CENTURY IMPOSITION OF WESTERN CLERICAL CELIBACY
A Monastic-Inspired Attack on Catholic Episcopal & Clerical Families
Joe Holland, 2017

PETER MAURIN'S ECOLOGICAL LAY NEW MONASTICISM
A Catholic Green Revolution Developing Rural Ecovillages, Urban Houses of Hospitality, & Eco-Universities for a New Civilization
Joe Holland, 2015

GLOBAL GOVERNANCE & UNITED NATIONS

SEEKING GLOBAL JUSTICE & PEACE
Catholic-Inspired NGOs at the United Nations
Emeka Obiezu, 2019

BRETTON WOODS INSTITUTIONS & NEOLIBERALISM
Historical Critique of Policies, Structures, & Governance of the International Monetary Fund & the World Bank, with Case Studies
Mark Wolff, 2018

PROTECTION OF RELIGIOUS MINORITIES
A Symposium Organized by Pax Romana at the United Nations and the United Nations Alliance of Civilizations
Dean Elizabeth F. Defeis & Peter F. O'Connor, Editors, 2015

PERSONAL WITNESS STORIES

"BETTER FOR BEING WITH YOU"
A Philosophy of Care
Sister Bernadette Kenny, MMM with Tauna Gulley, 2019

RUINED FOR LIFE
Post-Missionary Immersion, Reintegration, & Conversion
David Masters, 2019

PADRE MIGUEL
A Memoir of My Catholic Missionary Experience in Bolivia amidst Postcolonial Transformation of Church and State
Michael J. Gillgannon, 2018

WORLD RELIGIONS, ECOLOGY, & COSMOLOGY

A HIMALAYAN HOPE AND A HIMALAYAN PROMISE
India's Spiritual Vision of the Origin, Journey, & Destination of Earth's Environment & Humanity
Thomas Pliske, 2019

THE WHOLE STORY:
The Wedding of Science & Religion
Norman Carroll, 2018

LIGHT, TRUTH, & NATURE
Practical Reflections on Vedic Wisdom & Heart-Centered Meditation In Seeking a Spiritual Basis for Nature, Science, Evolution, & Ourselves
Thomas Pliske, 2017

THOMAS BERRY IN ITALY
Reflections on Spirituality & Sustainability
Elisabeth M. Ferrero, Editor, 2016

SPIRITUAL PATHS TO A GLOBAL & ECOLOGICAL CIVILIZATION
Reading the Signs of the Times with Buddhists, Christians, & Muslims
John Raymaker & Gerald Grudzen, with Joe Holland, 2013

THE NEW DIALOGUE OF CIVILIZATIONS
A Contribution from Pax Romana
International Catholic Movement for Intellectual & Cultural Affairs
Pax Romana / Cmica-usa
Roza Pati & Joe Holland, Editors, 2002

INSPIRATIONAL FICTION

SUNRISE STORIES & MOONLIGHT TALES
From the Mother's Garden
Thomas Pliske, 2023

Made in the USA
Monee, IL
23 December 2024

72150101R00236